The Avonmouth Line History and Working

Route indicator signal at Avonmouth Goods Yard, reading from Sidings to Up Great Western line.

The Avonmouth Line
History and Working

P.D. RENDALL

THE CROWOOD PRESS

First published in 2018 by
The Crowood Press Ltd
Ramsbury, Marlborough
Wiltshire SN8 2HR

www.crowood.com

British Library Cataloguing-in-Publication Data
A catalogue record for this book is available from the British Library.

ISBN 978 1 78500 437 7

Dedication
This book is dedicated to my parents, Reg and Jean,
who passed away within three months of each
other during the writing of the manuscript.

Typeset by Julie Laws, Stroud, Gloucestershire
Printed and bound in India by Replika Press Pvt Ltd.

Contents

Introduction

To many people, the history of the Avonmouth area of Bristol conjures up images of mass industrialization, belching chimneys, docks and trains. All reasonably accurate, but not on such a scale as might be imagined. The Avonmouth of 2017 is far more industrialized than it was when I worked there in the 1980s. True, the factory chimneys of Fisons and ICI have now gone, along with the factories themselves, but there are far more warehouses and industrial units along the riverbank today than ever before, stretching all the way to Severn Beach.

Most of the additional development has happened during the twenty-first century. Until then, even at its height, the industry covered a more limited area, along a strip just inland of the riverbank. Between there and the docks was the railway; the goods yards, sidings and stations of the London, Midland and Scottish and Great Western Railway companies almost dwarfed in size by the huge network belonging to the Bristol Corporation and the Port of Bristol Authority. Even so, there were plenty of green spaces and views across the factories to open fields. Driving to Avonmouth via Hallen village was still a country-lane experience until one or two fields short of the Philblack (later Sevalco) complex, where grass, hedges and streams began to turn black with carbon dust. The railway from Filton via Henbury ran through open fields nearly all the way to Hallen Marsh junction, with a few houses around Henbury.

Major change occurred with the advent of the Second Severn Crossing in the 1990s, which opened up the area and added another motorway to the Avonmouth junction. The Port of Bristol Authority sidings, lines and engines have long gone. The main railways have shrunk and changed, but they are still there and have a future, both in passenger and freight.

This book is mostly about the working and history of the Avonmouth lines *after* the 'Grouping' of the private railway companies into the 'Big Four' in 1923. In order to understand that history, however,

it will be necessary to lay the foundations as it were, by giving a short account of how the area developed. This account will set the scene, by taking a look at the birth of the lines and then recounting the history and working of them, from the 1923 Grouping up to the present day.

The book will cover only the 'main line' railway; dealing with the subject of the docks complex and all its changes would take a whole book in itself, and I shall refer to the docks railway only where it comes into contact with the main lines. Splendid coverage of the docks internal railway system can be found in the late Mike Vincent's book *Lines to Avonmouth*.

As ever, I am indebted to my ex-work colleagues past and present for their memories and photos of the line. Every effort has been made to credit photos to the people who took them, even if, after every endeavour has been made to track them down, that person can no longer be traced. Many of the photographs and diagrams are over fifty years old and the photos in particular were taken by ordinary working railwaymen during the course of their duties. The quality of the pictures may not be as good as those taken by photographers with access to more expensive cameras, but they are included here as they are an invaluable record of the railway. Indeed, some of them were taken from places where other photographers were not allowed to go.

Thanks are due to Wilf Stanley for use of his photos; Mary Gibbs for the use of John Gibbs' photo and Tim and Wendy Worrall for the use of the late Leonard Worrall's photos. Many of the diagrams are copied/adapted from diagrams once held by the Bristol District Signalling Inspectors and given to me some thirty years ago. Other information comes from my personal collection. I am also grateful to Valerie Lyons and her aunt, Mary Sheppard, for information about Alfred Allen, and the Wiltshire Records Office for their help.

P.D. Rendall
South Gloucestershire

CHAPTER I

The Beginnings

The story of the Avonmouth, Bristol line begins in the 1860s, at the height of Victorian engineering and the Empire. The Bristol City Docks were proving inadequate in servicing the needs of the rapidly developing shipping industry, and solutions had to be found. After a minor start with a riverside branch along the Avon Gorge to the mouth of the Avon, the railways expanded in tandem with the expansion of the docks. What is now usually referred to as the 'Avonmouth branch' became an important and busy complex of lines, both within and outside the docks themselves.

The River Avon flows through the City of Bristol and for around eight miles winds its muddy way out through a rocky gorge to the River Severn. Bristol has been a centre of trading for centuries and in the days when it boasted a castle, there were quays below the walls of that castle where ships could tie up to discharge and load their cargoes. By the time of Henry III, trade had grown so much that extra facilities were required. Commencing in 1239, the course of the River Frome was diverted where it met the Avon, and changed and straightened to form a deeper water channel known as St Augustine's Trench. After eight years' work, a new quay had also been built to replace the old Avon wharfs.

However, the Avon is tidal and over the following centuries, whilst the docks flourished, ships grew in size and captains were kept waiting for high tide, either in the docks or out in the Severn. Furthermore, because the ships were getting bigger, it was becoming more difficult for them to negotiate the sharp bends in the Avon Gorge and they often grounded on the narrow Horseshoe bend. They could also end up grounded when the tide went out; they were usually lost in this situation, breaking their backs, but even if they were in a fit state to be refloated, with assistance, a ship stranded on the mud inevitably caused delays to other shipping. Furthermore, ships were unable to load or unload at Bristol docks when the tide was out and were left grounded on the mud at the dockside until high tide.

In order to alleviate the problem, new docks were constructed a little way down the Avon, at Sea Mills. These failed to find favour with anyone as they were far away from the city with no means of transporting goods onwards. Another dock at Hotwells was equally unsuccessful, for similar reasons.

The tidal problem was solved by the construction of the 'Floating Harbour', which, by means of diverting the Avon through a new channel known (to this day) as the New Cut, and providing locks at each end of the docks, enabled water to be kept in the docks area all the time. Ships would enter and leave via the locks. The idea had originally been put forward in 1767 by one William Champion, a

Bristol's Avon Gorge is a tourist attraction today. If the Victorian idea had been taken seriously, this view would have included an area of commercial docks. The (now-singled) Bristol–Avonmouth railway can be seen.

large portion of its working life going to and from Liverpool docks instead – and Liverpool was one of Bristol's great rivals in the shipping trade. It was not just a lack of space in the city docks; the age-old problem of ships getting stranded in the mud and on the sharp bends in the Avon was ever present. Something needed to be done. Trade was beginning to suffer, with Bristol losing out to other British ports. In 1861 a plan was approved to build a deep-water pier at the mouth of the Avon. The idea was that large vessels could unload part of their cargo and then proceed upstream to the city docks, without the need to wait for the tide.

The plan, promoted by a company named the 'Bristol Port Railway and Pier Co.', also incorporated a railway line to run from Bristol to the area where the new pier would be built. Opened in March 1865, and named the Port Railway and Pier Line, it started at what is now Hotwells on the riverbank, at a spot just underneath the Gloucestershire pier of the yet-to-be-completed Clifton Suspension Bridge. A single line of rails would run for 5 miles 52 chains to the Avon estuary at Avonmouth. The new line thus did not connect with the Port of Bristol nor was there yet a completed pier at Avonmouth for it to use. There were stations at Sea Mills, Shirehampton ('for Pill'), Dock station (Gloucester Road) and the line's terminus, 'Avonmouth Station'. The latter had a run-round loop but was effectively in the middle of nowhere.

Avon Mouth, as the area was then known, had very little to attract people. There was a scattering of small farms and a few cottages, along with an artillery range, but that was about it. There was no specific reason at that stage for people in any numbers to want to travel to Avonmouth. Despite this, another enterprising company came into being and, in April 1865, opened a hotel complete with 'pleasure garden' on land adjacent to the terminus station. According to the records, the proprietor in 1881 was one Annie Woodrow, an Irish woman. Annie employed a Scot, Mary Wilson, as a barmaid and Jane Parsley from Almondsbury in Gloucestershire as a waitress. Sarah Foster from Winterbourne in Gloucestershire fulfilled the role

Quaker industrialist, but the 'powers that be' at the time thought it impracticable so it made no progress.

By the 1840s, ships had grown even more, and the larger, ocean-going 'iron-clad' ships found that they were unable to manoeuvre through the sharp bends. The debacle of the newly built SS *Great Britain* getting jammed in the locks, when an attempt was made to move it from the city docks where it had been built, prompted calls for a new dock. It was more than a little embarrassing when it was found that, once out of Bristol City Docks and along the Avon to the Severn, the ship was unable to return to Bristol City Docks. In fact, it spent a of domestic servant, whilst Henry House from Somerset was the ostler.

It was hardly surprising that the hotel failed to make any money. Passengers were the initial cargo for the new railway line but a day trip to what was a muddy, grassy area at the mouth of the Avon hardly drew in the crowds, even if there was, for the more morbid members of the public, the site of a gibbet pole on the marshy area known as 'Dunball Island', to the north of the estuary. It did not help that the 'Port and Pier' line, as it was popularly known, was not connected to the national railway system and was thus without the prospect of excursion traffic to and from the area.

The Victorians were nothing if not keen to seize on an opportunity however remote from its goal. Not far from the Bristol terminus of the Port and Pier line was another railway – one that was not visible to the public. The Clifton Rocks funicular railway commenced at a station near to Sion Hill, in Clifton, and ran in a tunnel through what was known as St Vincent's Rock down to the lower terminus adjacent to the river and a few hundred yards from the Port and Pier station. Opened in 1873, it was hugely popular for its first year and supplied to the Port and Pier curious passengers wishing to make a day out of travelling 'down' from the heights of Clifton to the Avon estuary. However, two white elephants do not add up to a going concern and, after the novelty of the first year, the Rocks Railway began to lose passengers in droves; by default, so did the Port and Pier. The Rocks Railway was a financial failure and by 1905 was in receivership.

Although the demise of the Rocks Railway was not the main reason for the lack of passengers wishing to travel to Avonmouth, it was perhaps not a surprise that the Bristol Port Railway and Pier Co. was also soon in financial difficulty. The directors recognized that, rather than standing alone, the Port and Pier would need to get connected to the growing national railway network. In 1867, the company applied for and received, by an Act of Parliament, permission to construct a railway from a junction on the Midland Railway's Bristol–Gloucester line near Royate Hill, Bristol. The junction with the Bristol–Gloucester line was, rather inappropriately, named Kingswood junction, although it was located nowhere near the district of Kingswood.

From Kingswood junction the line would run through Eastville to Narroways Hill, where it was to cross the GWR Bristol and South Wales Union line via a bridge, and onwards through Ashley Hill (where it would connect with a short branch from Narroways junction on the Bristol and South Wales Union line).

Continuing onwards through a short tunnel under Ashley Hill, the line passed through the suburb of Montpelier and through Redland to Clifton Down, where it would tunnel under the Durdham Downs to eventually meet the Port and Pier between Hotwells and Sea Mills. The junction was reasonably close to the nearby posh suburb of Sneyd Park, after which it was named.

As the Bristol and Gloucester was built to the broad gauge, so the line to Avonmouth was to be broad gauge. It would also be double-track from Kingswood and Narroways junctions through to the Sneyd Park junction; from there it would be single-track to Avonmouth.

Work commenced and staggered on for two years, after which the contractor failed and construction stopped. Meanwhile, a new dock had been planned by the newly incorporated Bristol Port and Channel Dock Company, at the mouth of the River Avon. To all intents and purposes, this new site for docks was the way forward – it would be easier for the increasingly bigger ships to dock there – yet, in spite of this, another scheme was put forward to build a dam across the River Avon near its estuary with the Severn and create one long floating harbour all the way downstream to the city docks. This somewhat novel idea was another that did not come to fruition. The city docks continued in use for smaller craft, but the focus shifted to building the new dock at Avonmouth.

Seeing a chance to gain control of what could be lucrative future docks traffic, both the Midland Railway and Great Western Railway companies stepped in and took over the work on the new railway. Now standard gauge (4 feet 8 and a half

Bristol City Docks in the 1960s before Avonmouth finally took all the shipping. (Len Worrall)

inches), the Clifton Extension line was completed in 1875 but trains were unable to run because the signalling at Sneyd Park junction did not meet Board of Trade standards when inspected. It was not until 1885 that the line was opened for traffic throughout, from Hotwells and Kingswood junctions to Avonmouth station. The delays were mainly due to the Port and Pier's permanent way being found to be unfit for the extra traffic expected. Eventually, the pier itself was completed and the railway, being laid into the dock area, gained a Pier station.

The line opened for freight traffic on 24 February 1877 and for passenger traffic on 1 September 1885. The new Avonmouth Dock also opened on the same date as the Clifton Extension, in February 1877.

The joint line opened with three new stations: Montpelier, Redland and Clifton Down, in addition to the existing Port Railway and Pier stations at Sea Mills, and the Shirehampton and Avonmouth Dock station. All the new stations were sited to attract passenger and freight traffic from the new Bristol suburbs. Clifton Down in particular was but a short walk from the zoological gardens and

Another 1960s view of Bristol City Docks. (Len Worrall)

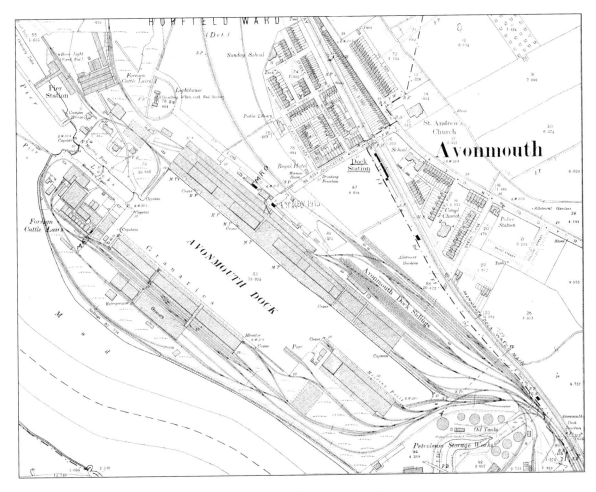

Avonmouth's first dock and pier (1901 OS map). 'Avonmouth Dock Sidings' became Old Yard.

the open spaces of Durdham Downs. Sidings were provided, mainly for coal traffic, at Montpelier and Clifton Down stations. There were signal boxes at Ashley Hill junction, Montpelier, Clifton Down and Sneyd Park junction (where the PR&P joined the Clifton Extension). Signal boxes at Shirehampton, Avonmouth Dock junction and Avonmouth Dock – where a small signal box was built adjacent to the level crossing where the line crossed Gloucester Road on its way to the terminus station – were already in use.

Signal boxes later opened at Horseshoe Point (1904) and Crown Brickyard level crossing (Avonmouth) (1892). The latter controlled a level crossing and also the sidings connection into the small brickworks, from which it got its name.

With the arrival of the MR/GWR Joint Clifton Extension in Avonmouth, the Great Western gained a share of both freight and passenger traffic into the docks from the south. Forward thinking was one of the Great Western's great attributes and it was already planning ahead. The company recognized that the new docks would inevitably expand and attract more traffic than the existing railway could handle, and that the area would also attract other industries. Not content to share access to the new docks with the Midland Railway, GWR was anxious to cash in on the traffic generated by the opening of its Severn Tunnel in 1886. It was clear that there was potential in a new line connecting South Wales to Avonmouth Docks, and GWR set its sights on its own links into the docks area. The question was, which route should it take?

North of the Avonmouth area, at Pilning, there were still the remains of the section of the Bristol and South Wales Union line to New Passage pier on the banks of the River Severn, which had been abandoned after the opening of the Severn Tunnel. The existing stub of the Bristol and South Wales Union line's original formation from a junction with the new line to the Severn Tunnel at Pilning was still in use as a siding, as far as the Severn Tunnel pumping station at Sea Walls. This could be extended to Avonmouth. The plan was therefore to use this formation for the new line and continue southwards, hugging the coastline.

To this end, the Great Western sought permission via an Act of Parliament to build a line direct from Avonmouth to New Passage, on the banks of the Severn, where it would connect with the existing section of the old route. The resulting GWR Act of 1890 authorized the company to construct the line between the junction with the BSWU line at Pilning and a junction with the Clifton Extension sidings at the Bristol end of Avonmouth. Known as the Avonmouth and Severn Tunnel Railway, it was single throughout.

It was to be a comparatively easy route, being more or less level all the way, and would run from Pilning straight towards the coast before turning 90 degrees south to Sea Walls, where the siding remained. The new route was to curve inland again before straightening and passing through the village of Severn Beach. From Severn Beach, it would run along the coast as far as Hallen Marsh, where, as the coast curved outwards, the railway would stay more or less straight for almost a mile before moving coast-wards to pass a matter of yards to the west of the Port and Pier terminus station at Avonmouth. It would then cross Gloucester Road on the level a hundred yards or so away from the Port and Pier Avonmouth Dock station crossing. The line was to be freight only.

The line was opened on 5 February 1900. There was no connection or interchange between the two lines, except through the dock sidings, until 1902, when a temporary connection was laid between them, south of the Port and Pier's terminus station.

The new century saw a continued rapid expansion of the facilities at Avonmouth. In 1897, it had featured so low down in importance on the list of places in the local *Street Directory* that it had been doubled up with nearby Shirehampton. All this was soon to change, however. The newly opened docks were attracting business at breakneck speed and new housing was springing up around the waterside. The need for further docks expansion soon became evident and by 1900 the docks committee had recommended to the council the building of an extension at the mouth of the Avon. A new dock would be built to the north of the existing dock, involving the requisition of the land upon which the GWR Pilning line ran and where the Avonmouth terminus station of the BPR&P stood. As the construction work commenced, a temporary connection would be laid, to enable traffic from the Pilning line to continue to run into the sidings at Avonmouth. Meanwhile, the GWR line from Pilning would be diverted from that company's Gloucester Road crossing to a new course further inland, rejoining its existing formation near what would later become Holesmouth junction.

Work on the new dock started in 1902, with the first sod being cut by the Prince of Wales. As work on the new dock progressed so the temporary connection between the two lines was closed and lifted by 1903. The Port and Pier line's terminus station was closed and demolished, the line being severed a few chains north of Avonmouth Dock station; its old formation beyond there was crossed by the Pilning line's new course inland. In effect, Dock station now became a terminus, with a headshunt running northwards over the level crossing.

As work on the new dock proceeded and the existing docks continued to attract trade, so the railway traffic became heavier. Avonmouth Dock station expanded. A new signal box was built at the

The first Avonmouth station and the hotel (1901 OS map).

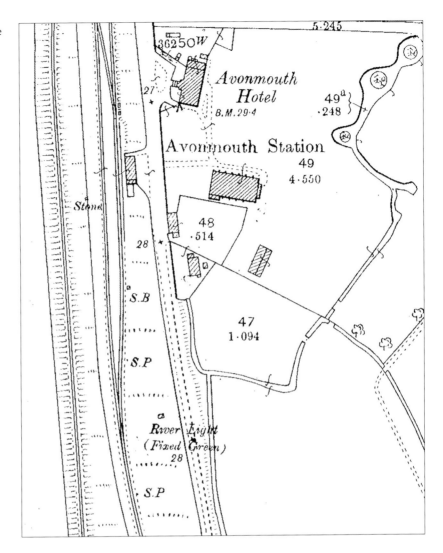

Bristol end of the platform and opened on 17 May 1903; the old one at the level crossing was closed, being replaced by a ground frame. The Down platform (then the only platform) was signalled for trains to both arrive and depart from here. In December 1904, a run-round loop was laid in and the platform extended to allow a bay line to be laid. This became an additional platform, known as the 'back platform'. A small loco shed was built and opened in January 1905, along with a turntable. A further storage siding was laid next to the bay line in July 1905. Down Midland passenger trains now terminated here, engines being able to run round and turn on the turntable before rejoining their train and restarting from the same platform. All this new work required new signalling and the signal box was equipped with a new lever frame in December 1904 to handle the extra burden.

Rail traffic increased further still and the single line between Sneyd Park junction and Dock station was doubled in 1906, coming into use on 6 January 1907. Such was the continued modification that Dock Station signal box was fitted with another new, longer lever frame for the opening of the double track. At the same time, the station was described as the 'GW and Midland Joint station'. A bay platform and run-round siding were provided on the down or arrival side of the main platform. Trains could arrive and depart back to Bristol from Avonmouth Dock, the loco shed which had opened in 1905 being equipped with a turntable.

The sidings at the southern end of the facility had already expanded and more was to come. Perhaps in anticipation of this, Avonmouth Dock Junction signal box had been replaced, in August 1903, by a new box a few chains nearer to Avonmouth. By 1907, the area of land between Dock station and the docks themselves was filled by a marshalling yard, the entrance to which was controlled by Dock Junction signal box. The marshalling yards at Dock junction comprised a group of six sidings owned by the Midland Railway Company between the dockside 'M' shed (which had its own three sidings adjacent to the shed) and a further four exchange sidings used by the GWR. There was then a further group of six sidings, again operated by the MR Co.

Avonmouth Dock junction was the junction for not only the docks sidings but also the Avonmouth Light Railway. This left its junction with the 'Down' main line and turned inland, passing through several exchange sidings before crossing Port View road and turning north, serving the new Kingsweston industrial estate. Originally, this freight-only light railway had been intended to run all the way along the inland side of St Andrews Road and rejoin the GW line near Holesmouth, but this extension never happened and the line terminated after about a mile. It was eventually taken over by the LMSR and GWR in 1927 and closed by 1938, latterly being shortened to a small section at the Port View road end, which served as a coal yard and was shunted by horses.

At the north end of the yard, connections ran into the docks complex from most of these sidings, before the line again became single and, joining with the GWR, continued over Gloucester Road crossing on its way to Pilning.

When completed, the new facility was the most up-to-date dock in the Avonmouth complex – all the sheds and warehouses were connected to the dock's internal railway system and the pier railway station was able to deal with both ocean passengers and mail. It was declared open by HRH Prince Edward, Prince of Wales, in a ceremony on 9 July 1908, and named the 'Royal Edward Dock'.

Avonmouth was now firmly established as a major port. As housing and industry sprang up around the docks area, further expansion of the railway facilities became vital and, as the docks internal railway system expanded, so Bristol Corporation Docks committee laid extra lines between the Crown Brickyard level crossing at the Shirehampton end of the older dock, to Gloucester Road. The signal box at Crown Brickyard, which had been replaced in 1906 by a new, MR-style box and downgraded to a crossing box, was now given a new lever frame and upgraded again to a Block Post. A rather complex junction was laid in and two new tracks laid from here, through the marshalling yard to Gloucester Road. These lines, known as the 'Joint Goods' lines, opened in September 1911; Crown Brickyard level-crossing box, which controlled the new junction, was renamed as Avonmouth Dock junction.

At the old Avonmouth Dock junction, the signal box, which had been replaced in 1903 by an MR-style box, was again replaced, this time by a larger MR box. New 'ladder' connections were laid in between the Joint Goods lines and new exchange sidings. The box was renamed 'Avonmouth Dock Sidings'. The sidings here served timber sheds, fuel storage tanks and warehouses.

Round at Gloucester Road, the signal box was given a new lever frame in connection with the doubling of the GWR line as far as Holesmouth, and with the opening of a new, single-platform GW station on the north side of Gloucester Road crossing. This platform was known as 'Avonmouth Dock' and opened in May 1910.

The Joint Goods lines were extended to Holesmouth junction; owned by the Bristol Corporation, these became known as the 'Corporation' lines. They opened between the new Avonmouth Dock junction and Holesmouth junction in June 1911, necessitating a new junction between the GW lines and the Corporation lines at Gloucester Road. The level crossing here had been controlled by a small signal box, which was removed, as the land on which it stood was required for the formation of the new goods lines. A new box opened on 9 May 1910 but, with the continued expansion of railway facilities in Avonmouth, there was soon a need to replace this with a larger box on a site to the river side of the new junction. This third Gloucester Road box opened just a year after the establishment of the second one.

From here, the four lines, two GW and two Corporation, turned through almost 90 degrees and headed inland. The line beyond the Joint Dock station had existed as a headshunt beyond the level crossing since 1903. It was not until 9 May 1910 that the short connection was made as a single line to join the GW at a new junction near the dock access road known as King Road, enabling the through running of Midland freight trains. The crossing ground frame at Dock station was opened at the same time. Initially freight only, this short section was doubled in August 1910. To the north of the Dock stations, the four tracks from Gloucester Road (GW/MR joint and Corporation) came together with the lines from Dock station, where there was a new double junction. Continuing as four lines, they passed over King Road, where a new level crossing was installed and a signal box known as 'St Andrews Road Junction' was constructed. Here, a further double junction between the main and Corporation lines permitted traffic to cross from Up and Down GW lines and Up and Down Corporation lines.

Half a mile further north towards Holesmouth, the GW and Corporation lines ran slightly inland from the Royal Edward Dock, where there were connections with the main GW lines. These were controlled from a Great Western-style signal box that also controlled connections to a small depot – the 'Avonmouth Town Goods Depot' – on the Down side between there and St Andrews junction. The signal box was named 'Avonmouth Goods Yard Signal Box', but was thereafter known by all as 'Town Goods'.

A junction on the Corporation lines at Goods Yard led to a group of half a dozen marshalling and exchange sidings for the Midland Railway. Whilst the Corporation lines now turned westwards, the GW lines continued straight on. A junction in the GW lines followed the Corporation lines and led into further sidings, where exchange of wagons took place between Port of Bristol and the Great Western. These sidings, known collectively as the Royal Edward Yard, were opened in 1911. In addition to the six Midland Railway marshalling and exchange sidings, there were twenty-three operated by the Port, and further sidings operated by the GWR.

The main GW lines carried straight on towards Holesmouth and, in 1917, St Andrews Road station was opened between the Royal Edward Yard and the main line.

At Holesmouth junction, all the docks and Corporation lines came together in a junction with the remains of the original GW line, which now served the huge complex of docks lines around the Royal Edward Dock itself. This junction was another odd one, with a shunting spur running through it. This spur was the scene of several collisions over the years, until eventually the layout was altered to be more conventional. After the junction the line, now double, then joined the main GW line. A short distance north of Holesmouth junction the line became single and then proceeded on its way to Pilning as a goods-only line.

CHAPTER 2

Avonmouth via Pilning

The GWR Avonmouth and Severn Tunnel branch to Avonmouth started at Pilning junction, on the main line to South Wales, at the point where a facing crossover in the main lines led to a connection in the Up main line. From the Up main there was a connection leading to a single line, which descended sharply westwards at a gradient of 1 in 100, crossing the lane known as Pilning Street by means of a level crossing. The signal box here was officially named Pilning Branch Signal Box, but always known as 'Low Level' to railwaymen. Up until 1928, the single line between the junction and branch boxes, being goods only, had been worked by means of a wooden train staff, but on Friday 22 June 1928, the branch became open for passenger trains as well. This working was withdrawn and superseded, with the single line henceforth being worked by special 'disc' Lock and Block instruments and the line being track-circuited. Beyond the branch signal box was a small, one-platform halt, officially known as 'Pilning Low Level', along with three loops. At the far end of these loops stood

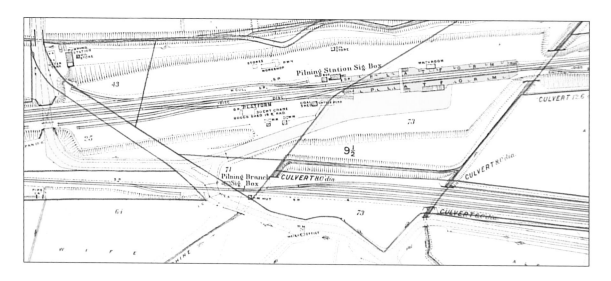

Plan of Pilning Branch signal box and platform, showing its relation to Pilning High Level (main-line) station. (Wiltshire History Centre)

GREAT WESTERN RAILWAY CIRCULAR 4077, PADDINGTON STATION, 21 MAY 1924

OPENING OF NEW STATION AT SEVERN BEACH

On Monday May 26th 1924, a new station will be opened on the Pilning and Avonmouth Branch at SEVERN BEACH, in place of Severn Beach Platform.

Accommodation will be provided for passengers, parcels, coal and other minerals and general merchandise traffic.

The distances from adjacent stations to Severn Beach are:

From	Miles	Chains
Avonmouth Dock Passenger Station	4	42
Avonmouth Town Goods Station	3	77
Pilning Low Level	2	20

Passengers, parcels and miscellaneous traffic by passenger train will be conveyed to and from Severn Beach via Avonmouth Dock only. Coal, other minerals and general merchandise will be conveyed via Pilning Low Level or Avonmouth. There will be no Goods shed, carriage shoot, crane, weigh-bridge or accommodation for livestock at present.

The company will not undertake Cartage to or from the station.

To ascertain the distance to Severn Beach for raising charges on passenger train traffic on a mileage basis, 4 and ½ miles must be added to the distance from your station to Avonmouth Dock Passenger Station.

Traffic from your station to Severn Beach must be treated as 'Local' and abstracted accordingly. Application for Passenger Fares and Rates for traffic by passenger train, must be made to your Divisional Superintendent, and for Goods Rates to your District Goods Manager.

R.H. Nicholls Superintendent of the Line
E. Ford Chief Goods Manager

---

a ground frame, released by means of a key from the signal box.

A Description of the Line

The train slows down as it approaches the large Hallen Marsh signal box where the driver collects the single-line token – the train's authority to be on the single line – from the post on which it has been placed, in a carrier hoop, by the signalman. Sometimes the signalman has not had time to place the hoop on the post and appears from the bottom door holding the token up for the driver. The driver snatches the token and, after checking that it is the correct one, hangs it on a hook in his cab. This done, the train steams off over the junction and on to the single line.

Once the junction is left behind, the line runs northwards, with the coast on the left and marshy ground on the right. On the right and slightly lower than the line is the site of the shell-filling munitions

Pilning Branch signal box. (Wilf Stanley)

factory. Some low-level buildings still remain. In spite of the Severn being a tidal river, the scenery is quite pleasant. The Welsh coast can be seen on a clear day and ships steam up and down the river to and from Sharpness Docks. If you are lucky, you can catch a glimpse of the Severn rail bridge way in the distance.

Soon, the Severn Beach 'Fixed at Caution' Distant signal is seen and the driver begins applying the brakes. Approaching the wooden signal box and sidings, the driver leans from his cab to hang the token on the post there and snatch the new one for the section 'Severn Beach–Pilning Low Level' as the train passes the signal box and runs into the long platform at Severn Beach. The train stops in the platform for a few minutes. There is no passing loop at Severn Beach; trains needing to be 'put away' for another train to pass are signalled into the bay platform, backing out again when they are ready to leave and the line is clear.

The level crossing, known as Ableton Lane crossing, is operated from a ground frame in a small cabin as it is too far away from the signal box. Once the crossing gates are closed to road traffic by a porter, the signals are cleared and the train can move off once again. Passing over Ableton Lane crossing, with its adjacent crossing keeper's cottage, the line now swings to the right in a long curve.

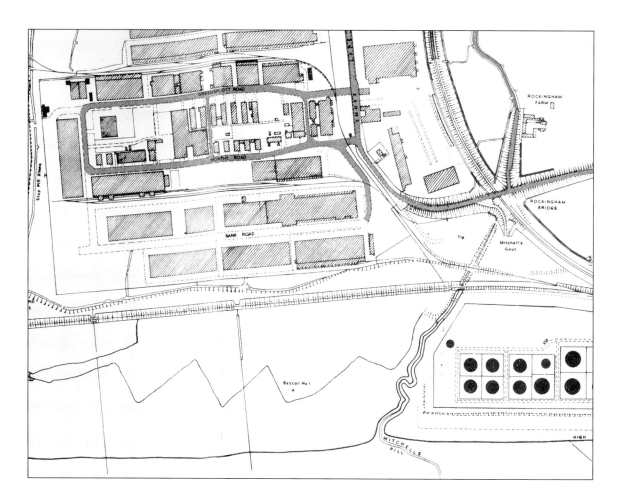

1974 plan of Chittening Trading Estate (site of the 1914 munitions depot) and Rockingham bridge. Top right on the line to Filton, Chittening platform is just seen.

About a quarter of a mile later the train passes over another level crossing, which takes a small lane over the railway. This is Green Lane crossing and it also has a crossing keeper's cottage next to the line. Soon after Green Lane crossing the line passes over the Severn Tunnel, but it is not possible to see the tunnel lines, even though the approach cutting to the tunnel is a matter of yards away from the line.

Just after crossing the tunnel and still on a long curve, we pass a siding on the left. It has a ground frame. A short siding leads towards the coast and a brick building. This is Sea Walls Pump House siding, which serves the English shore pumps that keep the water out of the Severn Tunnel; without these, and the Welsh side pumps at Sudbrook, the tunnel would soon flood. The pumps are still steam operated and a trip is made with a loco, coal wagons and brake van from Pilning to keep the pumps supplied with coal.

Still on a curve, the train arrives at New Passage halt. Nobody gets on or off, so the train moves onwards and shortly afterwards the line straightens and we slow down to stop at Cross Hands halt. No larger than New Passage, it serves the local community of Redwick, with the Cross Hands Inn close by.

Leaving Cross Hands, the line runs alongside a narrow country road and, approaching Pilning Low Level, an embankment can be seen on the right and soon a station. This is Pilning station, better known as 'High Level'. At Low Level there are three sidings, the points at the Severn Beach end being worked by a ground frame. Low Level has a small wooden platform and the brick signal box stands guard over yet another level crossing.

Here we will leave the branch line and resume the journey again at Hallen Marsh junction.

The Stations

St Andrews Road

St Andrews Road platform was initially opened as a workmen's platform on 1 March 1917. It closed in November 1922, but reopened again two years later, on 30 June 1924. The station buildings consisted of wooden shelters equipped with wooden, deep-valanced canopies. The station master at Avonmouth Dock station supervised St Andrews Road. Charlie Maycock and Bert Davis were porters here in the 1950s, before Maycock moved to Dock station as the 'ticket snapper'.

Severn Beach

The GWR Avonmouth and Severn Tunnel single line was originally freight only. What became 'Severn Beach' did not exist beyond a farm and a few isolated houses until the opening of the railway in 1900, which encouraged a certain level of development. Following the decision to develop the village of Severn Beach as a recreational resort, the GWR opened a platform here in June 1922. It was in use only during the summer season, with a seasonal train service for excursions being provided. In April 1924 a new signal box was opened, and from 26 May in the same year a passenger service was provided all year as far as the platform, with the line onwards to Pilning Low Level remaining as goods use only. In the mid-1920s the popularity of Severn Beach as a resort for the working-class people of east Bristol grew, with crowds flocking by train to the resident funfair. A new GWR station at Severn Beach opened in May 1924, consisting of a long platform to take the longest excursion trains and a new station building. This handsome building was unusual in that it was not on the platform but at right-angles to it, facing a track which was to become Station Road. There was a canopy provided on the front of the building; this canopy was of 'train-shed' proportions and covered the station concourse.

The odd thing about Severn Beach was that there was no beach there at all, just a shingle area on the coast. The cluster of dwellings is indeed on the banks of the River Severn, so that part of the name is correct, but many an unwary traveller has been caught out, hoping to find golden sands at the end of the line. After the Second World War, with the development of the nearby Severnside industrial area, the name 'Severn Beach' became even more of a joke. The nearby ICI chemical plant and Philblack's carbon black factory put this 'beach' into quite a different category from other holiday resorts. Railway staff would see hopeful holiday-makers arriving with their suitcases, then jumping straight back on one of the next trains out of there once they had seen what the place was really like.

The station master in the 1950s was Mr J.W. Hankey. He was a successor to a Mr Pew, who was remembered as a quiet, modest man. Mr Pew moved to Witham, Somerset, on the GWR West of England main line, where, after seeing a train off one day, he sat down in his chair and passed away. Mike (Hank) Michel was one porter here; his wife was the crossing keeper at Green Lane, where they lived in the keeper's house. Colin Hopes was a relief porter and Tom Neall was a regular porter.

Cross Hands halt in 1960. (Wilf Stanley)

New Passage and Cross Hands Halts

With the upgrading to passenger status of the Pilning Low Level to Severn Beach line, two new single-platform halts were provided for local inhab-itants, at New Passage and Cross Hands. The former got its name from the old jetty and hotel on the coast near by and the latter from a local inn. Both halts opened on 9 July 1928. The facilities covered just the 'bare necessities', consisting of a metal building similar to the corrugated metal lamp huts provided at signal boxes on the GWR, which served as shel-ters. New Passage halt came under the supervision of the Severn Beach station master, whilst Cross Hands was supervised from Pilning. No staff were employed at either halt; tickets were issued by 'agents' who lived close by.

Pilning Branch (Low Level) platform in 1960. (Wilf Stanley)

Pilning (Low Level)

The original platform at Pilning opened with the Broad Gauge Bristol and South Wales Union line to the coastal ferry at New Passage on the banks of the River Severn. When the line closed, in December 1886, with the advent of the Severn Railway tunnel opening for passenger traffic, so did Pilning Platform. The Avonmouth and Severn Tunnel Railway single line from Pilning to Avonmouth opened in 1900 as a goods-only line, so there was no station required, but when the line was upgraded to passenger status in July 1928 a new platform was provided on the site of the old one. The new platform, with a small wooden shelter, was named Pilning Low Level and opened on 9 July 1928. There was a female porter at Low Level in the 1940s.

The duties of supervising Pilning Low Level fell to the station master of Pilning station.

CHAPTER 3

Avonmouth via Henbury

With the advent in May 1903 of the new direct line from Wootton Bassett to a new junction with the BSWUR at Patchway, and a further new junction at Filton, the GWR finally put an end to the delays inevitably caused to trains to and from Avonmouth using the bottleneck at Pilning Low Level. The company constructed a new line to Avonmouth from the junctions at Stoke Gifford and Filton. From both Stoke Gifford and Filton junction, the new line was double track to a further new junction known as Filton West. Just a short distance towards Avonmouth the line became single. This new line was opened as a single line from Filton West to Holesmouth in 1910. These new junctions allowed direct through running from the new Badminton line to Avonmouth, whilst the new junction at Filton junction enabled GWR traffic to run to and from Bristol without using the Clifton Extension. The odd thing about this new work that there was no direct connection to enable traffic to run to and from the South Wales direction, to Avonmouth, until 1971.

Running from Filton, the new line passed through a short, 302-yard tunnel near the small village of Charlton (which was destroyed in the 1940s when Filton airfield was expanded for the development of the giant Brabazon prototype airliner) and the village of Henbury, before descending on an embankment across the flat, marshy ground towards Avonmouth. Arriving at Avonmouth, the single line ran parallel with the line from Pilning for a short distance before making a junction with it at Holesmouth.

The signal box at Holesmouth, originally opened in 1903 and closed in 1908, opened again in May 1910, controlling the junction between the new GW line from Filton and the existing GW line from Pilning.

The First World War brought extra traffic to Avonmouth and this in turn led to further expansion of the railway network at Avonmouth.

A Description of the Line

This time we leave Hallen Marsh on the double line to Henbury and Filton. The line climbs away from Hallen on a long right-hand curve before straightening and heading out across the moor on an embankment towards the distant hills. The line approaches a bridge and it is here, just before the embankment ends, that a signal box and fuel depot will be built in 1940 almost at the same place as the short-lived Hallen signal box, which opened and closed with the munitions factory in 1917. As we pass under Ison Hill bridge, we run into a cutting from which we emerge, pass under a road bridge and run into Henbury station. This is a pleasant, typical GWR country station with a couple of sidings.

Leaving Henbury, the line is still climbing gently and passes under another road bridge. Half a mile further on, the line runs into a cutting again and a tunnel looms ahead. Just before the tunnel was Charlton halt, which served the nearby small, scattered village of Charlton for five years, before its closure. It. Now we pass into Charlton tunnel – 302 yards of darkness – before emerging into a shallow cutting.

The line is not in the cutting for long and now runs between the grassy runway of Filton Airfield on the left, where a few biplanes stand, and a golf course on the right. The line has been dead straight for two and a quarter miles now and passes the site of Filton halt, then goes under the main Bristol to Gloucester road, before arriving at Filton West junction. Here we have the choice of going straight on to Stoke Gifford and the Badminton line, or sharp right to Filton junction and Bristol.

Trains from Avonmouth to the Midlands will go up to Stoke Gifford and take the Badminton line as far as Westerleigh West junction. There, they will turn off to the left and descend to Yate South, where they will gain LMSR metals.

The Stations

A short platform was constructed to the west of Filton West junction to create Filton halt, which was opened in May 1910. At the west end of Charlton tunnel a similar platform was built for Charlton Halt, and opened on the same date. Both halts closed in March 1915. Facilities at both were sparse, consisting in each case of a metal GWR pagoda-style shelter.

North Filton Platform

After the closure of the halt at Filton, a new 'station' was opened on the same site adjacent to the main A38 Gloucester Road, on 12 July 1928. This was important for workers using the nearby Bristol Aeroplane Company's factory and airfield. Two long platforms were built but there were no station buildings other than a solid brick structure, which resembled an air-raid shelter. The duties of station master here were covered from Filton junction. In 1958, this role was fulfilled by Mr T.L. Powell, who also covered Horfield station. Reg Watts was a porter there in the 1950s.

Henbury

Henbury station opened on 9 May 1910 as a single platform against the single line. Wartime exigencies saw the station temporarily closed in March 1915 but the advent of the munitions factory developments in 1917 led to the doubling of the line between Filton West and Hallen Marsh. During the time the station was closed, it was used for unadvertised workmen's trains. When Henbury reopened, in July 1922, it was as a double-track, two-platform station. On the Down side was a brick station building served by an approach road. The building contained the ticket office and waiting room. A brick-built waiting room stood on the Up platform and a solid brick signal box of typical GWR design stood at the Filton end of the Up platform. There were sidings on the Down side which served a coal yard.

According to the archives, a young lad from New Zealand got a porter's job at Henbury in the early 1960s. He told the signalman one day that he was fed up with the UK and wanted to return to his home country, but feared he would never have the means to do it, as the porter's pay was poor.

'What'll you do, then?' asked the signalman.

'I'm planning to get a job over there,' said the lad, waving a hand at the coal yard of Rudrum and Co. 'The pay is much better.'

Sure enough, a couple of weeks later, the lad resigned and started work in the coal yard, shovelling house coal into sacks for delivery. He and the signalman met again a month or two later. The heavy snows of winter 1962 to 1963 lay all around. 'How's the new job going?' enquired the signalman.

The lad admitted that it was not going at all well. The snow, ice and freezing temperatures meant that the coal was frozen and had to be broken up with a pickaxe before it could be shovelled into the sacks, which were also frozen.

'It's far harder than I bargained for,' admitted the lad, 'and because of the weather, we aren't working that many hours.' History does not relate whether the lad ever managed to return to New Zealand.

Mr L.H. Mogridge was station master here in the 1950s. He wrote in Gothic script and staff joked that it would take him 5 minutes to write his name! Frank Hughes was Grade 2 porter, as were Derek Eggleton and Ken Farmiloe. A Grade 2 porter earned £4 12 shillings and 6 pence per week before stoppages, and £4-7-7 after stoppages (around £4.62 before and £4.37 after). Albert Herbert was ganger here in the 1950s with Jim Steer as his sub-ganger. J.L. Steer was promoted to sub-ganger at Henbury in May 1957.

Chittening Platform

These long platforms were built in connection with the munitions factory development in 1917, and used for unadvertised workers' trains for the factory and the smelting works. Chittening closed in 1923 but reopened for unadvertised workers' trains again in October 1941, then to workmen only on 25 August 1947 and to ordinary passengers in May 1948. Platform accommodation on each side was a long corrugated iron 'fence' with a corrugated iron canopy. There were no goods facilities here. The platforms closed on 23 November 1964.

An unidentified class 46 hauls a mixed freight up from Avonmouth and approaches the site of Henbury station. 1982. (Author's collection).

CHAPTER 4

Avonmouth via Clifton

A Description of the Line

Leaving Kingswood junction, the line turned sharply away from the Midland main line and crossed the Coombe Brook valley and Royate Hill by means of a long, seven-arch viaduct, passing close to the expansive Victorian Greenbank cemetery. It then ran on embankment through the expanding suburb of Easton, parallel with the back gardens of Gloucester Street before crossing Fishponds Road by means of an iron bridge. After Fishponds Road, the line ran on embankment again for a short distance before entering on to another lofty viaduct known locally as 'Thirteen Arches'. After leaving Thirteen Arches viaduct and still on high embankment, the first Block Post was reached; this was Stapleton Road Gas Sidings signal box, opened in 1895. Both the Midland and Great Western railway companies had access to the large gasworks at Eastville, which opened in 1878 as the 'Bristol United Gas Light Company', and consumed huge quantities of coal.

Stapleton Road Gas Sidings box, which stood on the top of the embankment, was a small Midland Railway box, similar in size and looks to the one at Warmley on the Mangotsfield to Bath line (which has now been preserved). It was equipped with a twelve-lever MR frame and was provided with a Block switch. Access to the box was via a set of steps that led up the bank from a field, which in turn

was crossed by a footpath from the little track then known as 'Wee Lane'; nowadays, it is the busy commuter route of Glenfrome Road. There were several sidings on the south Down side of the lines and a connection into the gasworks.

Leaving the gasworks sidings behind, the Clifton Extension continued its progress on embankment and passed over Wee Lane (Glenfrome Road) by means of a skewed brick arch. Then the line ran behind Narroways Road and shortly after entered a deep cutting. Just before the cutting, on the south side of the line, stood the Midland Brick Works. Although served by its own little internal tramway, the brickworks does not seem to have ever had a rail connection to either the Clifton Extension or the gasworks sidings. This was Narroways Hill and the hill was also bisected by the GWR Bristol and South Wales Union line on its way up the incline to Filton and South Wales. Emerging from the cutting, the Clifton Extension crossed the GWR line by means of an iron bridge. The bridge was replaced by another steel bridge when the GWR lines were quadrupled in 1933. After crossing the GWR, the Clifton Extension entered another deep cutting which shallowed after a quarter of a mile further on and met with the GWR branch from Narroways Hill junction. This short section was the Great Western's own part of the Clifton Extension. The junction of these lines, the Clifton

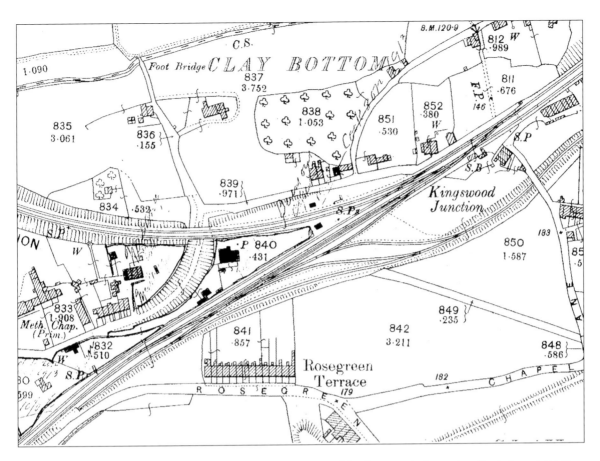

Map of Kingswood Junction (1901 OS). The lines curving up to the left are the Clifton Extension; the line curving off to the lower right is the branch to Deep Pit and the Atlas Locomotive Works of the Peckett company.

Extension and the GWR was named Ashley Hill junction.

Maximum permitted speed through the junction was 20mph.

Directly after passing Ashley Hill junction, the line entered a further deep cutting, which, after just over 200 yards, ran into the 288-yard long Montpelier tunnel. This tunnel curved to the right and emerged straight into Montpelier station. The station was built on a curve. Leaving Montpelier station, the line crossed Cheltenham Road by means of a viaduct, which partly consisted of a wrought-iron span bridge. Continuing on its way on the embankment high above the streets (useful

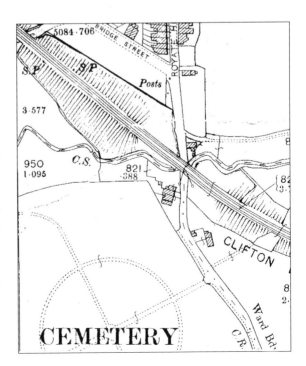

Map (1901 OS) of Royate Hill viaduct.

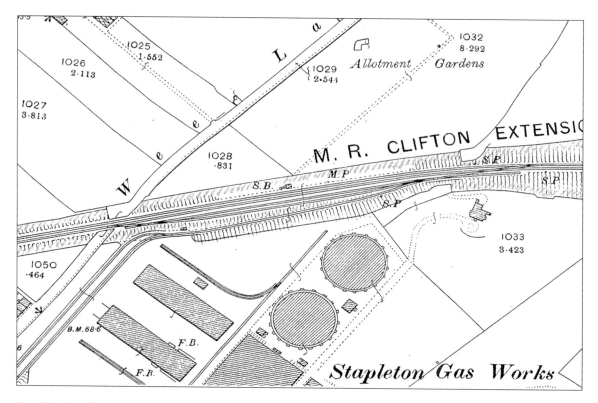

Plan of Stapleton Road gas sidings and Stapleton gasworks in 1901. (1901 OS map)

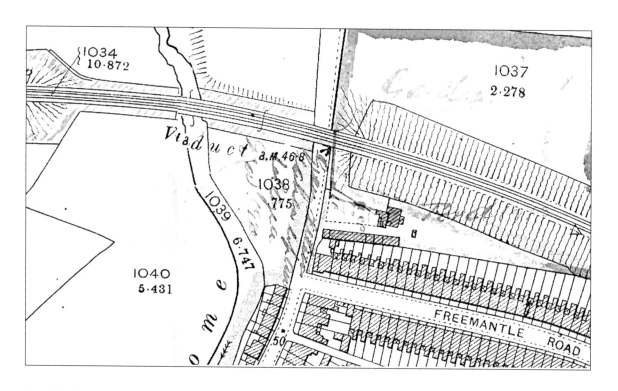

Plan of the Thirteen Arches viaduct crossing the River Frome. (Midland Railway Co. 1901 OS map)

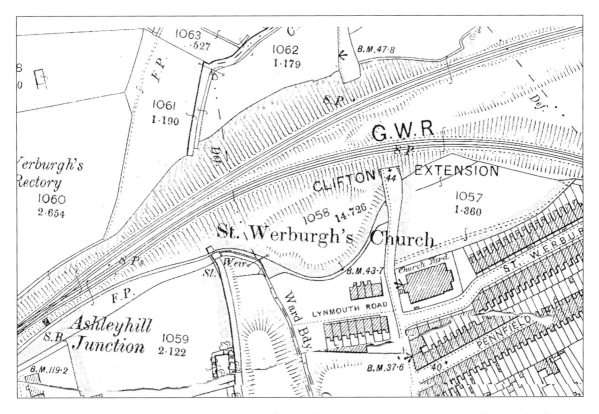

Plan of Ashley Hill junction, showing the Midland line coming in from top right and the GWR line from Narroways Hill approaching from lower right. (Midland Railway 1901 OS map)

for train crews to 'observe' the population), the line entered a gentle curve to the left and crossed Redland Road by means of a plain skew girder bridge, before entering Redland station.

Redland was then a very posh area to live in. Its streets were lined with large detached and semi-detached villas, in which lived a variety of gentry and ladies, mostly of private means, along with a smattering of reverends and retired military officers. The provision of tennis courts allowed those who enjoyed a life of ease to perfect their game on summer days.

The line passed from the small Redland station through more upper-middle-class Victorian suburbs, then ran dead straight through a deep stone-lined cutting, with the backs of the tall houses towering above the railway. Still in cutting, the line passed under Hampton Road and Hampton Park

before approaching Clifton Down station through cuttings. Again, it passed between tall Victorian houses, giving the impression of a somewhat suburban setting rather than a West Country town. The line then curved gently to the right, passing under Whiteladies Road and entering Clifton Down station.

This station was also built on a curve and the looming mouth of Clifton Down tunnel could (and still can) be seen from the overbridge at the far end of the platforms. The sidings and extensive coal yard stood on the 'town' side of the station.

Plunging into the tunnel, which took the line beneath Durdham Downs, the gradient steepened to 1 in 64. Overloaded Up MR freight trains frequently stalled in the tunnel, especially if they had one of the ubiquitous if underpowered 4F locos at their head. The loco, having wheezed and struggled

Clifton Down station, signal box and coal yard, after the closure and lifting of the sidings. (Author's collection)

Clifton Down tunnel ventilation shaft.

they would apply individual wagon brakes sufficient to hold the train, then uncouple the first portion of the train and bring this first portion up into the station where it would be shunted into the Down sidings. The loco would then return for the second portion, which would be brought up to the station and shunted into the sidings, where it would be coupled to the rest of the train. The journey could then continue.

Goods trains in those days were loose-coupled – in other words, the brake operated only on the locomotive – so on more than one occasion, the second portion did not have enough wagon brakes pinned down. The danger was that the action of the loco buffering up hard to it would overcome the wagon brakes and the guard's van brake and set it running away 'wrong line' back down the bank, to inevitable destructive derailment on catch points at Sneyd Park.

Much has been written about the Clifton Extension, particularly in respect of the famous 'clapper' in the tunnel. This was an old loco buffer suspended in a pit, which was struck by a 'hammer' when a treadle was triggered by the passing of an Up train. Its function was to remind train crews of their whereabouts in the smokey darkness of the tunnel. It also warned drivers to be prepared to emerge from the tunnel and look out for the position of Up signal 15, awkwardly positioned on the same bracket as the Down starting and shunt ahead signals.

its way up the bank from Sea Mills, would often have to stop here through lack of steam. The procedure in such cases was that, once the train crew had communicated with the Clifton Down signalman,

LMSR notice warning trainmen about the tunnel 'clapper'.

CLIFTON DOWN TUNNEL.

A clapper is fixed in the Up Line in Clifton Down Tunnel about 100 yards from the Clifton Down Station end to indicate to drivers of Up trains that they are approaching the end of the tunnel.

The clapper was not the only thing that sounded a warning at Clifton; the clock on the church opposite the station would chime hourly throughout the night, making it difficult for signalmen at Clifton Down box to catch a little nap during a lull in traffic.

Emerging from the Avonmouth end of the tunnel mouth, passengers were treated to a magnificent vista of the Avon Gorge – probably best seen when the tide was in, as the scene at low tide is an expanse of brown mud with a trickle of grimy water in the middle. On the opposite bank of the Avon, the Bristol to Portishead branch of the GWR could be seen.

After descending the 1 in 64 slope, the line almost immediately passed under a stone-built three-arch bridge and shortly after that approached Sneyd Park junction with its MR-style signal box. Here, the Clifton line had the straight approach whilst the Port and Pier line snaked in to the junction with it. In the early days, the Port and Pier line could be seen running between the Clifton Extension tracks and the river. After its closure, in 1924, the main road to Avonmouth – the Portway – was built on the Port and Pier's formation.

Shortly after passing Sneyd Park Junction box, following the river for a short distance, the Clifton line curved slightly inland. The line then took a curve to the right and ran into Sea Mills station. Leaving Sea Mills, the line crossed the River Trym inlet and a tidal basin where the Romans had a wharf, by means of a viaduct 88 yards long. The river here curves sharply round Horseshoe Point and the railway followed it, but, as the river bends sharper still, the line straightened and moved inland a little, where, after a short stretch of straight track, it entered Shirehampton station. On the right-hand side here was a goods yard with a coal merchant's. An MR-style signal box stood on the Down platform. The platforms were linked by an open lattice-style footbridge of the type seen at many MR stations, although the station buildings had a distinct GWR look about them.

After leaving 'Shire', as it was locally known, the line continued to curve inland before a tall, upper quadrant signal heralded the approach to Avonmouth Dock junction. Here, there was a gated level crossing guarded by an MR-style signal box. There was a junction too, where the goods lines branched off the main lines and ran parallel for a quarter of a mile or so before becoming lost in the mass of docks sidings now visible on the river side of the tracks. On the town side was the branch that

Shirehampton station footbridge in 1962. (Wilf Stanley)

Upper quadrant signal at Avonmouth Dock junction. This one lasted until the 1980s.

disappeared off through the houses as the Light Railway headed off to the industrial area.

Back on the river side there were oil storage tanks and an increasing number of warehouses and sheds. A tall MR signal box faced the sidings, then, as the line approached Avonmouth Dock station, both MR and GWR locos in company with Port of Bristol locos were to be seen at work in the Old Yard.

Avonmouth Dock station had two platforms and a bay line together with a turntable and a small, run-down wooden engine shed. At the end of the station was another gated level crossing, one of several in the docks area. It was controlled by a ground frame housed in a wooden cabin just off the end of the Down platform. At Dock station the direction of lines changed: what was the Down line from Bristol now became the Up line and the Down Line from Pilning became the Up line to Bristol.

After passing over this crossing, the line turned very sharply inland. Here the line used to run straight on, but the sharp curve is a legacy from the time when the land over which it ran was acquired to build the Royal Edward Dock. On the right a row of dockers' houses – Richmond Terrace – follows the line, which continued to curve as it approached St Andrews junction and another gated level crossing.

Had we followed the goods lines from Dock junction, we would have passed through Old Yard,

1974 plan of Avonmouth Dock junction and Earth Sidings.

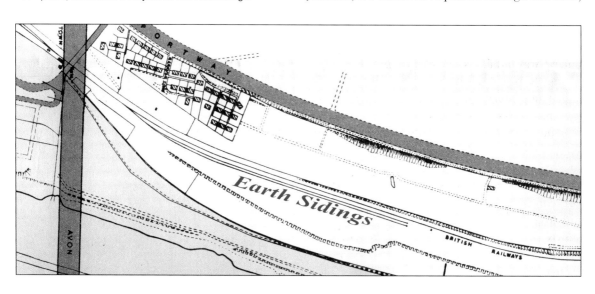

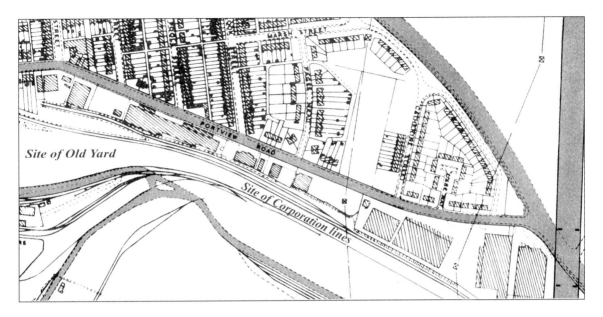

1974 plan showing the approaches to Old Yard.

with its mixture of MR and GWR sidings, and then, leaving the yard, over Gloucester Road crossing. The Down and Up goods lines split to become the Up and Down Corporation lines and the Up and Down GW lines. On the right-hand side, granaries, mills and animal feed warehouses loom over the lines. At Gloucester Road junction the direction of lines also changes.

From here onwards, as with Dock station, things take on a different look. This is now Great Western territory and everything – signals and signal boxes and railway buildings – is GW in appearance.

Just before the level crossing, with its large signal box in attendance, were the connections by which passenger trains could enter the docks to gain access to 'S' shed where the passenger terminal was located. At Gloucester Road the goods lines and Corporation lines became separate and from here they ran parallel as four tracks round the curve to St Andrews junction, where they met the line from Avonmouth Dock station. Trains moved slowly round the sharp curve, passing on the left the ship-repairing shed and the Port of Bristol locomotive depot. From St Andrews junction, where

there are connections to cross from Corporation to GW lines, the four roads continue northwards. The main lines are now designated Up and Down GW lines to Hallen Marsh and the Up and Down Corporation lines follow them as far as Avonmouth Goods Yard box.

On the right just after the crossing is the small goods yard known as 'Town Goods'. Here the signal boxes are close together and the next box can be seen. This is Avonmouth Goods Yard box, or 'Town Goods' as it is known to everyone. It is a large box as it has many sidings to deal with; some are behind the box where they lead into Town Goods Yard. At Goods Yard box the Corporation lines expand. The first group of sidings which split off into the docks are the LMS sidings. The Corporation lines now move away from the GW lines and, as St Andrews Road station is approached, they move away into the mass of sidings which constitute the Royal Edward Yard. Ships tied up at the Royal Edward Dock make a magnificent sight, especially when lit up at night.

After leaving St Andrews Road station, the line runs dead straight across marshy land with the

31

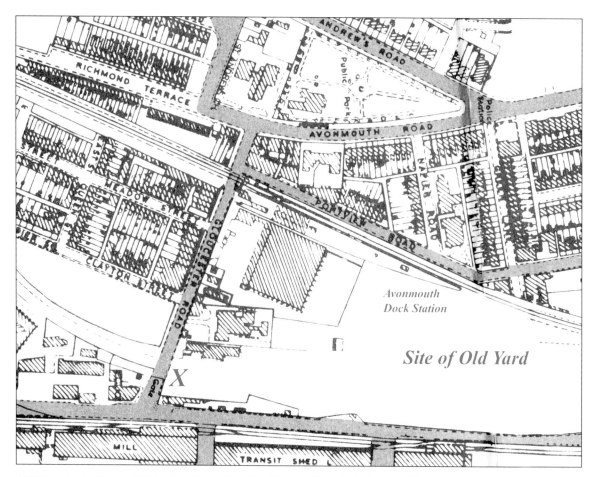

1974 plan showing the site of Old Yard and the location of Dock Station. 'X' marks the location of Gloucester Road signal box and crossing. Opposite is the old shunters' cabin and yard offices.

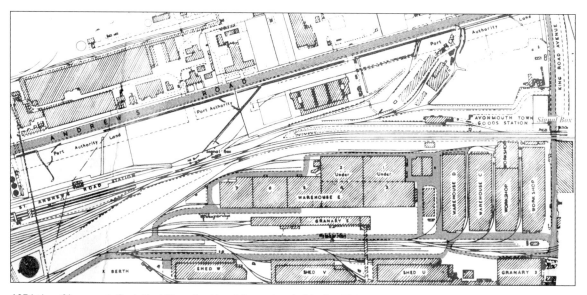

1974 plan of Avonmouth Goods Yard (Town Goods) and the south end of the Royal Edward Yard. St Andrews' signal box and level crossing is seen to the far right of the plan.

View of Royal Edward dock, ship and PBA wagons. 1980.

Royal Edward Yard still on the left side. A series of oil storage tanks can be seen. After about half a mile the line curves inland to the right and the Corporation lines once more approach from the left. Just on the curve, on the right-hand side, is Holesmouth Junction signal box, where the Corporation lines rejoin the GW lines and run for a few hundred yards before reaching Hallen Marsh junction. As Hallen Marsh is approached, a further level crossing is seen to the right.

Hallen Marsh is the point where the two lines from the Imperial Smelting Works (ISC) join the main line. These are known as the 'Inwards' (to GW) and 'Outwards' (to ISC) sidings. These cross the road known as 'Smoke Lane' via the level crossing just before Hallen Marsh.

Hallen Marsh is the junction also for the single line to Severn Beach and onwards to Pilning, and the Up and Down lines to Filton West via Henbury. There are a couple of long spurs alongside the Down line from Henbury and a tall water column stands by a siding.

The older line is the GWR Avonmouth and Severn Tunnel line to Pilning.

MV Etoric tied up alongside at Avonmouth in the 1960s, with a steam tug near by. (Len Worrall)

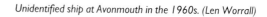

Unidentified ship at Avonmouth in the 1960s. (Len Worrall)

The Stations

Montpelier

The first station on the Clifton Extension line was Montpelier, opened on 1 October 1874 as 'Montpellier', like the town in the south of France. It also shared its name with a fashionable new suburb of Bristol, and the spelling was changed to 'Montpelier' in February 1888 and has remained as such ever since. The station master was provided with a house, to which was added the luxury of a coal shed in 1883 and an extra bedroom in 1887. In 1897, the station master at Montpelier was Henry Wells, who had been a porter at Eckington, north of Cheltenham. He lived in the Station House with his wife, son and two daughters. Mr Coates was a porter here in the late 1940s and 1950s.

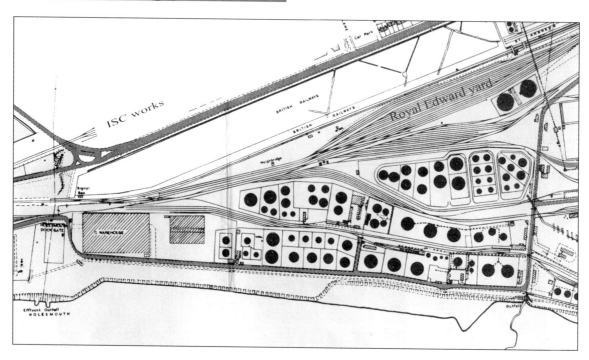

1974 plan of Royal Edward Yard and Holesmouth junction, showing fuel oil storage tanks along the coastline.

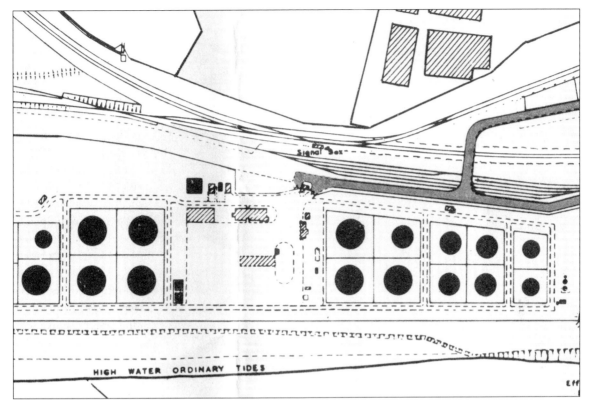

1974 plan of Hallen Marsh junction. The fuel depot belongs to Esso.

Small parcels and light goods were handled directly at the station. There was a small goods yard at the Clifton end, reached by means of a short bridge over the station approach road. The main traffic there was domestic coal. The coal merchants in the late nineteenth century were Alick Heyward, who shared the coal-yard premises with Milton and Co., coal merchants, Bird's coal depot (proprietor Oliver James Gullick), and Williams and Co., also coal merchants. Kingswood and Parkfield Collieries also had space here as did the Coalpit Heath Coal Co. Also in premises on Station

Montpelier station 2017.

Road Montpelier was Andrew Knowles and Co., builder's merchant.

Redland

The next station along the line was Redland, opened on 12 April 1897. This was one of two stations (the other was Sea Mills) on the Clifton Extension which had no goods yard. The main station building was on the Up side and consisted of a lovely brick building with a canopy, which was quite unlike any other on the line. On the Down side platform stood a brick waiting room with canopy and a small signal box stood at the Bristol end of this platform. On the Clifton end of the station, the quaintly named 'Lovers' Walk' crossed the line by means of a lovely wrought-iron footbridge and, just after that, Redland Grove crossed the line by a stone-built overbridge.

There were two porters at Redland in latter days and the Station Master's duties were covered from Clifton Down.

Clifton Down

Clifton Down was a typical Midland Railway design, built in what could be described as a 'standard' MR style. Large glass canopies covered each platform. The station was always well patronized – not only did it serve local people who wished to travel to Bristol Temple Meads or Gloucester and the north, but there were also plenty of Victorians who travelled to Clifton Down to perambulate on nearby Durdham Downs during summer weekends. In 1897 John Padmore was the station master. It is a commonly held view that people did not move around the country much until the advent of the motor car, tending to live and work within reach of their home town or village, but John Padmore was the son of a Shropshire farmer and had served as station master at Aberystwyth before moving to Clifton Down. He lived at nearby Cotham Brow with his wife, three daughters and a son. In the 1950s, Wally Beale was the station master at Clifton Down; he had previously been the Assistant Area Signalling Inspector for the west side of Bristol. The station master in 1958 was Mr G. Bennett, who also covered the duties at Redland and Montpelier stations.

The large coal yard at the station served the many residences in the area. The coal merchants who had premises here in the late nineteenth century were L. Twining and Co.; Williams and Co.; Dudley and Gibson; T. Paul and Co. and A. H. Milton and Co. John Snow and Co. also occupied premises on Whiteladies Road near the station, being merchants for 'Cannock Chase, Silkstone, Derby and Welsh Coals'.

Sea Mills

Sea Mills station was one of the original Port and Pier stations. Being originally on a single line, it had station buildings only on the Up side. The buildings were quite unlike anything else on the line, with the main one being built in a 'chalet' style. The station never had public or private goods facilities and came under the supervision of the Shirehampton station master.

Shirehampton

Opened on 6 March 1865, Shirehampton was one of the stations on the Bristol Port and Pier line from Hotwells to Avonmouth. With the coming of the Clifton Extension in 1885 the line grew in importance and was eventually doubled. The first station master was George Pinkerton, a Somerset-born man and son of a Railway Inspector of Works. He lived in Shirehampton with his sister, but by 1911 he had married a girl from Williton on the Taunton–Minehead line and moved to become station master at Borrowash, near Long Eaton on the Midland Railway. The 1958 station master was Mr A.H. Davies, who also supervised Sea Mills station. Tom Bullock was a porter in the 1950s.

Avonmouth Dock Station (Joint)

This station opened in 1885, with John William Lait, a local farmer's son, acting as station master from the start. Charles Parker, another local man, was employed as a porter. By 1901, Parker had left the railway and gone to work in the docks, as so many men did. He was employed at first as a general labourer and later got a similar job with the

Anglo-American Oil Co. In 1958, the Avonmouth Dock station master's duties combined with those of Old Yard; Avonmouth was designated as a 'Special Class' depot and yard/station master was Mr R.W. Thomas, who also supervised St Andrews Road station. Mr Thomas was remembered as a 'quiet' man who was always immaculately dressed. The office was on the Down platform and chief clerk was Arthur Richards who had at one time been in the Royal Air Force. There were two station foremen to cover the day shifts: Lloyd Beeton was one of them. Other staff included a parcels porter, ticket collectors and station foreman. The Avonmouth railway telephone exchange was based at Dock station and in May 1958, Miss F.H. Olsen, a telegraph clerk, moved to Avonmouth Dock to take up duties there. Cecil Long was a porter here, as were Charlie Maycock, who moved here from St Andrews Road, and 'Ginger' Parsons.

The main brick-built station building was on the Down side of the station where the platform was the only one until 1917, when it was extended towards Bristol and a new Up platform was built. Until then, Up trains reversed into the Down platform. With the new Up platform, a long timber shelter with canopy was built. There was a bay line behind the Down platform and shelter for passengers was provided by a canopy on the bay side of the main station building. The signal box, known as 'Avonmouth Dock Station', was built on the Down platform.

Avonmouth Dock (GW)

The small amount of information that is known about this short-lived GWR 'station' comes from the family of one of the signalmen from those early days. Alfred Allen was first appointed to Gloucester Road signal box and went on to be a respected member of the railway and local community in Chippenham, Wiltshire. Fortunately, he left a few documents and papers that give a valuable insight into the life of a railwayman in the early days of the docks.

Alfred Augustus Allen was born at Oake, Somerset, in 1892. His grandfather (who had been in the army at the time of the Indian Mutiny) was a railway guard; his father had been a signalman on the GWR and by 1901 the family were living at Norton Street, Norton Fitzwarren, Somerset. In 1906, young Alfred started his railway career, when he became a lad porter at Yeovil Pen Mill station. Like many railwaymen living away from home, he found lodgings at the home of another railwayman, in this case, Charles Ford, a goods guard. Four years later, Alfred transferred to Portishead station. From there he moved to Maiden Newton and then to Melksham. After Melksham he became porter/signalman at Montacute, near Yeovil. By 1914, Alfred joined his father in the signalling grade as signalman at

Alfred Allen and family. (Via Valerie Lyons and Mary Sheppard)

1904 line-up of staff at the GWR Avonmouth Dock station. In the background are the houses of Clayton Street. (Via Valerie Lyons and Mary Sheppard)

Gloucester Road, Avonmouth. He lodged at a local restaurant and attended Avonmouth Congregational Church, where he fell for the church organist, a pretty local girl who happened to be the daughter of the owner of his lodgings. Alfred Allen was at Gloucester Road for the duration of the 1914–18 war after which, in 1919, he moved to Pewsey. After a lifetime of work with the trade unions and Labour Party, Alfred Allen retired from the post of relief signalman at Chippenham, where he was also a Justice of the Peace.

The Avonmouth Dock station was intended as the terminus of the GWR new line from Filton via Henbury and comprised a single platform, a short wooden affair, served by a siding, which was entered via a facing connection on the Down goods line. Later, an extension was added to this siding, enabling the short trains that used the platform to back into the extension to allow another short train to enter. The station boasted a wooden hut as a shelter. It was opened to passengers on 9 May 1910 and closed temporarily in March 1915 due to the war. It finally closed completely on 28 April 1919.

Avonmouth Dock (GW) did not have goods facilities.

A view of Bristol, Narroways Hill Junction in the early 1960s. The two lines diverging away in the lower right corner are the Avonmouth lines. (Wif Stanley)

CHAPTER 5

The Avonmouth Line at War, 1914–18

When hostilities commenced in France and Belgium in 1914, the Avonmouth Docks complex found itself playing a major part in the war effort. The docks would serve not only as a place where foodstuffs and other war materials would be brought into Great Britain, but also a facility where troops and weapons would be despatched to the war zone. Nowadays, it would probably be termed a 'hub'. Lord Kitchener came to the docks in 1914 to assess its capabilities, and also to take due note of any land available around the docks area (more on this later).

With the British Expeditionary Force established in France, Avonmouth Docks became a key departure point for vessels carrying vehicles, weapons, fuel and troops to the war. The railways were essential in all this and both the yards were busy round the clock, with the signal boxes being manned full-time. Gloucester Road box, where the main connection into the docks left the GWR and Corporation lines, was kept very busy indeed, especially in the early months of 1915, when troop train after troop train arrived there. Ninety-two troop and military supply trains arrived at the docks during the early part of February alone. On arrival at the exchange sidings, the train engine would cut off and stand clear, after which the docks engine would emerge and be coupled to what was the rear of the train. The troop train

would be towed into the docks, where the soldiers and their equipment would disembark and make their way on-board troop ships that were waiting alongside the dock.

Regiments such as the Warwickshire Yeomanry, the Worcestershire and the Royal Naval Division all arrived by rail, as did more local regiments such as the South Wales Borderers and the Gloucestershire. As they scrambled off their trains, full of noise and laughter, and boarded troop ships such as the SS *Somali* and the Union Castle Line SS *Granbury Castle*, among others, the young soldiers had no idea where they were headed. The name 'Gallipoli' meant nothing to them at that time. It soon became familiar, however, to the many who returned to Britain on hospital ships; during the course of the war, over 36,300 wounded troops came back home to Avonmouth Docks in this way, to be loaded on to hospital trains and moved out to hospitals around the country. By 1917, Bristol alone had sixteen military hospitals, to which 69,000 wounded armed forces were moved by train.

It was not just supplies, men and equipment that passed through the docks. Assessing the area in 1914, Kitchener had observed that there was a significant amount of agricultural land adjoining the docks. What better place to build facilities for the war effort? First to fulfil this function was Shirehampton, where a 'Remount' depot was

A 1948 view of Hallen Marsh junction from Rockingham Road bridge: note the two spurs. (Wilf Stanley)

built. One of many such establishments across the country, the depot was a place where horses and mules were received and trained for the front line. Many of these animals were brought by ship from Canada. There was also a veterinary hospital on the site. When the time came for the horses and their handlers to move off to war, they went by rail to the channel ports, from which they would depart for France.

The other major contributor to the war effort was the munitions factory, which was built at Merebank near the northern end of the growing industrial area. It consisted of single-storey buildings spread over a large area on the coast. It was an ideal site, being detached from the inhabited part of Avonmouth, which was a mile or so to the south. While this isolation protected the general public from the potential explosions that were associated with munitions, it also meant that the site was not close to transport links. As the factory was just inland of the Holesmouth to Pilning single line, a platform, known as 'Chittening Factory', was constructed so that its staff could travel to work by train. The factory, known as 'No.23 Filling Factory', opened for use in March 1917. Exchange sidings were laid in, with access from the single line, and a network of internal sidings served the various buildings, using petrol locos. Access to the exchange sidings was by means of three ground frames, known as 'South', 'Middle' and 'North'.

As the war dragged on, the situation in France and Belgium became increasingly desperate. Conventional weapons were not solving the problem of the stalemate and there was a view on both sides that chemical weapons would be the answer. However, production of such weapons was thought to be 'uncivilized', and the Hague Conventions of 1899 and 1907 had explicitly forbidden the use of 'poison or poisoned weapons' in warfare. Nonetheless, the Germans had first used chlorine gas against the Allies in 1915 and had secretly developed, and used in September 1917, dichloroethyl sulphide, or mustard gas, also known as 'Yperite'. It was one of the most lethal of all the poisonous chemicals used during the war. It was almost odourless and took twelve hours to take effect. Yperite was so powerful that only small amounts had to be added to high-explosive shells to be effective.

One of the main components of mustard gas was sulphuric acid, which could be obtained through the process of smelting zinc. Prior to 1914, much of the zinc used in British smelting plants came from Australia and was smelted in Germany – the latter activity had of course ended with the outbreak of war. Halfway through the war, a decision was taken by the Allies to make use of mustard gas, and the Minister of Munitions Winston Churchill took many small smelting plants into public ownership under the banner of the National Smelting

Company (NSC). Avonmouth was proposed as a suitable site for the centre of production in the UK and the NSC was publicly commissioned to build a new zinc-smelting works and sulphuric acid plant there, at Chittening.

Construction of the chemical plant began in 1917, under the auspices of the Official Secrets Act. A new junction, known as Hallen Marsh, was laid in just north of Holesmouth and the single line from Holesmouth was doubled as far as here, which became the physical junction for the Pilning and Filton lines. From Hallen Marsh, two sidings were laid towards the new smelting works and a 'grid' of exchange sidings was also laid in. A new signal box was built and opened on 11 February 1917.

Although the smelting works plant came into operation from spring 1918, producing 22 tons of dichloroethyl sulphide, the first product did not arrive in France until September 1918, two months before the November Armistice. By November 1918, Chittening had produced 85,424 mustard gas shells, and was experiencing the human cost of this work. In December 1918, 1,213 cases of associated illness were reported among the workforce, which comprised mostly young females, including two deaths (although these were later attributed to influenza).

The construction of the munitions factory and its supply of lethal shells was too late in the war to achieve much. As it became increasingly obvious that the hostilities were approaching a conclusion, so the munitions factory became surplus to requirements. Production stopped and further development of the factory was abandoned in May 1917.

The single line from Filton to Avonmouth had been doubled in stages with further junctions into the proposed munitions factory extension laid in at a site just west of Ison Hill overbridge near Blaise hamlet. With the abandonment of the factory, this junction was never connected to the signal box (named 'Hallen' when it was opened in February 1917 and then 'Hallen East' on 22 March 1917, to differentiate it from the 'Hallen West' box, which opened in April 1917) and the rails were removed. This section of line had been doubled in April 1917, with the Hallen West signal box placed at the Avonmouth end of the new loop. A platform to serve both Hallen village and the munitions factory had been built and opened in March 1917, replacing the original Hallen halt, which had been close to Ison Hill bridge.

The doubling of the line onwards to Hallen Marsh junction continued, opening in May 1917. At the same time, Hallen East box was renamed 'Hallen', following the closure of the Hallen West box.

The docks and its railways played another part towards the end of the war, with 24,000 wounded troops being brought back by ship to Avonmouth in 1918 of which 13,000 were Commonwealth soldiers.

By 1920, there were 120 railway companies operating in the UK, most of which were losing money. The 1914–18 war had allowed the government to control the railways as a unified body and had shown that it would be more beneficial all round if this could be continued. Nationalization was not on the cards, but it was thought that combining the 120 companies into a smaller number might reduce the losses.

In 1921, Parliament, under Prime Minister David Lloyd George, passed the Railways Act, which grouped the 120 into four main railway companies: the London, Midland and Scottish; Great Western; Southern; and London and North Eastern. The provisions of the Act took effect from the beginning of 1923. As far as the Clifton Extension line and Avonmouth were concerned, only one company changed; the GWR remained the same and the LMSR took over the Midland Railway facilities.

By this time, most of the main railway facilities were in place and the situation would remain more or less the same until the closures of the 1960s.

CHAPTER 6

People

As with many places of work, it was the people who made the job. On the railways of a docks area, there were many different types of worker who added interest to both the day- and the night-time. Whenever a shop was in dock, there were sailors, mostly merchant seamen unless a royal or foreign naval vessel was paying a courtesy call. Once the ship was safely docked and their duties for the time being over, the sailors set out to find the world outside the docks.

I was on duty at St Andrews Junction box one evening when a shout was heard. I opened the window to see a group of around half a dozen merchant sailors there.

'Hey!' called one. 'Where can we find *girls*?'

I was a little taken off guard there, but directed them to one of the local public houses which had a 'reputation'. I had no idea whether they would find the type of entertainment they were seeking at this establishment, but they did not come back to complain so I assumed they were successful.

Railway staff became accustomed to seeing the same sailors at regular intervals when their ships were in dock. One of my colleagues recalled seeing a lone Indian sailor walking out of the docks gate reading a newspaper as he walked. Nothing so odd about that except that, eight months later, when his ship was in dock once more, the same sailor was

seen again, walking out of the docks still reading a newspaper!

There were often stories associated with the American sailors. When one US Navy ship was in dock, the crew went into town for drinks, with most of them slipping back through the docks gates before they were closed for the night. Some while after, the signalman heard a shout and, going to the window, saw an American naval officer there. 'Hey, buddy, how do I get back into the docks? I'll get into trouble if I'm late back on-board.'

The signalman replied, 'Just climb over the gates!'

The sailor went pale. 'I can't do that!' he cried 'I'll get shot!'

Holding back laughter, the signalman explained that the commercial docks in the UK were not guarded by men with guns and the sailor would be perfectly safe climbing over the gates and rejoining his ship.

Nervously, the American climbed over the dock gates and vanished into the maze of docks buildings.

The railway staff who worked in the area were numerous, especially when the docks railways were at their busiest, in the 1950s. Over the years after the war, the railways in Avonmouth and its lines were slimmed down and rationalized, but a structure of railway staff still remained, all performing their own particular roles.

The Signalman

Railways are regulated by rules and regulations, which make the system a safe place to work. Trains are kept apart by signals and these were worked by men (and sometimes women) in signal boxes along the line. It could be a comfy place to work – dry indoors when it rained, and warm in winter when others working outside were feeling the cold – but it could be hard work in a busy box. The signalman had to 'know the frame'. He had to be familiar with the function of every lever, and understand the bell codes that were used to describe trains between boxes. He needed to know how to operate all the other equipment, for example, ganger's keys, and single-line token machines where there was a single line. He needed to be familiar with tunnel regulations where there was a tunnel in the section. He needed to have passed competence tests on the *Signalman's General Instructions* (known as the 'Apple Green' after its green cover) and the *General Rule Book*, as well as the appropriate sections of the various appendices to the *Rule Book* and the Special Instructions for the particular signal box, or boxes, where he worked. He also needed to know what to do and who to call when something went wrong.

The working hours frequently covered seven days a week. 'Normal' shifts were 06.00–14.00; 14.00–22.00 and 22.00–06.00, but they could vary according to the traffic requirements. For example, Gloucester Road box worked normal shift but had no rostered Sunday duties. Avonmouth Dock Station box worked two turns and opened at 05.15. Shifts were changed at 14.15 and the box switched out at 22.30. Severn Beach worked two turns as well, opening at 06.00, changing shifts at 14.00 and closing at 22.15. Sundays at Severn Beach were 13.15–19.15 in winter and 13.15–21.15 in summer, to allow for excursions.

Signal boxes were graded for pay according to the amount of work done. This was calculated by awarding 'marks' for each piece of equipment – levers, bells, and so on – and for each lever

move made. The sum added up to the total marks awarded for the box and this determined the grade of the box. On the Avonmouth lines, Pilning Low Level, Severn Beach, Hallen Marsh, Holesmouth, Gloucester Road, Shirehampton, Filton West, Henbury and Blaise were all Class 4 boxes, whilst Town Goods, St Andrews, Avonmouth Dock Sidings, Dock Junction, Dock Station, Clifton Down and Ashley Hill Junction were all Class 3 boxes. The grade of box was important for pay: in 1953, a Class 4 job was paid at the rate of £5-6-0d per week and a Class 3 was paid at the rate of £5-10-0d per week. The average UK wage at the time was £9-5-0d for a 48-hour week. That could buy you sixteen pints of beer, or thirty-nine large loaves of bread.

The average signalman did not have a car. If he was able to get lots of overtime he might be able to afford a motorbike, but most would cycle to work.

The Clifton Extension line being a joint line, the Kingswood junction to Avonmouth Dock station section was signalled in Midland/later LMSR fashion with, at first, MR lower quadrant signals and, later, LMSR upper quadrant signals. The signal boxes were built either by contractors to the Midland Railway or by the MR itself, to its standard

BR cycling permit issued to Relief Signalman Brian Chaney in January 1962.

design. MR signal boxes were sparse, with little in the way of comfort; the Midland always believed that its signalmen came to work to work, not rest. Seating was provided by a settle-style wooden bench with hatches in the seat, under which was a small cupboard for the signalmen's personal possessions and rule books. The booking desk was a small sloping shelf fixed to the wall. The Midland also believed in saving money in other ways: why use one lever per movement if two movements could be coupled to the same lever? Thus, facing points (where they were used – generally, the MR did not like facing points) and point locks worked from the same lever. Some crossovers were not connected to the signal box at all, but were moved by a crowbar when necessary. Ground signals were not provided for every set of points.

The Midland always had the attitude that its workers went to work to do just that – work! They were not supposed to be too warm and comfortable. Even in BR days, the LMSR continued some of these old practices. In the Bristol area, the LMR relief signalmen had a particularly rough shift pattern: for example, it was quite normal for a Mangotsfield-based relief man to work a 22.00–06.00 night turn at Bath station (Green Park) followed by 'doubling back' for a 14.00–22.00 late shift at Yate South; this could even be followed by another double-back to 06.00–14.00 early turn at Bath station. It was hardly conducive to a good rest! They did get paid 'walking' or 'travelling' time if they worked away from their home station. On the LMR, this could work out like this: if a man worked nights at Rangeworthy box, then he booked walking time from his home station (for example, Mangotsfield). Likely as not, his next shift would be a double-back to lates at Westerleigh South, so he would book travelling time plus a lodging allowance (if there was no train service to get him to a box, he was allowed to book a lodge; if there *was* a train service, he was expected to use it). His next shift might be back at Bath station for an early turn, for which he could book travelling time only. On the Clifton Extension the LMR relief signalmen worked a similar shift pattern.

The LMR workers' opposite numbers on the GWR/WR got a much better deal. When Rest Days were introduced in the 1950s, Henbury signalmen, for example, like all others, were entitled to a day off per fortnight. Their shift was covered by a Rest Day relief signalman whose early turn roster was as follows: Monday, Holesmouth box; Tuesday, Hallen Marsh box; Wednesday, Gloucester Road box; Thursday, Coalpit Heath box (on the Badminton line); Friday, Filton West junction; and Saturday, Henbury box. The following week, the Rest Day man covered the late shift as follows: Monday, Holesmouth; Tuesday, Hallen Marsh; Wednesday, Gloucester Road; Thursday, own Rest Day off; Friday, Filton West; and Saturday, Henbury.

However, what with vacancies and sickness, there were often times when the Rest Day roster would be temporarily suspended. In such cases, 'resident' signalmen had to work on their Rest Days and the relief men covered the necessary turns needed. For example, on the week commencing Sunday 9 August 1959, one relief man began the week by working a Sunday shift 14.00–22.00 at Gloucester Road. He was back at work at 06.00 the following morning at Filton West box until 14.00. On Tuesday 11 August he worked 06.00–14.00 at Coalpit Heath box on the Badminton line, followed by 05.00–14.15 at Avonmouth Station box on Wednesday 12, Thursday 13 and Friday 14 August he worked 06.00–14.00 at Holesmouth followed by 06.00–14.00 back at Gloucester Road on Saturday 15 August.

On a week in May 1962, another relief man worked 14.00–22.00 at Gloucester Road on a Monday and his own double Rest Days at Kingswood junction 14.00–22.00 on Tuesday. Henbury was by now reduced to one shift only, so he covered this turn 11.30–19.20 on the Wednesday, Thursday and Friday, and 07.00–13.30 on the Saturday. Sunday was worked at Patchway Station box, 06.00–14.00.

Coverage of Green Lane crossing on the Severn Beach to Pilning line was usually 11.45–19.45. Considering that most relief men got to the job by bus or pushbike, it is clear that covering this many turns would leave them with very little free time.

Avonmouth Relief Signalmen

All signal boxes had relief signalmen, initially to take the place of the 'regular' man for holiday or sick leave. The relief man would also cover the duty when there was a vacancy. In the 1950s, British Railways agreed that signalmen should have one rostered day off every other week. This day was known as a 'Rest Day' and extra relief signalmen's posts were created to cover them. Among the Avonmouth relief men were: Doug Lock, Brian Chaney, Vernon Orchard, Ted Porter (who later went carriage cleaning), Geoff Sheppard (who came down from Stoke Gifford East after redundancy), and Dennis Harris. Dennis started his career as a shed labourer at Barrow Road steam shed on the LMR before joining the signalling grade at Redcliffe Swing Bridge. Well, sort of signalling grade – the bridge required stoking to get a good head of steam to enable it to be moved. From here, he graduated to South Liberty Junction box on the West District until that box closed in 1971. Following his redundancy, Dennis went to work as a shunter at Avonmouth's Royal Edward Yard, before returning to the grade as signalman at Holesmouth and then becoming a general-purpose relief man. I was also a relief man, as were Gerald Davidson and Dave Alley.

For a while, after the Bristol Resignalling of 1970–72, there were temporary relief signalmen in Avonmouth. These were Eddie Mann and Malcolm Eggleton (who later became permanent).

In addition to his normal duties, the signalman had to ensure that the box was kept clean and tidy and the levers, brasswork, windows and floor were polished. The floor was swept at the end of every shift and the coal buckets and kettle filled ready for the changeover. Polishing was normally done on Saturday afternoons, when there was less traffic.

The junction at Hallen Marsh could be a bottleneck when things got busy, with trains to and from Severn Beach, Henbury and Avonmouth all vying for their path through the junction. This was the case all through the working life of the junction and signal box. Things were busier in the 1950s when rail traffic was at its peak, even though the ICI works at Severnside had not yet been built. Even after the decline in rail traffic for the docks, other industries sprang up or changed and, with the passenger service staying almost the same as in the immediate post-war years, rail traffic through the junction remained busy.

What follows is a description of a typical day at Hallen Marsh signal box in the 1980s. The shift is the early turn and the details were recorded on

How a signal box should look inside: Hallen Marsh spick and span in 1985.

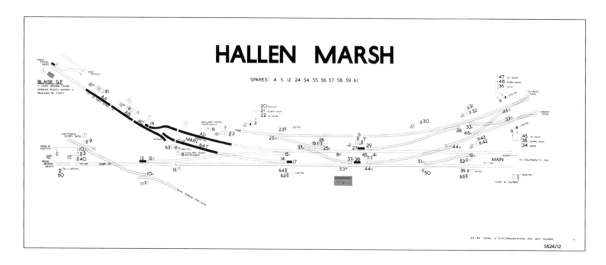

Hallen Marsh box track and signals diagram from 1972.

23 September 1983. It not only describes the movements of passenger and freight trains, but also gives an insight into the day of a man working a busy manual signal box, focusing on the human element that is so often neglected in railway histories.

Early shift at Hallen Marsh starts at 05.30, so it's an 04.45 rise for me, woken by the two alarm clocks by my bed; one set to go off slightly before the other: I'm no 'morning person' so getting out of bed at that time is difficult! The journey from my home to the

The way into Hallen Marsh box is through the pipes…

06.00 on a winter's morning at Hallen Marsh. The object in the distance above the loco roof is not a ship, but the Sevalco factory and chimney.

box takes about half an hour at that time of day and takes me through the northern suburbs of Bristol. It's just getting light as I park my car on the river-bank by the PBA sidings and opposite the Esso Oil terminal. Hallen Marsh box stands cold and silent in the early morning air, but a faint haze from the chimney tells me that the late turn man from the previous day has left the fire in, so it shouldn't be long before I can get the box warmed up.

I get my work bag from the car and walk across the PBA sidings to the box. To get to the box door I have to scramble through several lines of large pipes running behind the box, which carry aviation fuel from Avonmouth across country to various air-fields and bases. Producing the large GWR box door key from my uniform jacket pocket, I open the box door and step inside into the chill, clammy atmos-phere which always seems to be common to signal boxes which have been closed overnight. Although it's only September, being on the banks of the wide river, the air is quite cold. I shut the door behind me and hurry up the stairs.

First job is to open the damper and the ashpan door on the fire to start a draught on the embers. Dead on the stroke of 05.30 I turn the Block switch and pick up the phone to Bristol Panel. 'Hallen Marsh Open', I report to the sleepy panel signal-man who will shortly be off home to his bed. Next, I send 5-5-5 'Opening of Signal Box' to St Andrews

Junction box which has been open since 05.15. Then on goes the kettle and I turn my attention to the fire. By the time I've emptied the ashpan, raked over the embers and stoked up with coal, the kettle has boiled and I make myself a cuppa.

The bell from St Andrews rings once 'Call Attention'. I answer it and am offered the first pas-senger train of the day, the 05.15 Bristol Temple Meads to Severn Beach. Being a Class 2 service, the train is signalled 3-1. Moving the Block indicator to 'Line Clear' I now turn my attention to the Train Register. Heading up a new page I write the date and the time I booked on, followed by the time I opened the box. I enter the train description and the time I received and accepted the train, 05.40.

It's the practice at Hallen Marsh for the late turn man to leave the road set towards 'the Beach' before closing the box, so all I have to do is pull off the Up Main Home signal, No.65 and the Up Main to Severn Beach Starting signal, No.62. Then I release a token from the machine, which releases the Up Severn Beach Advanced Starting signal No.60, which I then pull off.

I place the token on top of the nearby cupboard and there's barely time for another cup of tea before St Andrews sends the two bells 'Train Entering Section' signal. It's 05.44.

Five minutes later, the 05.15 comes into sight. It's formed by a 3-car DMU and slows for the driver

GREAT WESTERN RAILWAY
Notice to SIGNALMEN, ENGINEMEN & others concerned

A considerable number of tokens are being damaged owing to the method of exchanging tokens with the picking up and setting down apparatus, and the attention of all concerned is called to the following instructions :—

ELECTRIC TRAIN TOKEN EXCHANGING APPARATUS.

1. In this apparatus the Token is fixed in a carrier to which is attached a hoop.

2. The post on which the Signalman places the Token, and from which the Fireman takes it before he enters the Token Section, is called the " Picking up " Post.

The post on which the Fireman hangs the Token, after passing through the Section, and from which the Signalman afterwards fetches it, is called the " Setting down " post.

3. To deliver a Token, the Fireman must hold it at full length, with the hoop facing, fairly and squarely, to the front.

On arriving at the " Setting down " post, the hoop must be passed over the projecting arm and the Fireman should be careful to release his hold of the Token IMMEDIATELY it passes on to the arm.

The Token should on no account be THROWN over the arm.

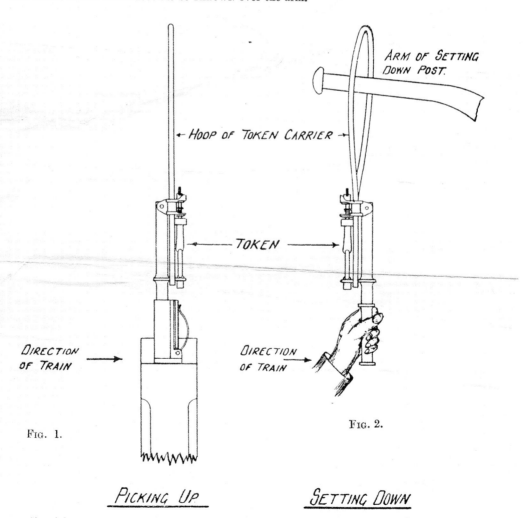

FIG. 1.

FIG. 2.

PICKING UP

SETTING DOWN

to collect the token. Although the official way to hand over the single-line token involves the train stopping and the driver collecting the 'key' from the signalman at ground level, in practice we lean out of the box window and hand the token to the driver at arm's length; the driver grabs the token without stopping the train and opens the throttle again.

With the DMU clattering over the junction points on to the single line, I send 2-1 'Train Out of Section' to St Andrews and throw the signals back to Danger. Next, I set the road for the DMU to return. This involves reversing point lever 16 'Up Main to Severn Beach Safety', then putting lever 13 'Facing Point Lock for 15' back in the frame and reversing lever 15 'From Severn Beach Facing/Down Main'. This is followed by pulling lever 13 again to lock 15 and then I hang the duster on the levers and sit down.

Ten minutes later, after a quick sandwich, it's time to get the road for the 05.58 Severn Beach to Bristol Temple Meads. I ask 'Call Attention' to St Andrews and when that's acknowledged send 3-1. This is accepted and 'Line Clear' pegged up. I pull the Home signal lever No.3 and the Down Main Starting No.7. While I'm entering the details in the Train Register, the sound of voices drifts up from outside. Then, one louder than the other calls, 'Mornin' Signalman!' I shout back an appropriate

greeting and walk to the window to see the figures of Chargeman Shunter John Duffy and Carriage and Wagon Examiner Pete Mead (known as the 'Venerable Mead'!) cross the tracks and head for their respective cabins alongside the Column Road. By the time I've put some more coal on the fire and closed the damper, the 05.58 can be seen heading towards the junction. I bang out two bells to St Andrews and head down the stairs to get the token.

The official way to exchange the token now is for the train to stop and the driver hand the key to me. But, as ever, we 'modify' the book and I stand by the trackside and grab the token from the guard who is leaning out of the cab window, one hand holding the token and the other holding his hat on. A successful grab and I'm heading back up the steps to the warmth of the box where I restore the token to the machine, throw the signals back to Danger and set the road back to the Beach again.

Whilst this is going on, the bells clang out 5-5-5. It's Town Goods box opening. I log this in the Train Register. After the 05.58 clears Town Goods at 06.09, there nothing on the Block for around half an hour, so I sit back in the chair and have a doze in front of the fire. The bell rings again at 06.35 and it's the next passenger DMU to Severn Beach. I repeat the moves I made for the first train and put the times in the Register.

Single-line key token: 'Pilning Low Level-Hallen Marsh', used when Severn Beach box was closed at nights.

Signalman (later Signalling Inspector) Jim Barnes demonstrating a way of collecting the token that was not shown in the Rule Book! *(Chris Goodman)*

The phone on the wall rings: one long ring for the box. It's the Venerable Mead.

'Two things,' he says. 'The tea's made and is the Tees about?'

The 'Tees' is a train of potash containers from Tees yard in the north of England to ICI Severn Beach. I answer in the negative and, grabbing my cup, head down the stairs and across the tracks to the shunters' cabin, where I help myself to yet another cuppa from the teapot there. 'The Tees will need examining when it arrives,' says Pete Mead, 'so keep it at No.2 please.' I nod agreement then hear the distant sound of two bells and hurry back across the walkway to the box, being careful not to spill my tea. I peg up 'Train on Line' and put the times in 'the book'.

This time, the DMU which forms the Severn Beach service squeals to a halt outside the box. While I lean out of the window to hand the token to the driver, the guard's compartment door opens and the figure of 'Mad Dave' McIlwain, the second shunter, climbs down. As the train heads off to the Beach, Dave crosses the tracks to the cabin, and I throw the signals back to Danger. The next service back from the Beach leaves there at 06.50 so I have some time to grab a bit of breakfast. I sit at the old motor-points generator table at the Severn Beach end of the box, so I can keep an eye on the single line for the return working.

At 06.55 I see the yellow front of the DMU appear in the distance and it's time to get the road again. Once I've collected the token, put the road back and restored the token to the machine, the Train Describer from the panel starts to buzz. This gadget is the TD which was once in Badminton box and moved to Hallen when Badminton closed. A description appears in the window '2B03'. I press the acknowledge button and reverse lever 19, the single- to double-line junction motor points, followed by lever 4 'Acceptance Lever from Bristol Panel'. Shortly afterwards, the first track circuit of the single line lights up and the Track Occupied bell rings. The train won't come any closer, for this is the celebrated 'Ghost Train'. Running under headcode 2B03, it's the train that runs into and out of Bristol

Temple Meads every morning and evening, carrying workers to and from the British Aerospace and Rolls-Royce aircraft factories at Filton airfield. The train – normally a 3-car DMU – runs into Filton North platform, a station that is not open for public use, and doesn't appear in any public timetable, hence its nickname. After 5 minutes, the track circuit light goes out and the panel sends me a 'cancelling' signal on the TD. I replace the acceptance lever and book the times.

The next move is at 07.11. The TD squawks out its urgent alarm and the number '6B51' appears in the window. This is the local trip headcode and the panel man rings me up to advise that this is the Tees potash. I pull the acceptance lever over, followed by lever 1 which is the Down Filton Home colour-light signal. This won't clear until the train has occupied the track circuit in the rear of the signal for a couple of minutes, as the road isn't clear beyond the Inner Home, No.2. I place a lever collar on lever 2 as the train will stand at that signal until it has been examined.

The line from Filton runs through the suburbs of North Bristol, through Henbury, and emerges from a cutting on to an embankment across the flat fields between Henbury and the River Severn. I keep an eye open for the train's appearance on the embankment as the Tees can produce a variety of interesting motive power.

Opposite the box, on the Column Road stands the BR brake van used by the shunters when they go off to shunt various sidings along the line between Hallen and Avonmouth Dock junction. John Duffy appears from his cabin and clambers up into the van. Shortly afterwards, a plume of grey smoke drifts from the stovepipe as John busies himself getting the fire going.

The Tees appears on the embankment and it's a Class 37-37304 on the front, so nothing special. I phone the examiner's cabin and tell Pete Mead that his train is on the horizon. Within 5 minutes the Tees appears from under Rockingham Road bridge and grinds to a halt at No.2 signal. It's 07.25. The examiner is seen briskly walking towards it, spanner in his hand as the driver leans out of his cab window. I replace lever No.1 although the colour-light signal automatically goes back to Danger once the train has passed it.

Things now begin to get busy. I'm offered the 07.00 Bristol–Severn Beach Up at 07.26 and as I'm setting the road for the Beach, so the TD goes off again and it's 7Z11 described. This is the Haverton Hill to ICI Severnside anhydrous ammonia tanks. I pull the acceptance lever again and place a reminder collar on lever 1.

The Up passenger passes Hallen at 07.35 and heads out towards Severn Beach. As I reset the road for its return, so the TD buzzes yet again. This time the description is 6Z68; this is the Immingham to Avonmouth, Fisons Sidings working, another load of anhydrous ammonia; this time in 100-tonne rail tankers. Eventually, this train will run to Fisons tank farm, situated behind the platform at St Andrews Road station and accessed at Town Goods box.

As the Haverton Hill is by this time crawling towards signal No.1, I replace the acceptance lever halfway and then pull it over again. This gives another acceptance to the panel and the Immingham can proceed on to the single line as far as signal DA115.

I can see that the Haverton Hill is headed by a Class 25 diesel and, shortly after it comes to a stand, the signal post telephone rings in the box. It's the driver of the Haverton Hill carrying out Section K 3.2.1 of the *Rule Book* by reporting his presence at HM1. I tell him that the Tees is ahead of him being examined and to 'wait for the signal'. I turn to the Train Register to book all this and see the nose of the 07.56 Severn Beach–Bristol appear in the distance. I ask 'Call Attention' to Town Goods and get the road. Pulling off I again turn to the Train Register and then the telephone from DA115 rings. It's the driver of the Immingham tanks carrying out Section K. I tell him, 'There's one ahead of you, driver; wait for

What better way to start work on a cold, snowy morning? Carriage and Wagon Examiner Pete Mead has just got the brake van fire going: note the paraffin can at his feet.

Fisons tank farm. 1981.

the signal to clear', then rush outside for the token, giving two bells to Town Goods on the way.

Outside, as I wait with my hand held up for the token, I hear the sound of a hurried 5-5-5 ring out from the Block bell. At the same time there's a 'crash' as the slot weight on the post of Hallen's Down Starter, No.7, returns to Caution as the DMU passes it and I grab the key. This is Holesmouth box switching in circuit.

Back up in the box I make the necessary entries in the Train Register and look around. There are now three freight trains waiting to be dealt with: 6B51, the Tees, at No.2; 7Z11, the Haverton Hill at No.1; and 6Z68, the Immingham at DA115. Holesmouth gives 2-1 'Train Out of Section' for the passenger and looking out of the window I see the examiner walking back to his cabin. He sees me and waves his hand in a gesture which I know means that the Tees is 'ready to roll'. Sure enough, within a minute the shunters emerge from their cabin, shunting poles held under arms like rifles at the ready. As Dave yells out, 'Run-round the Tees, Signalman!', I'm already heaving the locking bars over and pulling up the junction. Locking bars once again pulled, I slowly clear signal No.2. A roar from the loco exhaust and a blast on the horn indicate that the driver has seen the signal. Swiftly I call attention to Holesmouth and get the road for a five bells 'Fully Fitted Freight Train', advising my colleague in that

box that this is a 'run-round'. 'Line Clear' pops up on the Block instrument and I pull off the starter, No.7. As the train approaches the box, the driver shuts off power and slows a little for Mad Dave to leap on to the cab steps. The driver opens up 37304 once again and the train blasts its way towards Holesmouth. John Duffy walks slowly behind the train, ready to couple the loco on when it comes back. The Tees stops just beyond my crossover and John moves forward to take the air hose off its dummy. He opens the air pipe cock and this destroys the air pressure, enabling Dave to uncouple the brake pipes at the other end and then uncouple the loco.

Now that the line is clear ahead of HM1, I can clear that signal, allowing 7Z11 to trundle round to No.2 signal, where it, too, will be examined. Up the bank DA115 will clear automatically to a single yellow when the track circuit at HM1 is clear, allowing the Immingham to make its way slowly down to HM1.

At 08.13 I receive the 'Loco Arrived' 2-1-3 bell signal from Holesmouth followed by a 2-3 'Is Line Clear for Light Engine' on the Up road. Once accepted by me, Holesmouth puts it 'On Line' right away, but I leave the 'Line Clear' on the Block to give him time to pull off his signal. Once I see the loco heading back towards me, I can switch the Block to 'Train on Line'. I slowly clear the Up Home and 37304 shortly comes to a stand outside the box. I put the Home signal back and pull up the crossover points and dummy. 37304 drifts back over on to the Down line and buffers up to its train. As John Duffy clambers between the buffers to couple up the loco and the brake pipes, I put the dummy back to Danger and send 'Train Out of Section' to Holesmouth. Strictly speaking, at this point I should now send 'Blocking Back Inside Home Signal' to Holesmouth, because my Up main clearing point is about to be fouled by the Tees' next move, but this is seldom done. Instead, I set the road from the Down line across to the Up line and to Severn Beach. Taking a token from the machine, I pull off the signals: dummy No.52; signal 62 'Up Main Starting to Severn Beach' and the Severn Beach line advanced starter, No.60.

With a blast on the horn, 37304 gets the Tees on the move. Mad Dave leans out of the cab, arm outstretched for the token, which he takes from me with a flourish. The driver opens up the throttle and the diesel's exhaust rockets skywards as the heavy train rumbles over the junction and picks up speed. I replace the signals behind the train, reverse the crossover points and send 3-2-3 'Train Drawn Back Clear of Section' to Holesmouth, who acknowledges the signal and drops the Down line Block indicator to Normal.

It takes around 10 minutes for the Tees to reach Severn Beach sidings. When it gets there, Dave will use the token to unlock the ground frame and let the train into the sidings. Once in, he will put the points back to Normal (for the single line) and replace the token in the machine there. He'll phone the box to let me know he's done that and I'll make sure I can get another token out at my end, as it's been known for some unscrupulous shunters to keep the token with them whilst they go into the ICI factory, thus ensuring they have the road when they come out! All is well on this occasion and Dave runs round the train again and they descend the slope under the road and into the factory.

The 08.08 Bristol to Severn Beach passenger is due and in turn makes its way to 'the Beach'. When the DMU returns from Severn Beach at 09.13 I know the shunters will be waiting to come out of the sidings, so once I restore the token to the instrument in the box, I hold down the release plunger. The phone buzzes once; it's Dave. 'I've got a key,' he says. 'Loco for Stoke Gifford!'

This is where another of Hallen Marsh's anomalies comes in useful. The Up main line is signalled for bi-directional use for a short stretch. Movements from Severn Beach only can be signalled from the single line on to the Up main. From there they can either regain the Down Main via the crossover, points 51, enter the sidings, or reverse and run to Bristol via Henbury. As this latter move is the one required, I send the 'Blocking Back Inside Home Signal' 2-4 to Holesmouth and peg up 'Train on Line' for the Up main. Next I unbolt points 15 by putting lever 13 to Normal, then put back lever 15 and rebolt by pulling 13 again. Then I pull up the Safety point on the single line, 16. This done, I look out for the approaching loco.

The box door opens and John Duffy runs up the stairs. 'Run-round the Haverton Hill!' he cries and rushes back to ground level. I ask the road for a 4-1 on the Down line, tell Holesmouth it's another run-round, then pull off signals 2 and 7, rapping out two bells 'Train Entering Section' as I do so. Loco 25325 hauls the Haverton Hill tanks past the box as I lean out of the window to watch their progress. The last wagon passes and I see John neatly remove the tail lamp with his shunting pole.

Turning to the levers again, I pull No.1 to allow 6Z68 to draw forward to No.2. I can see that 37304 is approaching so I clear signal 40 to allow the loco to run on to the Up main and come to a stand outside the box. I reset the junction by putting back signal 40, reversing points 16 and locking bar 17. I pull up the Up main facing points 14, lock them with 17 and slowly clear signal 64, 'Up Main to Filton Starting', to indicate to the driver that he only has the road as far as the next signal. This is because 6Z68 is not yet clear of the single line. 37304 slides slowly off towards Rockingham Road bridge whilst I watch the track circuits on the single line.

Dave brings me up the token and dashes off to help his chargeman with the run-round. The single line becomes clear and I send the description '0F69'

('Light Diesel for Stoke Gifford') to the panel whilst reversing the motor points. With an audible 'click', the indicator shows a release and I can clear signal 63 to allow 37304 to proceed. The distant sound of a loco horn tells me that the driver has seen the colour-light change and I turn my attention to the run-round. Clearing the Block-back I'm immediately offered the light engine off 7Z11 and the run-round proceeds as before. I send 3-2-3 at 09.33 and this time it's John Duffy who leans from the cab to grasp the token from me.

Just to keep things moving, Dave yells from outside: 'Fisons!', which means that 6Z68, still trickling towards No.2, is ready to go. I get the road for a five bells and pull Nos. 2 and 7. Then it's over to the window to watch the train pass. I'm not just having a breather, but looking for anything wrong with the train, such as binding brakes. The train, headed by a Class 31, 31102, slows to pick up Mad Dave and as the last tank rolls by the figure of the Venerable Mead is seen crossing the tracks to the box. He comes up the stairs just as the Severn Beach ground frame phone rings. This is John announcing that the Haverton Hill is 'In Clear'. I test the token, tell him it's OK and go to the desk to enter the times in the book. Pete Mead puts the kettle on as the phone from the smelting works rings.

'Good Morning, yoong man,' says a voice, in a distinctive Birmingham accent. This is Don, one of the smelting works shunters. 'We'd loike to come up the Outwards to the spur to fetch our coke, please.'

The train of about thirty-five wagons of coke is brought over from Margam Sorting sidings in South Wales by service 6C10 every weekday evening and shunted into the spur for collection by the smelting works loco the next day.

As I tell Don it's OK to come up the sidings, a glance out of the window reveals the yellow smelting works diesel moving towards my signals, the barriers of the level crossing on Smoke Lane lifting behind it. As the points are already in the correct position, all I need to do is pull signal 36 to allow the loco on to the Column Road, then 23 'Spur Starting' to let it proceed on to the coke. The little yellow four-wheeled engine rattles up the Column Road, its driver sounding a greeting on the horn. Don is riding on the front step. The engine stops to attach our brake van and then pushes this on to the coke. I throw back 36 and 23 signals then pull No.20 (top of a stack of three dummies) to allow them back on to the Column Road; signal 30, 'Column Road to Outwards Starting' and the Outwards starter, 31. The train load of coke can now head back into the factory when it's ready. Thankfully I accept the cuppa offered by the examiner and, grabbing a packet of biscuits from my locker, fall into the chair, prepared for a chat with Pete Mead.

Three minutes later, at 09.47, the 09.15 Bristol–Severn Beach is asked up, so I have to get up and deal with that. The coke is rumbling past the box

1982: a mixture of carbon dioxide and ammonia heads for Severn Beach ICI whilst the Tees potash rolls in from Stoke Gifford.

6C10, the Margam sorting sidings – Hallen Marsh coke – rolls past Hallen Marsh box before setting back into the spur. 1983.

now, loaded wagons thumping out a slow beat over the rail joints. The little diesel is going for all it's worth to keep the heavy train on the move. I throw back the signals behind the coke and watch the Smoke Lane barriers lowering for its passage back into the factory.

The Block bell rings twice 'Train Entering Section', so I go to the shelf, acknowledge the bell, peg up 'Train on Line' and lean out of the window ready to hand out the token. The driver snatches the token and accelerates off to the Beach. Giving 'Train Out of Section' and dropping the Block to Normal, I'm straight away asked a 2-3, 'Light Engine'. Four buzzes on the box–box phone tell me it is a loco for Bath Road shed. I acknowledge this, peg up 'Line Clear' and set the junction for the Up Filton.

The smelting works four-wheel Sentinel shunter pulls the coke along the Column Road towards the Outwards siding and the smelter.

As I send the description 0F74 to the panel and get a release, so Holesmouth sends 'Train Entering Section' and I pull off all signals for the loco. 31302 slows to allow Mad Dave to drop off the step before powering away over the points. Dave comes up into the box and we give him a cup of tea.

The next move is the return of the passenger train so I reset the junction and have barely finished the booking when the factory phone rings again and it's Don wanting to come back up on to the Column Road with the brake van. I give him signal 36 and see the DMU approaching from Severn Beach, so rush outside to grab the token. Before I get back to the top of the box stairs, the Severn Beach ground frame phone is ringing!

I head straight to the token machine, knowing that John is waiting to come back from ICI with the Haverton Hill loco. The examiner has answered the phone, so, putting the token in, I hold down to give a release. I get a thumbs up from Pete Mead: John has the key and it's 'Loco for Bath Road'.

Now, the road is already set from the Beach to the Down Main, so I leave it that way. As soon as Holesmouth sends 'Train Out of Section' for the passenger, I ask him 3-3-2 'Shunting into Forward Section' and get an acknowledgement and 'Line Clear' back. The diesel is getting close already – this driver must be anxious to get back to shed – so I slowly pull signal 3. 25323 squeals to a stand outside the box and John jumps down from the cab. 'Which way?' he yells. 'Henbury!' I yell back over the engine noise and go back to the frame to pull lever 7 slowly.

John conveys this information to the driver. The engine's air brakes hiss and it moves forward to stand clear of crossover 51. I send two bells to Holesmouth, put signals 3 and 7 back followed by 13 and 17 locking bars and set the junction for the Up Filton again, pulling points 15 and 14, locking bar 17and crossover 51. I pull disc 52, then slowly pull signal 64 to indicate to the driver that signal 63, out of sight round the corner beyond Rockingham Road bridge, is still at Danger. 25325 sounds its horn and moves back over the crossover on to the Up main.

Whilst this is going on, John Duffy has come back up into the box and put the token on the table by the token machine. The smelting works loco is blowing up for the road back into the factory so I pull signals 30 and 31, put back disc 52 and send the description 0F74 to the Panel. Then I put back 64 signal as 25325 slowly makes its way to HM63. 'Shunt Withdrawn' is sent to Holesmouth at 10.15 and I now turn to the Train Register to catch up with the booking. There's still no release from the panel as I put 30 and 31 back behind the smelting works engine and pour myself another cup of tea, the first one being now cold.

The TD starts to chatter, squawks loudly and turns up 6B51. I press the acknowledge button to stop the noise, reverse the motor points and pull lever 4 to accept the train. I pull signal 1.

The HM63 phone rings; it's the driver of 25325 carrying out Section K. He's none too happy to learn that he will have to wait for a train to clear the single line before he can go on his way. All drivers think they have priority!

Dave announces that 6B51 will be the trip working from Stoke Gifford. This usually comprises 'roll-top' wagons from the Continent containing metals for the smelter, a few ferrywagons for Town Goods and wagons of chocolate destined for Rowntree's distribution depot at Avonmouth station. 'We'll shunt it when it arrives,' says John, who has previously seen the train consist (TOPS list) in his cabin.

The 10.08 Bristol–Severn Beach passenger is asked up at 10.36, shortly before 6B51 emerges from beneath Rockingham Road bridge. The driver of the DMU snatches the token from me and the unit clatters its way over the junction and off to the Beach. I send 'Train Out of Section' to Holesmouth and follow it by asking for a shunt: 3-3-2. I hear the 'Accepted' indicator from the panel click over for 0F74 but for the moment I'm giving the preference to the shunters. I pull off signals 2 and 7, send two bells to Holesmouth and then reverse the motor points and pull HM63.

The trip working, headed by 37304 for the second time that morning, rolls past the box as I reset points 19 behind the light engine now on the single line. I slam back 2 and 7 signals, pull over

Some of the wagons seen in
Avonmouth: two Belgian 'roll-tops' for
the smelter.

One of the 'curtain-sided' timber
wagons that were known to rail staff
as 'Elvises'.

Ferrywagons were used in several
locations around Avonmouth.

Suphuric acid tanks were converted from chlorine tanks by Tiger Rail, and ran between the smelting works and Swansea.

Let there be no doubt who uses this tank!

points 25 and dummy 26 and, as the shunters wave the train back into the spur, I busy myself with some more booking.

From outside, Mad Dave yells out a stream of instructions which I hasten to write down on a piece of paper: 'Spur-Down Henbury; Down Henbury-Spur; Spur-Column; Column-Outwards; Outwards-run round Column; Column-push down on to Outwards, from Outwards to Down Main-Down Main to Rowntree's.

We achieve most of this before the passenger is due back. The trip is pushed back on to the spur, where it attaches the brake van, towing the van and five wagons of chocolate back out on to the main line and then pushing them back on to the Down Henbury, where they are uncoupled. The loco and remaining traffic goes back on to the spur and then on to the Column Road, where the engine is uncoupled. This then runs round the traffic on the Column Road via points 28, 29 and 25, I reset the road, pull dummy 26 and signal 30 and 37304 pushes four 'roll-tops' and a ferrywagon for the smelter down on to the Outwards.

There we have to pause as the 10.50 from the Beach is due back, so I cancel the shunt and ask the road ahead for the passenger.

The DMU passes at 10.56 and battle recommences. This time the 37 needs to run from the Outwards to the Down Henbury. There's no signal for this move so when I've reversed points 28 and 29 and checked the road, I wave the driver back on to his train. As soon as Holesmouth sends me 'Train Out of Section' for the passenger, I ask the road for a 1-4, advising the signalman by phone that this is 'Rowntree's trip, 5 on and not calling at Town Goods on the way down'. The examiner ambles along the track and climbs up into the brake van. He'll ride with the trip to examine any wagons they fetch out of Rowntree's siding. Mad Dave swings up into the van, along with his shunting pole, whilst John clambers up into the loco cab. I reset 28 and 29, pull locking bar 27 and send 'Train Entering Section' to Holesmouth before dashing to pull lever 7 before it gets locked by the Block indicator. The Rowntree's sets off for Avonmouth station and I can at last sit down.

The door at the bottom of the steps opens and the well-measured paces of a pair of sturdy boots are heard on the treads. A flat cap comes into view. 'Mornin',' says a voice. It's Merv Jacobs, the Permanent Way ganger. He's just walked the line from Severn Beach. Merv places his rolled-up flags in the corner of the box and sits down in a chair, complaining that his feet are killing him. Naturally I sympathize with him and make a pot of tea. There's now a half-hour lull in traffic, so I take the opportunity to have a talk with Merv. He tells me that there's an engineers' occupation of the line between Hallen Marsh and Severn Beach on the coming Sunday and he will be the Person in Charge of Possession (PIP). I ask him how his prize-winning flowers are coming along and he replies that it's been a good year for them. Merv enjoys his cup of tea but he's a conscientious man and soon sets off to continue his patrol of the line. With a 'Probably see you on Sunday', he's gone down the steps when the Block bell rings again. It's the return of the shunters with the Rowntree's trip: 1-4 on the Block.

I peg up 'Line Clear' to Holesmouth and set the road for the spur by unlocking points 37 and pulling up points 25 and 37, locking 37 with locking bar 38. In order to gain access to the Rowntree's siding at Avonmouth station, the Rowntree's trip had to run to Avonmouth Dock junction where it ran onto the single line between there and Clifton. Dock Junction is the only ex-Midland Railway signal box left south of Birmingham and its Home signal is an upper quadrant. Once behind Dock junction's Home signal, the trip waited for the double- to single-line junction to be reversed and 'Line Clear' obtained from Avonmouth St Andrews box. As the trip will be stopping in the section to service Rowntree's siding, the trip is accepted 'Under the Warning' so the Home signal is cleared very slowly and a steady green hand signal exhibited from Dock Junction box. This tells the driver that the line is clear only as far as Rowntree's siding. Propelling its wagons and brake van now, the trip sets off slowly back towards Avonmouth station.

Back at Hallen, the trip is put 'On Line' and I wait until it is slowing down before clearing signal 39 to permit the train to run into the spur. The brake van rocks as it passes over the points followed by three wagons from Rowntree's and the loco. Dave leans from the brake van and yells, 'Loco to shed via Clifton!' I throw 39 signal to Danger and send 'Train Out of Section' to Holesmouth and, as I do so, the train describer starts up. I reset the road for the Up main and go to the TD. This time it's '6C36' which appears. This is the Westbury yard to Severn Tunnel junction freight, which runs via Avonmouth to pick up any traffic from the smelter, Town Goods or Rowntree's. I reverse the motor points 19 and pull the acceptance lever 4, followed by lever 1 so 6C36 can run all the way to signal 2. I collar up lever 2.

Sending 2-1 to Holesmouth now for the Rowntree's, I'm offered the 11.40 Bristol–Severn Beach passenger, which I accept. I set the road for the Beach and get a token out ready. Then I pull dummy 21 to allow the trip engine out from the spur to signal 7 and ask Holesmouth the road for a light engine, 2-3, buzzing four times on the box–box phone to indicate the loco is for Bath Road shed. It's 12.17 as 37304 accelerates out of the spur and I put it 'On Line' to Holesmouth.

A few minutes later, Holesmouth sends 2-1 for the loco and two bells for the Up passenger. By the time I've handed out the token, put the boards back behind the passenger and cleared back to Holesmouth, I glance up and see 6C36 coming to a stand at No.2. I give a quick phone call to the shunters to say, 'The Tunnel's here', and catch up with some booking. The shunters' instructions are to 'put the Tunnel up the spur'. This time there's no need to shunt into forward section as the Tunnel comprises just three wagons and will fit between the down starter and 25 points. I clear No.2 slowly and the Tunnel trickles down to No.7. Leaning out of the window I yell to the driver to set back up the spur. He waves to show he understands. Pulling 25 points and 26 dummy, I watch the short train set back into the spur against the three wagons brought back from Rowntree's. The shunters now want to run round but the 12.32 from the Beach gets priority so I set the road for that and get 'Line Clear' from Holesmouth.

6C36 forming up on the Inwards siding.

The passenger passes in due course and I run back up the stairs to put the token back in the machine. Then it's reset the junction and pull up 25 points again while waiting for the passenger to clear Holesmouth. As soon as I get 2-1 from Holesmouth I ask a five bells and put it 'On Line' straight away, telling my colleague at Holesmouth that this is a run-round. Then it's back to the frame and pull signal 21 and the starter No.7. The run-round takes 26 minutes in all, from the time I put the 'Train on Line' to the time I send 3-2-3 'Train Drawn Back Clear of Section'.

Nobody, it seems, is in a hurry – now.

6C36 departs Hallen Marsh at 12.51, bound for Severn Tunnel junction and at last I've got some time to myself. I use it to sweep and buff up the floor to bring up the shine in the polished lino, then rake out the fire and dispose of the ashes outside, put more coal on the fire and take the coal buckets to the coal shed and fill them up. After this I wash up the teacups and pack my belongings away in my locker.

It's the custom at this box to leave a freshly brewed pot of tea on the table for the man who relieves you, so on goes the kettle. It's also the custom for the crew of the next Up passenger train to Severn Beach to ring the Hallen Marsh signalman from Avonmouth station and ask for the kettle to be boiling when they arrive for the token.

The Up passenger is asked up as usual and I

set the road and pull off. At 13.40, Holesmouth puts the train 'On Line' and soon the DMU is coming to a stand outside the box with a squealing of brakes. The driver reaches up for the token. The guard's compartment door opens and the guard swings down to ground level, tea can in his hand. He climbs the steps to the operating floor and a time-honoured ritual now takes place. The guard hands over the tea can with a comment such as, 'I see they still haven't taken the roof off this place then, Signalman!' (meaning, if they let some fresh air into the box, you lot might wake up and not delay our trains!). Filling the can with boiling water, I suggest that the guard is merely a parasite who can't be bothered to make his own tea. Ritual complete, the guard thanks me very much and goes back to his train, which then departs for Severn Beach. While they wait there to come back, the train crew will enjoy their lunch with a cuppa. As I put the boards back behind the train, I see my relief's car pull up next to mine.

But I haven't finished yet. The smelter phone rings and it's Don again: 'We want to come up and put some traffic on the Outwards, mate.' I tell him that's OK and watch the Smoke Lane barriers rise and fall again behind the little yellow diesel, A rake of wagons moves slowly up the Outwards siding as far as my signals, then the shunting loco is off again, back across Smoke Lane into the factory. I book the move at 13.53.

The ISC Sentinel and traffic 'down in the works'.

My mate comes up into the box and I hand over to him with a brief outline of the current position of things. Then I'm off home, tired after a busy, but interesting shift.

The Porter

The duties of a station porter included the collecting of tickets, sweeping platforms, cleaning lavatories, loading and unloading parcels and light goods, and helping passengers with luggage and directions. At stations with goods sheds, the porter would also work the small hand-crane to load and unload wagons as required. Sometimes, they would help with shunting.

On the Clifton Extension and Avonmouth lines, where porters were provided, their turn of duty commenced before the first train of the day was due and ended after it had departed. This period was

37008 poses with (left to right) Pete Mead, Shunter Dave McIlwain and Chargeman Shunter John Duffy. Hallen Marsh 1985.

normally split into two shifts. However, when BR made cuts to staffing levels in the wake of Beeching, the number of porters and other staff at stations was drastically reduced and guards would issue tickets on the trains.

Up to May 1968, the duty roster at Avonmouth Dock station was as follows:

Leading porter No.1:
- Book on Duty at 05.14.
- Open up the station and switch on electric lighting as necessary.
- Attend to crossing gates as required.
- Sweep platforms daily. Clean lavatories daily. Clean station premises daily.
- Attend to parcels traffic.
- Read gas, water and electric light meters on Friday each week and enter reading in the record book.
- Assist as required.
- Book off Duty at 12.30.

Leading porter No.2:
- Book on Duty at 15.14 daily.
- Attend to crossing gates as required.
- Sweep platforms daily and dust around.
- Maintain windows of station premises in clean condition.
- Keep fire buckets on platform clean and filled with water.
- Attend to parcels traffic.
- Extinguish electric lighting and lock up station after departure of the last train.
- Assist as required.
- Book off Duty at 22.30.

Note: leading porter No.1 to rotate duty with leading porter No.2 week and week about.

Porter:
- Book on Duty 07.00 daily.
- Separate notices etc. for delivery to, leaving remainder of notices and correspondence in the wallet to be collected by the officeman.
- Deliver notices etc, together with any correspond-

ence from the Area Manager's Office, to Hallen Marsh to St Andrews junction inclusive, collecting time sheets and any other correspondence for the Area Manager. [Notices and time sheets from and for Avonmouth Dock junction were collected and delivered by a messenger.]

Meal interval is between 10.15 and 11.15.

- Depart to Shirehampton daily per 11.20 passenger train from Avonmouth Dock station.
- Clean Upside and Downside platforms at Shirehampton.
- Return to Avonmouth Dock per 11.54 passenger train from Shirehampton and relieve Leading Porter on early turn.
- Attend to crossing gates as required.
- Deal with parcels traffic.
- Maintain windows of crossing cabin in clean condition.
- Keep fire buckets at crossing cabin in clean and filled with water.
- Assist as required.
- Book off Duty at 15.16.

It should be remembered that at Avonmouth Dock station the porters worked the crossing gates ground frame.

During the same period the duty roster of the porter at Clifton Down was as follows:

Porter:
- Book on Duty at 08.00 daily.
- Inspect station premises and attend to any immediate urgent requirements.
- Depart per 08.36 passenger train to Sea Mills and perform cleaning duties there.
- Depart to Redland station per 09.31 passenger train and perform cleaning duties.
- Depart to Montpelier station per 10.56 passenger train and perform cleaning duties.
- Return to Clifton Down per 11.40 passenger train and perform cleaning duties.
- Fire buckets at all points to be maintained in a clean condition and filled with water.

- Meters to be read each Friday and readings entered in the record book.
- Assist as required.
- Book off Duty at 15.16.

After another cost-cutting exercise in May 1968, intended to make the line more profitable, the porters' duties were cut further. At Avonmouth Dock station the telephone exchange, which had until then been staffed by a leading porter grade on early and late shifts, was reduced to one Leading Porter working 08.30–17.30 Monday to Friday with a break between 12.00 and 13.00. The porters' duties between Montpelier and Avonmouth Dock were now to be covered by one man as follows:

Clifton Down porter, hours and duties:
- Book on Duty 07.00 (SX) and attend to any immediate requirements at Clifton Down.
- Book off Duty at 15.30.

Arrive	Station	Depart	Cleaning time etc.
	Clifton Down	07.24	
07.28	Montpelier	08.27	59 minutes
08.29	Redland	09.24	55 minutes
09.26	Clifton Down	10.36	34 minutes
(Take meal break 10.00 to 10.30 hours)			
10.41	Sea Mills	11.49	68 minutes
11.59	Avonmouth Dock	14.15	2hr 16 mins*
14.30	Clifton Down		60 minutes

(*Also provides cover for level crossing)

By the 1980s, the duties of the porters had gone and the Avonmouth lampman was given the responsibility of sweeping the platforms along the line.

The Lampman

The 1948 Avonmouth Signal lampman's area covered the lines between Henbury (inclusive) and Pilning Low Level via Hallen Marsh to Gloucester Road inclusive. He was also responsible for the lamps at Pilning station booking office and signal lamps to Severn Tunnel East box's Up Distant. Filton West Up Starting and Down Distant signals, plus the stop blocks in the carriage sidings, was covered by the Patchway lampman. The rest of the Filton West signals were covered by the Lawrence Hill lampy. The line between Avonmouth and Kingswood junction was covered by an LMR lampman.

Wally Cotterell used to be the Avonmouth lampman and was succeeded in the 1970s by John Hawkins. When Hawkins went into the signalling grade, his job was taken by Len Fynn, who had previously worked at Temple Meads and Bristol St Philips goods depots.

By 1980, the duties of the Avonmouth lampman were as follows:

- Monday: clean, trim, refill and light all signal lamps at Avonmouth Dock junction
- Tuesday: clean, trim, refill and light all signal lamps at St Andrews and Avonmouth Goods Yard boxes
- Wednesday: clean, trim, refill and light all signal lamps at Ashton junction signal box (on the south side of Bristol and the only other remaining manual box in the area)
- Thursday: clean, trim, refill and light all signal lamps at Holesmouth and Hallen Marsh
- Friday: sweep all station platforms. Drive to Bristol West depot and clean, trim and refill the sidings stop block lamps

The lamp on the stop blocks at Severn Beach platform was, by this time, electric.

When a 'lampy' was on leave or off sick, the relief signalmen used to cover the lamping duties on overtime – not an easy number. I well remember climbing the tall signals at Dock junction and St

Happy in his work: Lampman Len Fynn.

Andrews, carrying a lamp or two. At St Andrews Up Home signal, the wooden planked platform at signal level was covered with a slippery green algae-like growth, which made movement precarious, especially when there was a gale blowing! And you tended to go home smelling sweetly of paraffin...

The Shunter

The job of shunter was a busy one. On the go for most of the shift in a busy yard, his duties were to make up trains for departure and 'break' up trains on arrival. For example, a long train arrives on the Outwards road in the Royal Edward Yard. Ten of the wagons in the middle of the train are destined for the PBA. The shunter, armed with the details of the train by the guard, walks along the train until he identifies where to make the 'break'. He signals

to the crew of the loco to 'ease up' if the couplings are tight and then signals to the driver to 'destroy' the vacuum in the braking system. This done, he scrambles between the wagons and uncouples the vacuum pipes. He then unwinds the coupling tensioner and lifts the heavy coupling off the drawbar hook. Climbing out from between the wagons, the shunter signals to the driver to 'Draw ahead', thus parting the train.

As the train pulls forward, the shunter is running alongside and, when the wagons are clear of the points to the siding he wants, he signals to the driver to stop. Pulling the hand point lever, he then waves the train back on to the siding. The pilot loco may be waiting on the siding and the wagons are pushed gently against the pilot and its 'backer' (shunter's truck) and the shunter, with a flourish, whips the coupling over the hook using his long shunting pole. There is no need to couple the vacuum pipes as the wagons will be shunted on to the PBA reception line.

Waving the driver forward again, the shunter runs along the train and repeats the manoeuvre, in reverse this time, to get the train engine and wagons back against the main train. Once the train has buffered up to its remaining wagons, the shunter dives between the wagons once again, lifts the coupling and drops it over the hook, then winds up the tensioner. He couples the vacuum 'bags' together, slips the safety clip through and dives out again. Then he stands at the trackside and, fist clenched, pumps his arm up and down. In some contexts, this could be construed as a rather rude gesture, but in a railway situation it means 'Create vacuum' (or 'Air', if the train is air-braked).

There's a creaking and groaning as the train's braking system is exhausted of air and the vacuum recreated.

The shunter walks to the rear of the train and, if there is a guard's van, tells the guard to make a brake test. The guard, in his van, moves the vacuum brake handle to the full brake application position and watches the vacuum brake gauge drop to zero. He then restores it to the running position and watches the vacuum rise again.

Pete Mead and Shunter Bernie Reid.

In the absence of a brake van, the shunter would advise the guard to make the brake test, which would be done by removing the rearmost brake pipe from its 'dummy' to destroy the vacuum. The driver would sound his horn when the vacuum had been destroyed and the brakes applied. The guard would then replace the vacuum pipe on its dummy again and wave (or show his handlamp) to the driver to recreate vacuum. Once the test had been done successfully, the shunter would advise the signalman that that particular train was ready to leave for its destination.

The job is not over for the shunter, as he now has to supervise the pilot and wagons to move on to the PBA reception sidings.

This is just a small sample of the work required of one train. Sometimes, the wagons that needed to be shunted out were in several different parts of the train, in which case, several 'cuts' were needed. In a busy yard, the work went on round the clock, in all weathers, including wind, rain, snow or fog. It was a dirty, greasy job and the postholder needed to be very fit, as he would usually walk (or run) several miles during the course of a shift.

The Carriage and Wagon Examiner

The carriage and wagon examiner, or 'rolling stock technician' (RST), as they were known in the 1980s, was just as the name implies – a person who examined trains. Trains had to be checked at specified places on the railway system – mainly in goods yards – and the job of the examiner was to look for defects and, if any were found, decide whether the wagon concerned was able to run back to its place of origin at normal or reduced speed, for repairs, or whether it had to be 'red-carded'. If the latter, then the wagon was shunted out of the train and placed on a siding for later attention by the local carriage and wagon fitters or by a mobile repair gang. Most goods yards had one or two 'cripple' sidings, where

wagons which had been red-carded would be kept until they could be worked on. Minor repairs – such as replacing a frayed vacuum pipe or tightening up a loose bolt – were carried out on the spot by the examiner.

C & W staff were allocated to both Old Yard and Royal Edward, but after the closure of Royal Edward the examiner was allocated a cabin at Hallen Marsh. Once the examiner knew that a certain train was approaching, he would advise the signalman at Hallen Marsh to 'keep the train at No.2 signal' whilst he examined it. The signalman would keep signal 2 at Danger and place a reminder collar on the lever to prevent it being moved.

On arrival at Hallen Marsh (one of several places where trains could be examined), the train would come to a stand and the examiner would advise the driver that he was examining the train. Then he would commence a slow walk along the side of the train, looking at every vehicle for defects: damaged or leaking buffers, damaged couplings, broken springs, worn brake blocks, and overheated axle boxes would all came under his close scrutiny. Having reached the rear of the train, he would walk slowly along the other side back to the locomotive. If all was well, he would shout out to the driver that

Hallen Marsh signal box with (left to right) Shunter Tom Gallop and C & W Examiner Dick Cuff. Signalman John Gibbs leans out of the box window.

he could move when instructed by the shunters and signalman; if not, he would make his way to the shunters' cabin and advise them which vehicles needed to be shunted out of the train.

When the Rowntree's trip ran, the examiner usually travelled with the train to the Rowntree's depot at Dock station in order to examine the loaded wagons before they left the depot, in case any faults had occurred during loading.

Pete Mead and Dick Cuff were two of the examiners. The relief examiner, who stood in for the regulars when they were on leave or off sick, was Geoff Breakey, who had been signalman at Uphill junction near Weston-super-Mare until made redundant there in 1972.

The Signal and Telegraph Lineman

Signal boxes, being full of signalling equipment, needed regular maintenance. This was the job of the signal and telegraph linemen (later called 'signal and telecommunications technicians') and their assistants. The Avonmouth line S & T men were based at Avonmouth Dock station, where they had a cabin at the end of the Up platform. Reg Talbot was lineman in 1950s, with Ron Smith as his assistant; Bob Theobald was lineman in the 1980s; his brother, Ken Theobald, had been assistant lineman at Avonmouth, starting work there in May 1956.

The S & T would make a weekly call at each signal box in turn and check batteries, cables, signalling instruments, signal wire pulleys and points. There was one occasion when one of the assistants, a young lad, went under the box to check some relays in one of the cabinets there. The rest of his gang and the signalman were putting the world to rights on the operating floor when there came a scream and a loud crash, followed by the sound of the locking room door slamming shut. Everyone thought there had been some sort of accident, but the lad was seen standing outside the box, taking deep breaths. It turned out that he was afraid of spiders and, when he took the door off the cabinet, he had come face to face with a rather large and fierce-looking specimen! He just shrieked, threw the door away and ran out of the box!

The S & T men were also called for when any failure of equipment occurred, often in the case of block failure or a signal wire breaking. In later years, vandalized signal post telephones were another common 'fault'.

When more trains passed in one direction over the single line than in the opposite direction, the result would be an imbalance in the number of tokens at one end of the section. In such cases the lineman would be called for, to open the token machine at the end where there were more tokens, extract the right number to balance the system and

Signal and telecommunications staff at work repairing signal wire pullies. Clockwise left to right are Steve, Adrian and Jon, watched over by Technician Bob Theobald.

take them to the signal box and place them in the machine at the other end of the section. This would all be dutifully recorded in the Train Register in both signal boxes, along with the number of tokens transferred.

The Permanent Way Department

The maintenance of the track, points, ballast and drainage were all part and parcel of the work carried out by the Permanent Way (or P. Way) department. To ensure regular inspection of the track, the line was split into lengths, each of which then became the responsibility of a gang of men. Each gang was supervised by a 'ganger', and it was his duty (or that of the designated 'patrolman') to walk his length every other day and inspect the track and points. He would carry a set of flags – one red, one green – with him. He would be looking for broken rails, loose sleepers, 'spreading' track (track that was becoming 'wide to gauge'), 'rail burn' (where a locomotive had suffered wheelslip and damaged the rail surface), sleepers 'pumping' (where the ballast was thin and the sleeper able to move up and down under a train, pumping slurry

out of the void), as well as many other defects. Everything would be noted down in a notebook. If a serious defect was found, the patrolman, who would know the time of the next train and the direction from which it was due to come, would head in that direction displaying a red flag. When he had covered a quarter of a mile without coming across a telephone, he would place three emergency detonators on the rail and walk on until he found a phone or arrived at a signal box.

'Routine' defects would be noted in his book and a report sent to his supervisor, who would bring it to the attention of the monthly engineering planning meeting. It would be discussed and, if necessary, an occupation of the line would be arranged for a coming weekend or night shift. Sometimes, if the job needed doing urgently, the ganger would discuss the defect with the signalman and arrange a local occupation to fix it. This meant that the gang would arrive either later that day or the next and the ganger and signalman would arrange for the work to take place between trains.

Sometimes, it was necessary for a permanent speed restriction to be put in place for various

Smudged notice of weekly engineering at Fisons siding.

Wrong Line Order issued for loco 6630 to travel 'wrong line' between Gloucester Road and Avonmouth Sidings boxes in October 1956. Signalman John Brazneill issued the order and it was countersigned by Harold Eady, his colleague at Sidings box. This was probably due to engineering work.

reasons, including sharp curves or subsidence. A Permanent Restriction of Speed (PRS) was advertised in weekly train notices and indicated by warning boards at the lineside. There was no excuse for a driver exceeding the speed limit and, if caught, he was usually disciplined.

On 8 March 1956, the 09.00 Temple Meads to Avonmouth, hauled by 'Prairie' 2-6-2 tank loco No.5528, was caught out. The driver failed to realize that a speed-recording machine was conveyed as part of his train and was logged passing through a 40mph PRS between Clifton Down and Sea Mills at 53mph, and through the PRS of 20mph between Sea Mills and Shirehampton at 31mph.His defence was that he had not been aware of the presence of the speed recorder and that he had failed to notice that

he had made up lost time between Clifton Down and Avonmouth. Exceeding speed limits on the railway is always considered to be potentially dangerous, and disciplinary action duly followed.

In order for the Permanent Way department to be able to carry out routine and planned or emergency work on the single line to Severn Beach and Pilning, there was a system in place whereby the gang could use a motorized trolley on the line. They had to get permission from the signalman concerned to put their trolley on the line, which was done by means of a 'ganger's key'; these were kept in instruments at intervals along the single line, where telephone communication with the signalman was also provided. There were two sections: Hallen Marsh to Severn Beach and Severn Beach to Pilning Low

By the 1980s, the Permanent Way gangs no longer worked from cabins; instead, they were 'mobile gangs' and had lorries with mess facilities. Dock junction 1983.

Level. The Hallen Marsh to Severn Beach section was known as Group A and there were two places where key instruments and telephones were sited: Box No.1 was at 13 miles and 54 chains (just to the Hallen Marsh side of the old Chittening Factory platform) and Box No.2 was sited at 12 miles 62 chains, which was at the lineside near to where the stream outlet known as 'New Pill Gout' ran into the Severn. The phones at both these locations communicated with the Hallen Marsh signalman.

The Severn Beach to Pilning Low Level section was known as Group B and ganger's key instruments and phones were sited at 11 miles 24 chains (near Pump House Siding ground frame) and 10 miles 24 chains (the Pilning side of Cross Hands halt). Group B phones communicated with the signalman at Severn Beach box, unless this box was closed, in which case the phones connected with Hallen Marsh.

The ganger's key was his authority to be on the single line and operated in much the same way as a single-line token or train staff. In the event of a ganger needing a key and the boxes at Pilning Low Level and Severn Beach both being closed,

Sleeper changing between trains. Visible (left to right) are: Bill Thatcher, Mervyn Jacobs and Johnny Buckley.

Returning to Bristol East depot after sleeper changing at Fisons: in the brake van, the lad with flaming hair is Rob Tudor.

both sections came under the control of the Hallen Marsh signalman.

The Hallen Marsh to Pilning junction single line came under the control of one Permanent Way gang, Gang No.149. Tom Cannard was the ganger at Hallen Marsh in the 1950s (he was said to be 'old' in 1949!) and Reg Martin was in the gang. After the Second World War, the Pilning Low Level ganger was Mr Williams.

In 1897 the Permanent Way Inspector at Shirehampton was Mr E.E. Baker. In the 1980s, the P.W. Inspector based at Stoke Gifford was Mr Wiseman and the supervisor was Arthur (Art) Fortune. Another supervisor frequently seen in charge of work at Avonmouth was Fred Webb. Mervyn Jacobs was the ganger in the 1980s based at Avonmouth. The gang consisted of Wilf Robbins, Bill Thatcher, Rob Tudor, Bert Lippiatt and Wayne Spence. The Clifton end of the line from Clifton Down to Avonmouth Dock station was patrolled by ganger Charlie Anderson and patrolman Johnny Buckley.

The Permanent Way staff carried out more than just track maintenance. They also took on the duties of 'snowmen' in extreme weather conditions, keeping points and other equipment clear of snow.

This was a cold and wet task and not as easy as it sounds; once the man had swept the snow out of the point blades, a strong wind and further precipitation would often ensure that he had to start again straight away. And if the wind did not cause the problem, the passage of a train would do it. Luckily, most of the Avonmouth area was never far from a signal box and the 'snowmen' generally stationed themselves in the box and worked as directed by the signalman. In other areas the men were stationed some distance away from the box, but still signed on there before trudging along the line to their cabin.

Another task carried out by the P. Way was to act as 'fogmen'. When visibility was reduced to the point at which the signalman could no longer see his 'fog marker' (usually the backlight of a signal around a quarter of a mile from the box), he would call out his fogman, either by telephone or by sending a porter to the man's house if the box was at a station. The fogman would report to the signal box and be allocated his duty – usually walking to the Distant signal of a signal box and staying there. All the time the signal was at Caution, the fogman had to keep one detonator on the rail and display a yellow hand signal or light. When the signal was

After working hard clearing the snow from the points, the Permanent Way gang pose for the camera. They are (left to right) Bert Lippiatt (rear), Wilf Robbins, Wayne Spence (rear), Ganger Mervyn Jacobs and Bill Thatcher. Wayne Spence was a talented artist and later went to work on Temple Meads station.

As it was located right on the banks of the River Severn, Hallen Marsh was a place where early-morning mist could soon turn to fog.

FOG AND WIND DUTIES

Extract from Train Register at Severn Beach Signal Box, 29 January 1958:

Snowmen on Duty 7.15am: H.H. Samsun and G.R. Tudor
Snowmen off Duty 7.15pm: H.H. Samsun and G.R. Tudor
A twelve-hour shift. All trains ran normally with no recorded delays.

Extract from Train Register at Severn Beach signal box, 29 November 1957:

Fog. Down Fogman on Duty 7.15am: H.H. Samsun. Up Fogman on Duty 7.16am: R. Palmer
Down Fogman off duty 11.00am: H.H. Samsun.
Up Fogman off Duty 11.00am: R. Palmer
Just under four hours' duty before the fog cleared. All trains ran normally and on time.

Extract from Train Register at Gloucester Road signal box, 30 January 1957:

Station advised 1.00pm that Windmen required.
Windmen on Duty 1.15pm
Windmen off Duty 5.30pm

LOCATION OF CATCH POINTS

Catch points were 'deliberate derailers' – points provided to throw any runaway trains or vehicles off the lines, in order to prevent disaster. Avonmouth being on the coast and therefore at sea level was accessed by lines that ran up and down gradients. Catch points were provided at the following locations:

- Henbury: 580 yards in the rear of the Up Home signal.
- Blaise: 870 yards in the rear of the Up Home signal.
- Filton West: 446 yards in the rear of the Up Starting signal.
- Clifton Down: 412 yards in the rear of the Down Home signal and 283 yards in the rear of the Up Home signal.
- Sea Mills: 437 yards in advance of the Down Intermediate Block Home signal.

Clear, the detonator was removed and the hand signal withdrawn.

Because of their proximity to the Rivers Avon and Severn, the Avonmouth lines were often affected by fog. The signal boxes being close together meant that many Distant signals were fixed to show a permanent Caution, so the detonator was on the line for the duration of the duty.

'Fogging' was another cold and damp job and the fogman was unable to enjoy the warmth of the signal box. However, there was normally a tiny wooden or concrete cabin sited at a Distant signal, with a small coal stove, so the man could brew tea or warm food (and himself!). In the later years of semaphore, 'double block' working was used when it was foggy and it was no longer necessary to call out fogmen. This meant that a signalman would not accept a train from the box offering it forward until he had it accepted by the box in advance. This could add time to train journeys but was usually worked so that delays were minimal. During the times it was foggy, staff were treated to the mournful drone of the docks foghorn: it was just a question of getting used to it...

The P. Way department also supplied staff to act as 'windmen' for the extra-long level-crossing gates at Gloucester Road and St Andrews junction. (The job was sometimes done by station staff, if available.)

CHAPTER 7

Signal Boxes

Kingswood Junction

Kingswood opened as a junction in October 1874 and was controlled by a Midland Railway signal box. It is unlikely that the signal box that stood there until 1965 was erected at the time when the junction opened. Presumably, an older MR-style cabin was used at first, as the 'standard' design of MR signal box did not arrive on the system until the 1880s. The wooden Kingswood Junction box possibly dated from the latter time; it had a twenty-four-lever MR frame and a Block switch was provided. It controlled the junction between the Bristol–Gloucester line and the Midland Railway's Clifton Extension to Avonmouth, as well as the entrance to Deep Pit colliery and the Atlas Locomotive works, home of the famous Peckett company, builders of industrial steam locomotives.

A ground frame, released from the signal box, worked the trailing connection leading into the sidings from the Down main line. At the Fishponds end of the sidings, a connection was made via a single slip into the main-line crossover. There was a single slip connection in the main diamond crossing of the junction and this acted as a mains crossover. Without a normal crossover, Kingswood junction used the crossover slip in the junction for such moves as crossing locomotives. In such cases it was rare, for example, for a loco from the Avonmouth lines requiring to go to Barrow Road shed (which would require crossing over at Kingswood junction) to get a clear road from Ashley Hill junction (or Stapleton Road Gas Sidings box if it was open), as the lines up and down Whitehall bank from Bristol's Lawrence Hill junction to Fishponds were so busy. In MR and LMSR days, it was normal practice for the Kingswood Junction signalman to refuse such a move from Ashley Hill junction (or Gas Sidings) until he could give full 'Line Clear'. In BR days, provided the line from Avonmouth was clear as far as the Home signal at Kingswood junction, then Regulation 5, the 'Warning Arrangement', was authorized. On receipt of the 'Is Line Clear?' bell code, the Kingswood Junction signalman would respond with the 3-5-5 bell signal. The Ashley Hill Junction (or Gas Sidings) signalman would then be required to caution the locomotive crew that the line was only clear to Kingswood junction's signal.

One signalman recalls the day when the bank was quiet and he was able to give full 'Line Clear' to his colleague at Ashley Hill junction for a light engine for Barrow Road shed. This turned out to be a 9F 2-10-0 and it steamed through the junction and came to a stand on the Up main. From here it had to be crossed through the slip to the Down branch before the slip was returned to normal and the engine waved back on to the Down main. Once 'Line Clear' had been obtained from Lawrence Hill junction, the loco was then able to steam off to shed. Such ease of movements was not normal.

In another unusual working, a train was booked 06.30 from Bath Midland Bridge road sidings to Westerleigh sidings, then from Westerleigh sidings to Bristol St Philips yard, where, having detached its train, the engine and brake van would run to Kingswood junction. Here, the engine and van would halt before reversing back on to the branch and onwards to Avonmouth. The crossover (slip) in the main lines was removed in August 1960, and the diagram shown here was current from then until closure of the LMR section of the Clifton Extension along with Kingswood Junction signal box, on 14 June 1965.

Unusually, the 'Up Main Starting' signal lever brass read 'Starter to Birmingham' rather than 'Up Main Starting'.

In the 1950s, Roy Langley, Jack Coles and Dave Boston worked here as signalmen. Wilf Stanley also worked here, as relief signalman.

Ex-Somerset and Dorset 2-8-0 loco 53802 propels a brake van back over Kingswood junction en route from Stapleton Road gas sidings to Westerleigh yard for the second 'Stapletons' trip of coke. (Wilf Stanley)

Stapleton Road Gas Sidings

Although fulfilling an important function when it opened, Stapleton Road Gas Sidings box became unstaffed on a regular basis between the two World Wars. 'Gas Sidings' as it was popularly known, was 'open as required' from the 1920s; even in the 1950s, a typical signalman's shift consisted of booking on duty at 07.30 and opening the box at 09.30 for the coal traffic. A usual day's working consisted of two coal trains into the sidings; the engine and brake van off the first would return to Westerleigh sidings for the second and haul that to Gas sidings.

Coal empties were almost always taken out via Stapleton Road GW sidings. At 12.10 the box would be switched out of circuit and the signalman would take his meal break until 12.40. From 12.40 until the end of his shift, at 15.20, the signalman would busy himself making out and attaching destination labels to empty coal wagons stabled on the sidings.

In its last few decades of use, Gas Sidings box was really little more than a ground frame, and as such it was musty and seldom, if ever, cleaned. The box always smelt damp and the lever brasses were dull.

All levers remained in use until closure. It closed permanently on 14 June 1965.

Relief signalmen known to have worked this box as required are Ray Whiteford, Wilf Stanley, Jim Barnes, Brian Lockier.

Ashley Hill Junction

Opened in 1874 with the MR's Clifton Extension line, Ashley Hill junction was controlled by a signal box built in a cutting by contractors MacKenzie & Holland to their design. It was equipped with a thirteen-lever MR Co. tumbler locking frame with levers at 6in centres and a Block switch was provided. All thirteen levers remained in use throughout the box's life. When wartime bomb damage necessitated single-line working between Ashley Hill and Kingswood junctions, a crossover was laid in on the Clifton side of the junction. This was never coupled to the signal box; in order to move the points, a crowbar was usually employed. The crossover was clipped and padlocked out of use when it was not needed.

Although the passenger services over the Kingswood junction–Ashley Hill junction section had been withdrawn in 1941 and freight traffic was sparse, the nationalized British Railways decided to replace the signal box when extensive repairs became necessary. Accordingly, a new signal box was built approx 63 metres towards Stapleton Road (GW), and the old Ashley Hill Junction box closed on 10 May 1959.

The second Ashley Hill Junction box was built to a British Railways 'Type 16B' design, a modern design in brick and concrete similar in style to the boxes at Tenby and Ashchurch. The new box opened on the same day as the old box closed. It had a twenty-three-lever five-bar vertical tappet locking frame with levers at 4in centres, plus a small two-lever frame for the detonator placers. The GWR-design five-bar VT frame was situated at the back of the operating floor, which meant that signalman worked with his back to the trains. This was LMSR practice and was widely adopted by British

Paxman-engined 'Teddy Bear' 0-6-0 No.D9502, having been backshunted on to the Up Midland branch to accommodate a passenger train, now moves off again with a freight for Avonmouth Old Yard. 5 April 1965. (R. Cuff)

Railways in their new signal boxes. However, the GWR style of signalling the layout was used, with the Distant signals occupying the ends of the frame (LMS practice was to have running signals in the middle of the frame). The 1941 crossover was coupled to the box and provided with ground signals. The detonator placer levers were provided on a separate small frame, although the main frame had four spaces and could have accommodated these two levers.

Montpelier signal box was closed at the same time as the old Ashley Hill junction, and the sidings there were operated by a new ground frame released by the signalman at the new Ashley Hill Junction box. A Block switch was provided. The opening times in 1953 were: 07.00–midnight on Monday, and then 07.00–01.00 Tuesday to Saturday. The morning turn was 07.00–15.00 for the signalman, with 15.00–17.00 being covered by a Montpelier porter/signalman. The remainder of the day was covered 17.00–01.00 by the late turn signalman. The Sunday turn of duty was 09.00–18.00.

In later years the box would close after the passage of the 23.30 Old Yard to Gloucester (known as the '11.30 Midland'), which passed Ashley Hill junction at approximately midnight. When the train had passed, the signalman would ring Gloucester Control and ask if anything else was about. The answer was invariably 'No', so, when the 'Train Out of Section' signal was received from Kingswood junction for the 23.30, Ashley Hill Junction box switched out.

A plunger in the signal box operated the platform bells at Montpelier and Redland stations. Three rings meant a Down (to Avonmouth) train was imminent; two rings meant an Up train.

Signalmen Bert Hopgood (ex-Shapwick box on the Somerset & Dorset Highbridge branch) worked here in the 1950s, and Jim Barnes and Wilf Stanley are known to have worked here as relief signalmen.

Ashley Hill Junction box was a victim of the radical rail closures of the 1960s, and stopped its operations on 27 February 1966, with some of its signals being added to the Stapleton Road (GW) box.

Montpelier

Contractors MacKenzie & Holland built several of the signal boxes on the Clifton Extension, including the small signal box at Montpelier, which used their own design. Opened in 1874, it was equipped with a sixteen-lever MR tumbler locking frame, with levers at 6in centres. Signals 1, 2 and 3 were rotary locked and there were no detonator placers here either.

The signal box special instructions called for the Up Distant signal, No.1, to be left at Caution when the box was switched out. This acted as an additional Distant for Ashley Hill junction.

In 1953 the box opening times were 06.15–22.15 Monday to Saturday. The box was manned by a signalman 07.00–15.00, then during the 1950s it was worked by a porter/signalman between 15.00 and 17.00; one of these was one 'Spud' Murphy. From 17.00 to 01.00 the box was again staffed by a signalman, and it was switched out 01.00–07.00. One of the regular signalmen here started his career as a porter on the LMSR.

As with the box at Ashley Hill junction, the last train was the 23.30 Avonmouth Old Yard–Gloucester freight, and before switching out at night, the signalman had to phone Gloucester Control to make certain that there were no more freight trains for the Avonmouth branch.

The layout at Montpelier underwent little or no change throughout its existence. The sixteen-lever signal box closed on 10 May 1959, and was replaced by a two-lever ground frame released from the second Ashley Hill Junction box.

Relief Signalman Wilf Stanley worked here on several occasions during the 1950s.

Clifton Down

The signal box at Clifton Down stood at the Avonmouth end of the Down platform. Designed and built by contractors MacKenzie & Holland, it was fitted with an MR twenty-eight-lever tappet locking frame with levers at 6in centres. The frame was laid out in typically Midland fashion, the shunting levers being all on the left side of the frame and the main running signals on the right. Again, there were no detonator placers. There were several alterations to the layout at Clifton Down over the years, starting with signal 15, which was renewed as a normal straight post signal, 159 yards from the

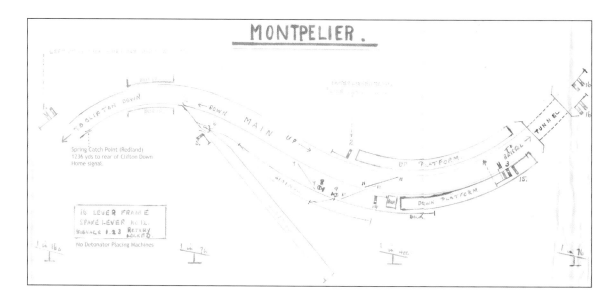

In the 1950s, Bristol District signalling inspectors made drawings of all layouts under their jurisdiction: this is one of Montpelier.

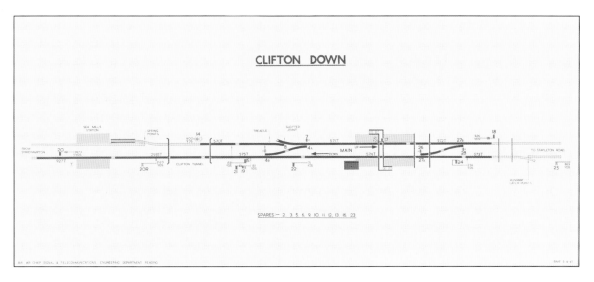

Clifton Down signal box track and signals diagram. 1970.

box, in December 1952. On Sunday 24 April 1960, the Up Distant No.4 was renewed as a two-aspect colour-light, 600 yards from the box. This signal was situated in the tunnel itself and was 2 feet 5 inches high.

Slip connection 10, together with shunting signal 9 and main-line signals 16 and 23, was taken out of use between 2 and 4 July 1967. By 1970, the connections into the yard had gone: points 2 and shunting signal 3 were recovered. Crossover 11, discs 12 and 13 were also removed.

Clifton Down was fitted with MR Rotary Block for most of its working life, hence the treadles to the rear of catch point No.8 and outside the box. For this reason, no engineering trains were permitted to work in the wrong direction on either line. Western Region '1948' pattern commutator block was provided in 1961.

Because of the Intermediate Block Section (IBS) at Sea Mills, the normal instructions for signalling trains were amended. When 'Is Line Clear?' was asked from Ashley Hill junction (or Montpelier), and the train was accepted by Clifton Down, the latter signalman cleared his signals without asking the train forward to Shirehampton. When 'Train on Line' was received from Ashley Hill junction,

Clifton Down then asked the train forward. 'Train Approaching' (1-2-1) was sent to Shirehampton when the train passed Clifton Down box; 'Train on Line' was sent when the train passed the IBS Starting signal.

Originally, a Block switch was not provided, but one was installed in the early 1960s. The 1953 opening times were: 05.00 Monday to 23.45, Sunday but in later years Clifton Down box was open continuously.

The 05.10 Down train from Bristol Temple Meads to Avonmouth was the first train and the 23.30 ex-Avonmouth goods for Gloucester was the last one up.

The platform bell at Clifton Down for the benefit of station staff was operated by the signalman. Three rings meant a Down train was approaching; two meant an Up train was approaching. A bell was also provided at Sea Mills station, remotely operated by Clifton signalmen. In this case, three rings on the Sea Mills bell indicated that a Down train was approaching that station.

Seventeen out of twenty-eight levers were still in use when Clifton Down signal box closed under Stage 6 of the 1970 Bristol Resignalling scheme, on 17 October 1970.

Shirehampton station and signal box. (Wilf Stanley)

Signalmen known to have worked at Clifton Down include Johnny Tetsall, who worked here in the 1950s and 1960s; Wilf Stanley, Jack Coles, John Gibbs, Johnny Tuckfield, Dennis Smith, H.E. (Harry) Bond, who left to take up a post at Filton Junction box in September 1955; B.J.M. (Benjy) Davies, who left Clifton Down in May 1957 to become signalman at Bristol East Depot, Austin Potter and Malcolm Eggleton.

Sneyd Park Junction

Little is known about this signal box, which was built in 1875 by railway signalling contractors McKenzie & Holland for the Clifton Extension. It is thought to have had a brick or stone base and wooden upper floor. It controlled the junction between the single-line Port and Pier railway from Hotwells and the Clifton Extension. When the Port and Pier line was closed, in 1922, there was little reason for Sneyd Park junction to exist; despite this, the box stayed open until 26 May 1935, albeit with the 'junction' part of its name removed.

Shirehampton

The Shirehampton box covered here was the second signal box at Shirehampton, opened in 1903. The signal box stood on the Down platform and was a small, pleasing box built to 'standard' MR design. It was equipped with a twenty-lever MR frame.

MR-style Rotary Block was in use here until it was replaced in the early 1960s by WR pattern instruments. With the Sea Mills IBS section, a similar method of working to that of Clifton Down was used to signal trains on the Up line.

The sidings, which had once served a small goods yard, were used in later years by an oil company. On closure of the signal box the points were connected to a ground frame released by Avonmouth Dock Junction box.

The 1953 opening times were 06.40–22.40 Monday to Saturday and 12.00–20.00 on Sunday. A Block switch was provided.

Men who are known to have worked at this box include Sam Small, Wilf Stanley and John Gibbs.

Shirehampton signal box was closed under Stage 6 of the 1970 Bristol Resignalling scheme.

Avonmouth Dock Junction

Avonmouth Dock Junction box was another Midland Railway box. It had a twenty-eight-lever frame with MR tappet locking and levers at 6in centres. Opened in 1905 and originally named 'Crown Brickyard Level Crossing', the box was made a Block Post and renamed when the Joint Goods lines from there to Avonmouth Old Yard and

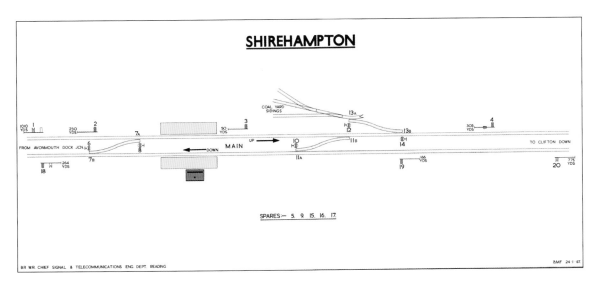

Shirehampton track and signals diagram. 1967.

the Docks were opened, in 1911. The box underwent quite a few layout changes and lasted until the rationalization plan of 1988.

The layout as originally signalled was an interesting one, with many unusual moves to be seen and made. There was, for example, in the 1950s, a run-round move, whereby a freight arriving on the Down goods line would detach its locomotive, which would be crossed to the Up goods line at the sidings box. Signalled as a light engine, the loco would arrive at Dock junction and be given signal 7 towards the spur. Having come to a stand on the spur, the loco could proceed back on to its train via the spring points without any further move

Avonmouth Dock Junction signal box in 1984 after extensive renovation work had been carried out. Four years later, it was closed and demolished.

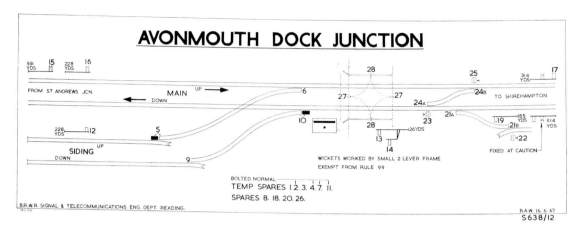

Track and signals diagram of Dock junction showing the Earth Sidings (points 21), and the Corporation lines reduced to sidings. Note the crossing still has its gates.

by the signalman. This particular end of the layout was subject to several changes (as can be seen in the second diagram). The changes were certainly due to the various mistakes made at the junction between the main and goods lines, which caused more than one derailment over the years.

The goods lines between Dock Junction and Dock Sidings signal boxes were worked under the 'Telegraph Bell' ('TB') system. When a train was required to enter on to the goods line, the signalman would tap out the required code on the bell for the line concerned. There were no Block instruments. Drivers were required to proceed over the goods lines at a slow speed and be prepared to stop short of any obstructions or other trains. This rule applied as far as Gloucester Road junction.

On the Shirehampton side of the level crossing, a couple of sidings were laid in during 1940. These were known as 'Earth Sidings' and were accessed directly through connections controlled by Dock

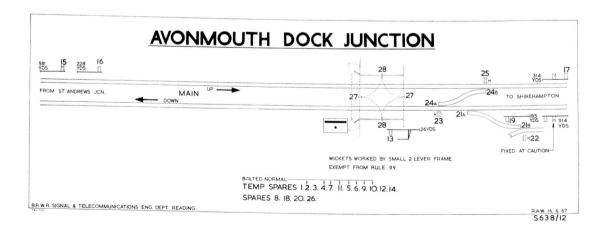

A later diagram of Dock junction. The Earth Sidings and gates are still there but the Corporation lines have gone.

junction. Movements to Earth Sidings were made under the auspices of a 'wrong direction' move over the Down line.

As befitted a bustling docks entrance in the 1950s, the level crossing was busy, with a police post situated just behind the box. The latter was very useful for providing witnesses when a lorry or car driver ignored the warning lights and attempted to use the crossing when the barriers were being lowered, often with damage being caused to the barriers. Before the installation of full lifting barriers in the 1970s, the signalman's duties involved filling and trimming the crossing-gate lamps on Tuesdays.

Avonmouth Dock junction succumbed to rationalization in the Beeching years, losing the goods lines to Sidings box in 1967 (although they were retained for a short stretch as sidings), and Earth Sidings in 1969. The railway's greatest rival of the 1960s was the motorway – Dock junction saw its layout dwindle as the M5 was carried on a bridge right over the box.

With the advent of the Bristol Resignalling, Dock junction was to have been reduced to the status of a crossing ground frame, controlling the crossing only, whilst colour-light signals controlled from the new panel box at Bristol would be installed. However, it was not to be; the proposed Stage 13 of the resignalling did not come off and Dock Junction became instead a fringe box to Bristol Panel when Stage 6 came in. The line to Clifton was singled, and trains signalled by Track Circuit Block (TCB) worked with an acceptance lever in the box. The direction of the line was also changed at this time, with the Up direction being redesignated as being from Bristol to Avonmouth. The old Avonmouth Light Railway sidings, once controlled by Sidings box and now renamed 'West Sidings', were accessed via a ground frame released from Dock Junction box.

As the line between Clifton Down and Dock junction was now being worked under Track Circuit Block regulations, a special instruction was issued. This concerned the working of the first two trains over the single line on a Monday morning after the box had been closed on the Sunday. If the first train

Dock Junction box in 1981: it was never quiet with that motorway overhead.

ran in the Down direction (which was unusual), then it had to be stopped at Dock Junction box and the driver and guard instructed that the train be brought to a stand at Bristol signal B358 at Clifton for the Bristol signalman to be advised that the train had arrived complete. Likewise, the first Up train was to be seen to be complete at Dock junction.

During the 1980s, when the Leyland R3 railbus was trialled on the Bristol to Severn Beach services, this unit was so bad at operating track circuits that the instruction for the R3 was amended. It now had to continue all the way to Lawrence Hill station, where it was to stop and the driver was to advise Bristol Panel box that the thing had arrived there. Only then could Dock junction accept another train from St Andrews junction. This caused many long delays and staff were happy when the R3 was moved off the branch.

On Thursday 5 April 1979, the siding at Dock station, which gave access to the Rowntree's factory built on the site of the back platform there (*see* 'Avonmouth Dock Station'), and controlled by a ground frame until then released by St Andrews junction, was added to Dock junction's layout. Access was only by means of running from Avonmouth on to the single line then propelling back to the factory.

After the closure of Shirehampton box in 1971, access to the private sidings here for the oil company was by means of a ground frame released by Dock Junction box. This siding was served by trains in the Down direction only (which was towards Bristol after 1971). The Bristol Panel signalman had to be advised if the loco or locos from the sidings move would run to Bristol after working at Shirehampton or return to Avonmouth.

All sidings had gone by the time the box closed in January 1988.

Special bell codes were used here: 2-3-4 denoted a light engine bound for the Royal Edward Dock; 1-2-3 was a light engine bound for Severn Beach; 1-6 was 'Backing Down Up Main' (used for shunts to the Light Railway at West Sidings); and 4-2 meant 'Backing Up Down Goods' (for wrong-direction moves to the sidings box along the goods lines).

One interesting working was the latter-day Rowntree's shunt. The train, consisting of up to six wagons and a brake van, would run normally to Dock junction, where it would be signalled to Bristol Panel as a freight train and the panel would advise it was a shunt. The train would proceed as far as the Bristol side of the upper quadrant Down Home signal and stop. The signalman would reverse the junction and signal the train forward to St Andrews as 2-2-3 'Freight train wishing to stop in section'. St Andrews would reply with the 3-5-5 bell signal, indicating that the train had been accepted 'under the warning', as the level crossing at Dock station was still open to road traffic. The Dock Junction signalman would clear the Down Home signal slowly and lean out of the box window exhibiting a green flag held steadily. The driver was supposed to acknowledge this hand signal with a toot of his horn and the train now propelled slowly back past the box on the Down line, with the guard, shunters, and frequently the carriage and wagon examiner as well, all leaning over the balcony of the brake van. It would propel the wagons to Rowntree's siding to work there, afterwards continuing to Town Goods or Hallen Marsh as required.

Once the movement was clear of the single line again, Dock Junction box cancelled the move to Bristol Panel.

As it was a level-crossing box, a Block switch was not provided. 1953 opening hours were 05.15 Monday to 23.45 Sunday. In the 1980s the box was opened between 05.05 and 22.40 Monday to Saturday (or when the last train had cleared Clifton). There was no regular Sunday duty.

Leyland R3 railbus approaching Dock junction from Avonmouth; it certainly played its part in dissuading people from using the line. Nothing could follow it towards Bristol until the driver had phoned Bristol Panel box at Lawrence Hill station to report 'Train arrived complete'. Sometimes they forgot, causing more delays…

There were several attempts to preserve the box after closure, but none came to fruition and the structure was destroyed. The diagrams shown here are for 1948, 1955 and 1985.

Signalmen known to have worked here include Brian Rivers, Mick Munden (who came to Dock Junction from Henbury box), Wilf Stanley, Fred Carpenter (who was Signalman at Dock Junction before leaving BR to work in the docks), Peter Grimstead, Malcolm Eggleton, John Turton, Dave Alley, Dennis Harris, Brian Chaney, Peter Purdom, and the author.

Avonmouth Dock Station

Dock Station box, built on the Down platform at Dock station, was officially the last box on the Clifton Extension. It was another MR design and was equipped with a thirty-six-lever MR Co. tumbler locking frame, with the levers set at 6in centres. Opened on 17 May 1903 and sited on the Down side of the line, this box controlled an interesting layout. Trains from Bristol could start back to Bristol from the same platform, which was designated as a 'Down-Up' platform. If steam-hauled, the loco would run round via the level crossing and main crossover; if it was a GW or BR diesel railcar or a DMU, all that was required was for the driver to change ends.

Similar procedures applied for the Bay platform.

Until 1924, engines could use the loco shed but when that was closed, and after it had been demolished, engines still used the turntable.

When the bay lines and turntable had been removed, the Rowntree company built a distribution depot on the site of the bay lines. This was rail-served and shunts were made daily during the week. A ground frame, released at first from St Andrews box but later from Dock junction, operated the points. The turntable pit was still visible in 1985.

The last passenger train of the day was the 23.40 Avonmouth to Bristol TM via Clifton. The 1953 opening times were 05.15–23.40 (or until last train had cleared) Monday to Saturday and 05.15–23.30 on Sunday.

Because of the level crossing at the end of the platform, certain rules applied to the working of the box. A Down passenger train *not* stopping at the station had to have had 'Line Clear' from St Andrews junction before the signals could be cleared. In the event of St Andrews not accepting the train, then the train had to be brought to a stand at signal 36/33 until 'Line Clear' was received for the train, after which the signals could be cleared.

In foggy weather (of which Avonmouth, being on the coast, had more than its fair share), Down stopping trains not yet accepted by St Andrews were again brought to a stand at signal 36/33 until the platform staff had given the signalman a verbal

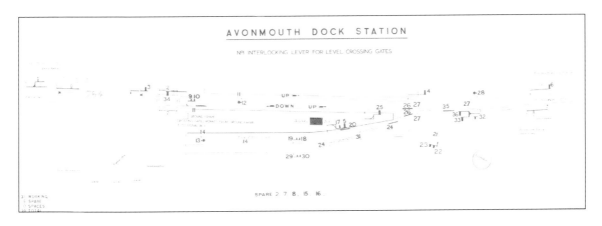

Avonmouth Dock station track and signals diagram. Note the bay platforms and turntable.

assurance that the Starting signal 34 (operated in conjunction with the level crossing ground frame) was still showing Danger. Then signal 36 could be cleared slowly and the train allowed into the platform. All this was because of the sharp curve after Dock station, and the level crossing and junctions at St Andrews.

Staff known to have worked at this box include Ern Taylor, who was a regular man here, Cliff Ball, and Jim Barnes, who was porter/signalman here in 1949–50, in his first railway job. At that time the box was worked by a signalman between 05.00–13.00, then by a porter/signalman between 13.00–16.00, then again by a signalman 16.00–00.01. After a spell at Dock Station box, Jim Barnes went to Holesmouth junction as signalman and then to Ashley Hill main line, after which he became a relief signalman at Pilning. Jim retired from the railway as Area Signalling Inspector (by then with the more modern job title of 'Area Movements Leader'). Dick Clark was signalman at Avonmouth Station box for a while in the 1950s before he got the post of station master at Patchway. He later emigrated to Australia. His brother, Derek, was a relief signalman on the Bristol East district. In July 1955, Ron Broomfield moved from Clifton Bridge box to Avonmouth Dock station as signalman, and later went to Bristol St Philips box. K.G. Davis transferred from Avonmouth Dock Station box to Ashley Hill junction in December 1957.

Avonmouth Dock Sidings

Taking the route along the goods lines, the next signal box after Avonmouth Dock Station is Avonmouth Dock Sidings. Originally named Avonmouth Dock Junction, this box became Avonmouth Sidings when the Joint Goods lines from Dock junction were opened, and the rail entrance to the docks was moved to the latter box. This was the largest of the MR boxes in Avonmouth and controlled the goods lines, the main lines and the docks sidings, in addition to the shunting from both the Midland and Western yards. Avonmouth Sidings box was another Midland Railway box. It had a fifty-six-lever MR Co. tappet locking frame with levers at 6in centres. The levers faced the rear of the box and the box itself faced the goods yard.

As far as ordinary passenger and goods trains were concerned, Avonmouth Sidings was little more than a 'passing box'. Trains were asked on to Sidings and Sidings passed them on to Dock station, then pulled off the signals for the main line. Once 'Train Entering Section' was received from either Dock Junction or Dock Station boxes, it was barely a minute before the train passed behind Sidings box and the signalman there had to send 'Train Entering

Section' onward to the next box. Meanwhile, he would be busy with shunts, or pulling off to let the docks loco, or 'Docky', come out into the yard to collect empty banana vans.

Opposite the rear of Sidings box, on the main lines, was the Light Railway sidings. Moves to these sidings were made via Dock junction, then set back 'wrong line' to the sidings, the train returning the same way. Locomotives working trains in from the Midlands (or Somerset & Dorset) nearly always needed turning before returning via Clifton and Kingswood junction. This was done on the turntable at Dock station. (Engines could run via Gloucester Road, St Andrews, Hallen Marsh and Stoke Gifford to Westerleigh West junction on the Badminton line to return 'Up North' if the train crews had route knowledge.)

With the passenger and freight trains of two companies to deal with, shunting moves and docks 'trips', the signalmen at Dock Sidings certainly earned their wages. However, the actual shunting moves were not like those undertaken at a marshalling yard; rather, they were shunts in and out of the docks and actual trains starting and terminating in Old Yard.

On the signal gantry adjacent to the box was sited a klaxon horn, the purpose of which was to 'facilitate the movement of trains shunting in and out of the Inwards sidings'. It was operated by the shunter in charge of shunting movements by means of a bell push fixed to a post near the Inwards shunters' cabin.

There was also a siren, on a post adjacent to the Docks East gate, which was operated from the docks weighbridge. It was used to advise all staff that a loaded and weighed banana train was ready to leave the Docks and propel into the yard.

Special bell signals were used here too: 1-6 meant 'Backing Down Up Main' and was used

Avonmouth Dock Sidings signal box and an impressive array of traffic in Old Yard. 27 August 1964. (R. Cuff)

Port of Bristol Authority steam loco No.S11 returns to the PBA sidings from Old Yard. 27 August 1964. (R. Cuff)

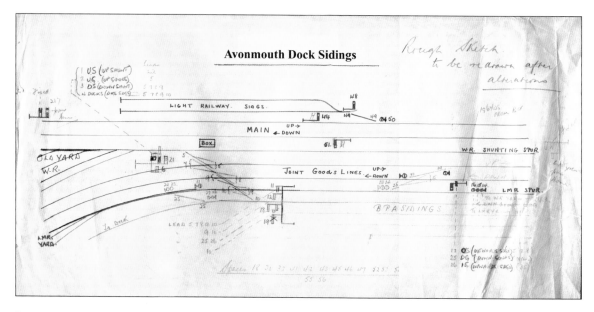

Diagram of layout at Avonmouth sidings, after a drawing by the Bristol Signalling Inspector.

between Sidings box and Dock Junction for moves from the Light Railway (West Sidings); 2-4 was used between Dock Junction and Sidings box for moves 'Backing Up Down Goods'.

The 1953 opening times were: 06.00 Monday to 06.00 Sunday.

It was all very busy, until Elders & Fyffes pulled out of Avonmouth Docks and the banana traffic was lost. Dr Beeching and Barbara Castle swung their axes, and the busy yards were suddenly closed and the freight transferred to the roads.

Like Dock junction, the layout underwent several changes during its life. The one shown being before the alterations to the 'ladder' connections which took place in the mid-1950s and then remained current until the closure of the yards and box in 1967.

Dock Sidings box closed on 19 January 1969 after presiding for little over a year over a layout which had become a shadow of its former glory.

Signalmen known to have worked here include Harold Eady, Austin Potter (who had started his career on the GWR at Clifton Bridge box on the Portishead line), Dennis Smith, Wilf Stanley, Les Hogarth and Dick Harris. Dick Harris had been signalman there in the 1960s but moved to Filton Junction after the closure of Sidings box. After Filton Junction closed in 1971, Harris went to work on the buses. In May 1957, Austin Potter left Sidings box to become a relief signalman on Bristol West District.

Gloucester Road Crossing

Gloucester Road was the largest signal box on the Avonmouth lines. It was equipped with a seventy-lever GW locking frame and controlled the goods lines to and from Avonmouth Sidings box, the junction where the Up and Down goods lines split and became the Up and Down Corporation lines and the Up and Down GW lines (otherwise known as the Joint Goods lines.) All four tracks ran to St Andrews and beyond. The direction of the lines changed here, the Up Goods becoming the Down Corporation, the Down Goods becoming the Up Corporation, and the 'main' lines changing from Up to Down GW and Down to Up GW. On the Dock Sidings side of the junction was the GW yard on the Up side and the LMSR yard (No.8 siding) on the Down side.

D6353 trundles along the main line between Dock junction and Dock sidings with a mixed freight bound for the Royal Edward Yard. It is just passing Dock Sidings Home signal No.51. (Author's collection)

Midland Railway
— BEDFORD NORTH JUNCTION —

One day, the Avonmouth sidings signalman decided to clean the glass of the track diagram, and this is what he found behind it. The MR wasted nothing.

The goods lines between here and Avonmouth Dock Sidings box and to Dock junction were worked under the 'TB' system, with trains simply being belled to the next signal box and drivers proceeding with caution. The GW lines between Gloucester Road and St Andrews Road were signalled under the Absolute Block system, with bells and Block instruments. The Corporation lines to and from St Andrews were under the 'No Block' system and were treated as sidings as far as the stop signals provided.

Here also was the junction into the docks, where passenger trains gained access to Port of Bristol territory and 'S' shed, where the passenger terminal was. If the train was to meet the arrival of a ship, then the empty coaches which formed the boat train – usually hauled by a tender loco, frequently a 'Hall' or a 'Grange' – would arrive in Avonmouth via Henbury and run to Gloucester Road via St Andrews junction and the Corporation lines. The train would run into the GW sidings, where it would come to a stand clear of the level crossing and the train engine would be uncoupled. The docks policeman would appear and open the dock gates for the docks loco, known as a 'Docky', to come out. The 'Docky' would emerge and attach to the rear of the empty train before hauling it into the docks. Once the passengers had boarded the train, the boat train was hauled out of the docks on to the GW siding again, where the waiting loco (which had been on the spur) would back down and couple up. When ready, it was then 'Right Away' via Henbury to Bristol and beyond as a four bells (express passenger train).

The reason for using the GW siding was because the facing point giving access to the sidings was fitted with a facing point lock, or FPL (point 27, FPL 26 on the diagram).

A boat train coming from the Clifton and Dock sidings direction on the Down Goods was under instruction to stop at signal 70 where the engine would be uncoupled. The loco would then run forward to a position on the Up Corporation line next to the signal box (this was known as 'under the

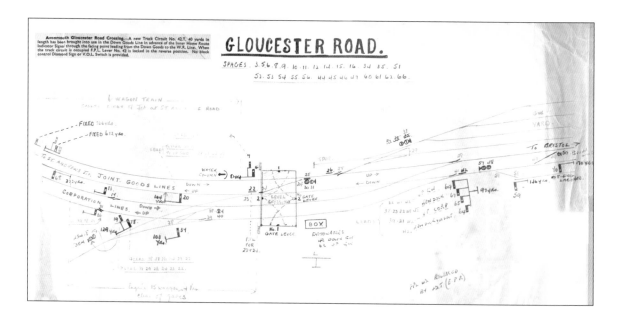

Gloucester Road layout and signals from a Bristol signalling inspector's diagram. To the lower left is the line into the docks. Boat trains leaving the docks would be hauled into the GW sidings (top right) by a 'Docky' and the main-line loco would move on to the rear of the train. Once the train had gone via St Andrews and Henbury, the 'Docky' would return to the docks.

box'). The points would be replaced to the reverse position and the road set for the 'Docky' to steam out and couple to the train. When ready, the boat train would be hauled into the docks.

When the train was ready to leave, it would again be hauled out of the docks by the 'Docky' engine and would stand on the GW siding. The train engine meanwhile would have been shunted from its position 'under the box' back on to the Up Goods. From there, it would run over the level crossing and stand behind signal 20, which was an elevated disc signal. When the crossover was reversed and signal 20 cleared, the train engine could back into the GW sidings and on to its train.

Boat trains were not frequent and the points and signals for these moves were difficult to operate as they were rarely used. Loaded boat trains were signalled as a four bells (express passenger train).

All passenger-train moves into and out of the docks were supervised by the Avonmouth Old Yard Master at the point of exchange, that is to say, Gloucester Road junction. The Corporation lines at Gloucester Road were also often used to stable freight trains in order to make room in the Old Yard.

After the Second World War, the 1948 British Nationality Act conferred the status of British citizen on all Commonwealth subjects. It is well known that the first immigrants from the West Indies arrived at Tilbury Docks on the MV *Empire Windrush*, but subsequently the point of entry for many people coming from the Caribbean was Avonmouth Docks. When the train pulled out of the docks, the Gloucester Road signalman and other staff were well aware of the gaze of the bemused passengers, getting their first views of Britain and British life. The bright and colourful clothing of the West Indian women contrasted starkly with the drab, dark uniforms of the railway staff.

Gloucester Road itself was a main docks entrance with a police post just inside the dock gate, which was just beyond the level crossing which carried Gloucester Road over the four lines of railway. The crossing gates at Gloucester Road were, of necessity, very long, being required to span four tracks, and could be difficult to move in strong winds.

Possibly because of its position adjacent to docks utilities, Gloucester Road signal box had electric lights as early as the 1950s, when Hallen Marsh, Holesmouth and Town Goods boxes were lit by paraffin Tilley lamps and St Andrews had gas lights. Strangely, there was always a smell of gas at Gloucester Road even though there was no gas to the box. When Area Freight Manager Ted Barrett entered the box for his weekly visit, he would often

Inside Gloucester Road box in the 1960s. Note the gate wheel. (Author's collection)

sniff the air and observe, 'This box will blow up one day!' In fact, the smell did not come from any gas supply to the box, but from the nearby animal feed mills.

It was the task of the day shift signalman to ensure that the oil lamps on the crossing gates were refilled and the wicks trimmed every Monday, Wednesday and Friday. The lamp hut was at the rear of the nearby goods offices.

Signalmen known to have worked at Gloucester Road include Alfred Allen, ex-Guardsman John Brazneill, and Gilbert Moore, who worked at Gloucester Road before going to Stapleton Road box. Moore had been a paratrooper in First Airborne division. Later still, he went to Gloucester panel box, from where he retired. John Gibbs first went to Gloucester Road box in 1955 after completing his National Service in the Army. He is remembered as having learnt the box whilst still wearing his Army uniform – from which all the badges had been removed! He later went to Shirehampton for a while before going to Filton Incline and later St Philips relief. He was a Bristol East Side relief signalman and after redundancy, when the Bristol Resignalling took place, moved to Hallen Marsh box. When that closed, in 1988, he moved to St Andrews box, from where he retired. Other regular men were Fred Austen, Arthur Hood, and Fred Nichols. After Gloucester Road closed, Austen left the service, Hood became a goods guard at Bath Road and Nichols became a shunter at Temple Meads. Bill Snell (who lived at Shirehampton) was a signalman at Gloucester Road and is remembered for having only a few glowing embers of coal in the box fire grate during a cold winter.

Malcolm Eggleton, Jim Barnes, Jack Davies, Gordon Holmes, Wilf Stanley, Ted Law, Ray Whiteford and A. MacDougall also worked Gloucester Road on occasions.

St Andrews Junction

St Andrews Junction signal box opened on 9 May 1910. It was a 'typical' GWR wooden box and had a fifty-one-lever three-bar horizontal tappet locking frame. It stood adjacent to the level crossing where King Road crossed the railway to enter the docks. Here, as at Gloucester Road, there was a four-track layout and a junction. Four roads, the Up and Down Corporation lines and the Up and Down GW lines led to Gloucester Road and the Main lines took the sharp curve to Avonmouth Dock station. From the Up Corporation line a connection led to a siding, which ran as far as Avonmouth Goods Yard and the Royal Edward Yard. From the Down main line a connection trailed into the Town Goods sidings.

Special bell codes were used here for routing purposes and these sometimes needed to be changed at St Andrews. If the code received on the

---

EXTRACT FROM 'RULES FOR THE MOVEMENT OF TRAINS AND LOCOMOTIVES', ISSUED BY THE PORT OF BRISTOL AUTHORITY, JANUARY 1963

Rule 40: All loaded passenger trains must be hauled, not pushed, by a locomotive.

Rule 41: The speed of passenger trains whether loaded or empty between the Gloucester Road junction and the passenger terminal at 'S' shed must not under any circumstances exceed 6 miles per hour.

Rule 43: Ten minutes before the departure of trains from the Gloucester Road junction or from the terminal point on the docks as the case may be, the Foreman shunter or in his absence a man specially deputed in writing by him to perform this duty must walk over the lines over which the train has to pass to ensure that:

(a) The road is clear of all vehicles or other obstructions and that the Junction Cut bridge (in the docks) if to be crossed, is in 'rail position', and
(b) All connecting lines are clear of vehicles or other obstructions within fouling distances and that the nearest vehicles standing on such lines are safely secured to prevent them being accidentally moved.

Rule 47: When a Port Authority's engine is attached to a passenger train and before the vacuum pipe is attached to the train, the brakes must be released by pulling the vacuum valve on each coach after which vacuum must be restored by the Port Authority's engine; not less than 20 inches of vacuum must be maintained.

St Andrews Junction signal box in 1976. The gates have been replaced by full lifting barriers.

Up main line was 3-1, then this was an ordinary passenger train destined for Severn Beach and St Andrews would offer it forward as a 1-3. Likewise, an Up Ordinary Passenger train for the Henbury line was received as a 3-1 and sent forward as a 3-1 (the destination being advised by Dock Station box). A Down Ordinary Passenger train was received as a 1-30, whether it came from the Severn Beach or Henbury lines, but was forwarded as a 3-1.

An express passenger train was signalled as a four bells.

Any Down passenger train that was not calling at Bristol and was routed via North Somerset junction was signalled through Avonmouth as 5-1.

Goods trains were also subject to differing bell codes between signal boxes. On the Down line, a goods signalled as just three bells was for Gloucester Road; if it was signalled as Headcode – if it was Class 5, 6, 7, 8 or 9 – then it was signalled appropriately.

If a three bells was received from Gloucester Road, then the train was bound for the Royal

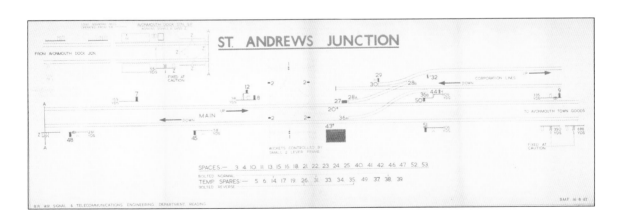

Track and signals diagram of St Andrews junction. The Corporation and GW lines to and from Gloucester Road have gone.

Edward Yard. A light engine for Severn Beach was a 1-2-3 and a light engine for the Royal Edward Yard was 2-3-4.

From the beginning of the Corporation lines, there was a certain amount of 'demarcation' between the Midland Railway (later the LMSR) and the Great Western. Midland trains could use the Corporation lines between Dock junction and Old Yard, but only GWR trains could work on the GW lines. There were exceptions, of course: In order to reach the LMS sidings at Avonmouth Goods Yard box, Midland trains were permitted to run from Dock station to St Andrews junction, where they were permitted to cross to the Corporation lines. Likewise, Midland trains from the LMS sidings at Goods Yard were allowed to leave the Corporation lines at St Andrews and run to Dock station and beyond.

In December 1964, the Up and Down Corporation lines between Gloucester Road and St Andrews were closed. The Up and Down GW lines continued in use until August 1967, when they were closed at the same time as Gloucester Road box. From then on, the main lines between Dock station and St Andrews became known as the Up and Down GW lines.

In 1970, the old Up and Down lines were brought back into use between St Andrews and stop blocks

were put in near Gloucester Road and used as sidings. A year later they had been closed again and they were lifted after.

The siding from Town Goods depot was removed in 1969.

Those wide wooden level-crossing gates were replaced by full lifting barriers on 8 October 1972.

Signalmen known to have worked at St Andrews include regular men Morris Munster (an Irishman who had started on the GWR in 1944 at Avon Crescent box on the Bristol Harbour lines, then went briefly to Henbury box before going to St Andrews, from where he retired in the 1980s) and Mike Heary, as well as Percy Watkins, Harry Holmes (uncle to Relief Signalman Gordon Holmes), Dennis Smith, Roy Mitchell, and Wilf Stanley (who went there after redundancy from Bristol East relief in 1971. He replaced Roy Mitchell, who went into the handsignalmen's 'pool' at Bristol.) In the 1980s, ex-milkman Roy Smith worked there, as did I, Dave Bower, Tony Justin and Dave Alley. Signalmen Eggleton and Gibbs went to St Andrews when the remaining Avonmouth boxes closed in 1988. Both retired from there. The box remained open, with John Hawkins (ex-Holesmouth) moving there with Phil Rogers.

An unidentified BR 9F 2-10-0 shuffles off the Up GW line with a short transfer trip from Old Yard to the Royal Edward Yard. The signals show it will run via the Up Corporation line. (Wilf Stanley)

Avonmouth Goods Yard (Town Goods)

Although this box was officially named 'Avonmouth Goods Yard', it was always referred to as 'Town Goods'. It opened on the same day as St Andrews and to all intents and purposes looked identical. It had a three-bar horizontal tapper locking lever frame. The box controlled the Up and Down Corporation lines (opened in 1911) and the Up and Down GW lines. There was a junction on the Up and Down Corporation lines where the lines branched off into the MR (later LMSR) sidings and another junction in the Up and Down GW lines, which led into the Royal Edward Yard. Both were on the Up side.

On the Down side was a connection into Avonmouth Town Goods depot. A further siding led from this siding into premises used by Hill, Leigh timber merchants. Later, the freight company called Isis Link used the sidings.

The Second World War brought expansion to the docks and the railways. In 1941, following the building of a new Ministry of Works cold storage depot on land behind Town Goods box, a series of connections were brought into use to enable trains to enter and leave the cold store from the Royal Edward Yard. A shunt spur ran from the new connections back as far as St Andrews Road platform. Town Goods box was extended and a new sixty-eight-lever GW five-bar vertical tappet locking frame installed. The Up and Down GW line signals were not 'locked by the block' and signalmen had to keep a close watch on what they did to ensure that two trains did not enter the section ahead. The signals were at last locked by 'Line Clear' in the mid-1980s.

The lower floor of the box was rebuilt in brick as an air-raid precaution, with a brick blast wall also being built to protect the door to the box.

Post-war development saw Fisons fertilizers moving into Avonmouth and building a liquid ammonia discharge depot and tank farm on the old cold store shunting spur. Ammonia emanating from the depot permeated the sea air with its delightful smell. One day, a small leak at the tank farm caused the collapse of a signalman walking to duty at Town Goods box along the platform from the car parking area at the far end of St Andrews station. He was briefly overcome with the fumes but did recover to tell the tale.

Avonmouth Goods Yard signal box ('Town Goods') in the 1960s. (Wilf Stanley)

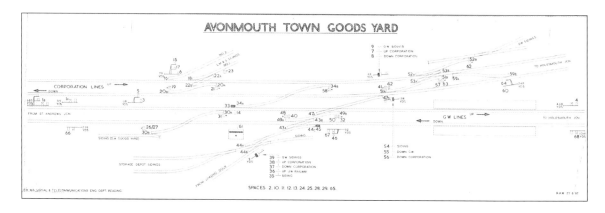

Town Goods track and signals diagram, showing the LMSR sidings (left) and the GWR sidings (Royal Edward Yard) to the right. The very lowest sidings on the diagram, labelled 'Loading Dock', later served the premises of Avonmouth Cold Storage.

Signalmen who worked here included Sam Small, Len Tuck, Austin Potter, Dave Alley (ex-Hewish X-ing), Geoff Sheppard, Gerald Davidson, Paul Smith, Steve Wring, me, Brian Chaney, Malcolm Eggleton, Richard Lewis and Geoff Harcombe. Harcombe left to go to Teignmouth box. Sam Small later went to Hallen Marsh and, later still, moved to Bristol West District as a relief signalman.

Holesmouth

Holesmouth signal box was another typical GWR wooden box with a slate roof. Built and opened in May 1910, to replace a temporary structure, it had a forty-five-lever three-bar horizontal tappet locking frame. Holesmouth was one of the GWR boxes where an addition to the lever frame was marked by some strange numbering; in this instance, when

A lovely view of the south end of the Royal Edward Yard. In the foreground are the LMSR sidings. The Corporation lines run past before turning left into the yard. The wooden steps provide a platform for guards and shunters to give hand signals to drivers. (Wilf Stanley)

Inside view of Town Goods box in the 1960s. (Wilf Stanley)

the Up GW line Distant signal became worked rather than fixed at Caution, the additional lever at the beginning of the frame was numbered '0', making the frame length 46.

At Holesmouth, the Up and Down Corporation lines met again with the GW lines and the lines from both the Royal Edward Yard and the Port of Bristol Authority sidings. There were in effect two junctions: the Corporation lines leaving the GW lines and then the PBA lines split off from the Corporation lines a short distance towards the yard.

During the Second World War, following some bomb damage, the box was rebuilt on a site slightly to the north side of the original. Much of the original structure was utilized in the rebuild, but the roof was re-made with gabled ends and, instead of slates, roofing felt. From this time until it closed, Holesmouth box always had a slight 'wobble' to it when levers were pulled. Although it had been damaged by the bombing, the lever frame was also re-used in the rebuilt box. The damaged lever brasses showed the scars to the end.

View out of the back window of Town Goods box in 1980. 45020 shunts Fisons tank farm.

Holesmouth junction from the south in 1979.

The layout at Holesmouth changed little until the 1950s when the PBA sidings which connected to the Corporation lines here were extended to run northwards to a small 'fan' of five sidings behind Hallen Marsh box. From there, a single line ran to the new trading estate built at Chittening on the site of the First World War munitions factory, crossing the Severn Beach line as it did so. Signal No.10 (*see* diagram) was always kept in the 'Off' position to enable PBA to shunt to and from the sidings as they pleased. However, in the event of a 'Docky' going to the Chittening trading estate, then the signal was placed at Danger to prevent any further moves until the 'Docky' had passed Hallen Marsh, when it was again cleared.

Holesmouth junction had, at one time, two Down Distant signals from the Henbury line: the Inner Distant, situated under Hallen Marsh box's Down Starting signal was lever 45, and the Outer Distant, situated beneath Hallen's Down Home signal, was lever 46. These two Distants were later operated together from lever 45, becoming designated 45a and 45b respectively. This may have happened in 1970 when the Down Distants became motor-worked. Holesmouth's Distant signal from the Severn Beach line was fixed at Caution.

The facing point, No.27, was secured by a locking bar until September 1960, when it was replaced by a facing point lock; for more information regarding locking bars, *see* 'Hallen Marsh'.

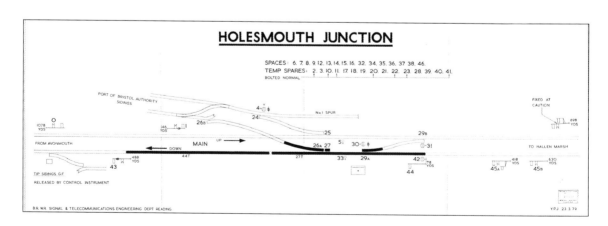

Holesmouth junction track and signals diagram.

ABOVE: Lever brass No.33 at Holesmouth, showing scars from the 1941 bombing.

RIGHT TOP: PBA 0-6-0 Sentinel No.39 scoots past Holesmouth box on its way to shunt Chittening Estate. 1982.

RIGHT BOTTOM: Holesmouth box and the main lines in the middle distance are separated from the PBA sidings by the fuel pipelines. 1984.

The signalmen at Holesmouth were instructed to give two rings on the yard phone when all Down trains bound for the Royal Edward Yard were approaching, to give the shunters time to get in position to deal with the train.

In 1955 Holesmouth was listed as having a Block switch, but here, as at Goods Yard box, the Up Starting signals on both the GW lines and from the yard were not locked by the Block.

When BR pulled out of the Royal Edward Yard (officially in December 1977, although the sidings – mostly PBA sidings – were used into the 1980s), the layout at Holesmouth changed. Although the Corporation lines were still in use at this end of the docks complex, all stop signals were removed and the yard and Corporation points at Holesmouth converted to hand operation. The signal to the shunting spur (which was accessed from both Down and

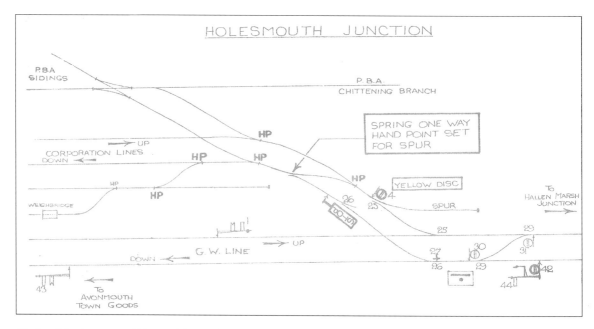

BR plan of the alterations to Holesmouth layout after the official closure of the Royal Edward Yard.

Up Corporation lines – the junction between all three had been the site of several derailments over the years) was replaced by a yellow ground disc. Yellow signals may be passed at Danger for shunting purposes only.

In April 1978, it was agreed that BR would infill the marshy land it owned between Holesmouth and St Andrews Road platforms. Accordingly, a programme of reclaiming the land for future development began. In September 1978, a 'tip siding' was installed on the Down GW line between Holesmouth and Town Goods, with an entrance near St Andrews station. It was controlled by a ground frame released from Holesmouth box and was used for the unloading of spoil trains, usually carrying spent ballast from engineering works.

Ex-LMSR Stanier 2-8-0 pulls out of the Royal Edward Yard at the north (Holesmouth) end, with a train of box vans, grain hoppers and open wagons for the Midlands via Westerleigh West junction. (Wilf Stanley)

A Class 31 pulling out of the 'closed' Royal Edward Yard in 1982.

The last coal train into the docks – until the advent of the bulk-handling terminal over 10 years later.

Tip trains from weekend engineering works would be combined at Stoke Gifford, leading to some of the longest trains ever to be seen in Avonmouth. Such trains were dealt with by a 'Shunt into Forward Section', the shunt being withdrawn when the tip train was shut in the siding 'In Clear' of the GW line. Some trains were so long that it was not unusual for the Town Goods signalman to need to lower his Home signal to allow the train to clear the siding points. Indeed, one was so long that Town Goods had to ask it forward to St Andrews junction as a freight train and lower the Down Starting signal as well, and St Andrews had

to lower the crossing barriers and lower Down his Home signal, too.

Holesmouth junction signal box closed on 22 January 1988.

Signalmen who worked Holesmouth over the years include Jim Barnes, who went to Holesmouth junction in May 1956 after a spell as porter/signalman at Avonmouth Dock station; Mike Sorrell; Len Tuck, who moved to Holesmouth from South Liberty junction on the west side of Bristol; Tom Bullock (reportedly a 'wizened little man', who had been a porter at Shirehampton and got the vacancy at Holesmouth in the 1950s, but did not stay long);

Looking towards Holesmouth from St Andrews Road station footbridge: the tip siding and ground frame is on the right. The signal is Town Goods Up GW Starter with Holesmouth Distant (No. 0) beneath.

The one-lever tip sidings ground frame.

The Annetts key machine at tip sidings ground frame, still labelled 'GWR' in 1984. It would seem that BR did not waste anything.

Ron Singer, who was signalman at Holesmouth as was his father, Frank, before him; Ron later moved to Severn Tunnel East. Ken Souter started on the railway as a porter at Stapleton Road station and later became signalman at Holesmouth. When Bristol Panel came in with the Bristol Resignalling in 1970–72, Ken was displaced by a senior man under redundancy and moved to a shunter's job in the Royal Edward Yard. Living in Kingswood, he found the travelling plus the 12-hour day and night shifts too much, and decided to leave the service. In 1972, after redundancy moves had been made, the Holesmouth signalmen were Bill Dearing, John Gibbs and L. Davies. Dearing later went to Hallen Marsh and from there to the panel handsignalmen's 'pool'. Malcolm Eggleton worked here as relief signalman. Dave Withers was signalman here in the early 1980s before going to Swindon Panel box. John Hawkins, who had at one time been the Avonmouth lampman, was resident man at Holesmouth in the mid-1980s, by which time it had been reduced to a one-shift job, 08.00–16.00. I also worked at Holesmouth several times during the 1980s as relief signalman.

At the end, in January 1988, Richard Lewis did some shifts at the box and, after the closure, Relief Signalman Len Ball was there as 'caretaker' for a few days.

Hallen Marsh

Hallen Marsh, a GWR box of wooden construction dating from 1916, was the last signal box on the line to be built. It stood on the eastern bank of the River Severn and had inside stairs.

Hallen Marsh box controlled the junction between the Avonmouth–Severn Beach–Pilning Low Level line and the line to Filton and Stoke Gifford via Henbury. There was a junction into the Imperial Smelting Works at Hallen Marsh and behind the box were sidings belonging to the Port of Bristol Authority. From these sidings, a single line crossed the line to Severn Beach on the level and ran into the nearby Chittening trading estate. From the smelting works sidings, a line ran parallel to the main lines and alongside the Filton line into a long spur ending in buffer stops.

There was a facing and trailing connection into this spur from the Up and Down main lines. The section of track between these connections and the works sidings was known as the 'Column Road' after a water column that used to stand there in steam days. (The stump of this column remained after it was demolished.) The box controlled the junction for the Henbury lines and the single line to Severn Beach and Pilning as well as the Inward and Outward sidings from and to the smelting works. Ex-GWR diesel railcars were forbidden to use these sidings for any purpose. On the Down side of the line, opposite the box, were connections to two shunting spurs which ran alongside the Down Henbury line. One spur was out of use when removed in 1949. The spurs were connected to the 'Outwards' by a short siding at the side of which stood the water tank and column; this led to the siding being known as the 'Column Road'. The name continued to be used until the layout was changed in 1988, even though the water column had long gone, along with the steam locos it once served. Locos came from the Royal Edward Yard to take water here.

Hallen Marsh box was equipped with a sixty-five-lever GW three-bar horizontal tappet frame from its opening in February 1917 to its closure in January 1988, by which time the box was a working museum piece; facing points were equipped with locking and fouling bars and several ground discs had plunger detection. The method of signalling between Hallen Marsh and Holesmouth was by Absolute Block and originally the same working

applied between Hallen Marsh and Henbury. Single-line working by Electric Train Token (ETT) was used between Hallen Marsh and Severn Beach boxes, with a different token in use between Hallen Marsh and Pilning Low Level when Severn Beach box was switched out of circuit.

Latterly, three different railway systems were served by the box: British Rail, the Imperial Smelting Company (or ISC), and the Port of Bristol Authority (PBA) lines. (The ISC had previously been known as the National Smelting Works, or NSC, and, from 1957, as the Imperial Smelting Works. Later still, it was known as Commonwealth Smelting, until it was taken over by Pasminco in 1992.)

By 1971, three different types of signalling were employed here: Absolute Block between Hallen Marsh and Holesmouth box; Track Circuit Block (single line worked by acceptance lever) to and from Filton West; and No Signalman Key Token working (NSKT) to Severn Beach. There was an intermediate token machine at the ICI sidings at Severn Beach, where trains could 'shut themselves in', leaving the single line clear. When Stage 7(b) of

For the Great Western 150 celebrations in 1985, BR repainted a three-car DMU into GWR 'chocolate and cream' livery. It is seen here passing Hallen Marsh box on its way back from Severn Beach.

Hallen Marsh, showing the 'Column Road' with the water column and a Stanier 8F. (Wilf Stanley)

the Bristol Resignalling abolished Filton West box, and the junction to the single line at that end was taken over by Bristol Panel box, Hallen Marsh lost its token machines at HM1 and No.2 signals.

After 1971, whilst the area immediately surrounding the box was a forest of ex-GW and BR semaphore signals, there were anomalies; a form of modified Track Circuit Block working applied on the single line to Filton West, several automatic signals being installed along the line, which was now designated as the Up and Down Avonmouth. One of these, DA115, a two-aspect signal, wasn't really fully automatic nor was it a semi-automatic signal. The signal stood normally at Danger, showing a red aspect, and only cleared upon operation of the acceptance lever No.4 at Hallen Marsh, when it would show green or yellow depending on the occupation of the line ahead of HM1. However, by being there it meant that trains could proceed down the bank and, if the line was 'full', it was possible to have a train standing at Hallen Marsh No.2, HM1 and DA115.

In the early 1980s, in order to permit trains to shunt into the tip sidings at Stoke Gifford, which were accessed from the single line, a Block switch was installed at Hallen Marsh. When Hallen was switched out at night, this switch gave a permanent

ADDITIONAL INSTRUCTIONS FOR THE SIGNALMAN AT HALLEN MARSH SIGNAL BOX IN CONNECTION WITH THE WORKING OF SMOKE LANE LEVEL CROSSING

No movement is to be allowed beyond signals 31/32/42/43 on the Inwards and Outwards sidings without the permission of the Smelting Works crossing keeper and his assurance that the barriers have been lowered OR traffic is at a stand. When no crossing keeper is on duty, No movements are allowed beyond signals 31/32/42/43 EXCEPT: The ISC loco to the private siding for wagons on the BR side of the gates; OR a light locomotive to the private siding for the purpose of running-round the Column Road.

acceptance to the Panel, enabling them to clear the signal at Filton West junction and run trains into the tip.

All in all, Hallen Marsh must have been unique. It worked three different types of Block working, controlled three different companies' railway systems, maintained its original frame, and locking, still had signals with plunger detection, had locking and fouling bars, was a fringe box and switched out to a major panel box.

Hallen Marsh had a ganger's key instrument for when the Permanent Way department needed to carry out maintenance on the single line between Hallen Marsh and Severn Beach or Pilning Low Level. This device comprised three slides: the Control slide; the Occupation Key Group A; and the Occupation Group B. Group A was for the section between Hallen Marsh and Severn Beach and Group B was for between Severn Beach and Pilning Low Level. Both were connected to Hallen Marsh when Severn Beach and Pilning Low Level boxes were switched out of circuit. The instrument was sited at the end of the box operating floor and had a megaphone for communication, sited at the top of the stairs. There was no button to press; when someone called, the operator simply spoke into it. When the ganger called up Hallen Marsh to ask if the line was clear and whether he could have an occupation key, the signalman would communicate with his counterpart at Severn Beach box (or Pilning Low Level if Severn Beach was closed) and, once it was agreed that the occupation could take place, the appropriate slide was pulled out. The ganger could then take a key from the instrument at his end.

Token working could not be used while a ganger's key was released. Once the work was complete and the key had been replaced in the instrument at the lineside, token working could recommence.

The single line to Severn Beach was at first just a goods line and worked by train staff. By the 1920s, holiday excursions were being organized during the spring and summer months to the new holiday resort of Severn Beach. Eventually, the GWR accepted that there was a demand for a through passenger service to run via Pilning and accordingly the line between Severn Beach and Pilning junction was upgraded to passenger status in June 1928. The line was then operated by Electric Train Token to and from Severn Beach box. On nights when Severn Beach box was closed, Hallen Marsh then worked Electric Train Staff to Pilning Low Level. Later, this was changed to Electric Train Token between Hallen Marsh and Low Level.

In 1955, Hallen Marsh was recorded as having a Block switch whereby the box could switch out of circuit to Holesmouth and Henbury boxes. On such occasions, the Severn Beach line was closed. In 1966, this switch was removed when the lines to Henbury and Filton West were singled, but by 1981 Hallen had another Block switch, this time to enable the box to 'switch out' to Bristol Panel box. Operation of this switch gave a release to the Panel for signals B441 at Filton West; B318 at Patchway and B320 at Stoke Gifford, allowing shunts on to the single line as far as signal B322, to gain access to the tip at Stoke Gifford.

The layout at Hallen Marsh changed little over the years. The PBA did pay BR for a diamond crossing to be laid in across the single line just towards the Severn Beach side of the single to double line junction. This was brought into use in May 1951

Token machine at Hallen Marsh.

Signalman Wilf Stanley in Hallen Marsh box in 1950. Hanging up are the hoops for the tokens and train staff. (Wilf Stanley)

and connected the PBA sidings behind Hallen Marsh box with the Chittening trading estate.

The line to Filton was double until 1966, when it was singled. The major change to the layout took place over the weekend of 22–23 May 1966 when the line between Hallen Marsh and Filton West junctions was singled. The line taken out of use was the Down line between milepost 113 and a quarter at Filton West and milepost 118 at Chittening. A new, two-aspect colour-light Up Starting signal, designated 'HM63', was provided at the double- to single-line junction at Hallen whilst in the Down direction a new three-aspect Down Main Home colour-light, 'HM1', was provided on the Henbury side of the same junction. Located 2,358 yards further out towards Henbury was the two-aspect colour-light Distant signal

for HM1, which was designated 'HM1R' (with 'R' denoting 'repeater').

The new junction points at either end of the single line were motor-worked, with power supplied by means of a hand generator in each signal box. The line was worked under the Electric Train Token system and tokens were inscribed 'Hallen Marsh–Filton West'. Blaise signal box was closed at the same time and access to the Ministry of Petrol sidings was via the existing trailing point, now controlled by a ground frame released by the single-line token.

At that time, two-aspect colour-light signals had been installed at either end of the single line, with colour-light Distants. Block working was by single-line token with auxiliary instruments being installed at new colour-light Up Main Starting

The view from the PBA siding to Chittening Estate via the flat crossing with the BR line to Severn Beach. In the left background is the ICI stack, which must have been having a maintenance shut-down as it is not spewing yellow smoke!

The ground signal shows 'Off' as a PBA Sentinel bounces over the flat crossing en route to Chittening Estate.

signal HM63, and existing semaphore Inner Home signal, No.2.

When the Bristol Resignalling brought about the closure of Filton West box, Token working was removed and the line was worked under the Track Circuit Block system between there and Bristol (Stoke Gifford/Filton junction/Patchway junction.) Hallen Marsh was provided with an acceptance lever, which was pulled right over to accept a train from the above location. Should another train be required to follow the first down the single line (controlled by the signals), the lever (No.4) was replaced halfway then pulled over again. Train description was by a four-character train describer, which had come from now-closed Badminton box.

In common with the boxes at Holesmouth and Town Goods, Hallen Marsh was still lit by Tilley lamps in the 1950s. Equally old-fashioned were the ground discs with plunger detection, and the locking bars. (The latter is a facing point lock and fouling bar combined. A 'ramp' is sited on the inside edge of the facing points; when it is depressed by the flange of a train or engine wheel, the points cannot be moved until the train has gone.) Hallen Marsh had locking

1966 BR notice of the singling of the line between Filton West and Hallen Marsh.

bars and the old-type discs until closure, making it something of a working museum piece.

Many signalmen 'graduated' from Hallen Marsh box over the years, including Jack Wheeler, who was there in 1947 until 1951, along with Eric Jones. The third shift was a vacancy – Cecil Long at Avonmouth station performed the role, but he could not be released from his main job, so Wilf Stanley took it on on a temporary basis. Cecil Long did come to Hallen later to learn the box and, after a few weeks, the District Signalling Inspector Charlie Old came to assess him. After watching him make a few moves and asking him a few rules, Charlie was incensed when Cecil told him that he had decided to leave the railway!

Ray Allen came shortly after and took the vacancy and Wilf Stanley moved to Saltford as regular man. During 1952, Ray Allen and Welshman Percy Priest were signalmen at Hallen Marsh. Allen was on duty shortly after an RAF Vampire jet had crashed into the marsh a short distance opposite the box, killing the pilot. It took a week or so to recover the wreckage, and the RAF recovery men found the nearby signal box useful for getting a kettle of boiling water to make tea.

Signalmen Percy Priest, Steve Moore, Mike Pugsley and Ronnie Broom all worked at Hallen during the 1950s, with Broom leaving the railway in 1953 to become a postman. Malcolm Eggleton became signalman there in 1953, and Reg Owlett worked there in the 1960s, as did a southern Irishman called Dermot Orr.

When the Bristol Resignalling came in during 1970–72, redundancy moves brought Bert Edmunds to Hallen for a while after the closure of Bedminster box. He later moved into the Bristol handsignalmen's 'pool' and his place was taken at Hallen Marsh by Jim Barnes. When Jim gained promotion to Bristol Panel box (later becoming Assistant District Signalling Inspector), his place was covered by reliefmen. Stan Horn went to

PRIVATE AND NOT FOR PUBLICATION   Notice No. S.2496

BRITISH RAILWAYS

(WESTERN OPERATING AREA)
(For the use of employees only)

SIGNAL ALTERATIONS AT HALLEN MARSH JUNCTION AND FILTON WEST JUNCTION

Between 07.30 hours on Saturday, 30th April, 1966 and 17.00 hours on Sunday, 1st May, 1966, or until completion, the Chief Signal and Telecommunications Engineer will be engaged in taking out of use Blaise Signal Box and singling the existing double line between Hallen Marsh Junction and Filton West Junction.

The following new signals will be brought into use at Hallen Marsh Junction and will bear an identification plate as indicated. In each case the bottom aspect will be 12 feet above rail level.

Form	Description	Position	Distance from Signal Box
HM IR	Down Main Distant	Down side of Single Line	2358 yards
HM I	Down Main Home	Down side of Single Line	1038 yards
HM 63	Up Main Starting	Up side of Up Main Line	770 yards

The existing semaphore Down Main Distant and Up Main Starting signals for Hallen Marsh Junction will be taken out of use.
All signals and associated equipment at Blaise will be recovered.

Hallen under redundancy and when he left to go into Bristol Panel box, Sam Small took his place. Bill Dearing took over from Stan Bowes, who went into the handsignalmen's 'pool'; when Hallen Marsh lost the night shift in 1974, Dearing followed him into the 'pool'. John Gibbs went to Hallen Marsh box from St Andrews and was the last signalman to work the box along with Wilf Stanley who had done a redundancy swap with Steve Wring.

In 1982, Brian Rivers moved to Hallen for a short while from Dock junction but moved back to Dock junction again after a short period and I took his place. When I moved to Bristol Panel box, in October 1985, my place was taken by Signalman

Steve Wring from Town Goods yard box. When a vacancy occurred in the Panel at Bristol in 1986, Wring moved to Bristol and his place was taken by Signalman Wilf Stanley, who returned again to Hallen Marsh to fill the vacancy.

On the last day of working at Hallen Marsh, I was present in the box for the closure, with John Gibbs, Jim Barnes and several members of the Permanent Way department, and again when the junctions were taken out on the Sunday after closure.

Severn Beach

Severn Beach signal box opened on 15 April 1924 when Severn Beach station was built, replacing the excursion platform that had previously stood there. When the new station officially opened on 26 May 1924, the single line between Hallen Marsh junction and Severn Beach was used for both passenger and goods services. Goods trains only ran beyond Severn Beach to Pilning Low Level. With the opening of Severn Beach box, trains were able to use the Bay platform and the new carriage sidings, the latter being on the Avonmouth side of the signal box.

Severn Beach was equipped with a thirty-two-lever locking frame. Twenty-four levers were in use; There were spaces in the frame at lever positions 8, 9, 10, 12, 26, 27 and 28. The lever for switching the box in and out of circuit was No.11.

Full passenger working throughout to Pilning junction was instigated in June 1928.

The box at Severn Beach being almost a quarter of a mile from the level crossing at the station, this crossing was worked by a ground frame (*see* 'Level Crossings'.) There was no crossing release from Severn Beach box, but the Down Starting signal and the Up Home signal which protected the crossing were slotted by Ableton Lane crossing ground frame; neither signal would show 'Clear' until both the appropriate signal box and ground frame levers were reversed.

The layout remained the same until 1963 when, on 16 June 1963, preparation work having been done over the previous few weeks, new sidings and signals were brought into use at Severn Beach in connection with the opening of a new chemical fertilizer plant by ICI. The existing carriage sidings became a siding and reception siding from which a new branch ran southwards then turned east and passed under the road from Avonmouth to Severn Beach before entering the ICI works sidings. Two 'Janus' industrial diesel shunting locomotives worked here, but BR locos also brought traffic into the works sidings.

This new work necessitated changes to the locking frame at Severn Beach box. As an extra connection to the sidings was laid in nearer to Hallen Marsh, new signals were required for access to and leaving the sidings. Together with new points and point locks, the spare levers in the frame were taken up, with only levers 12 and 19 remaining spare after the alterations.

As goods trains were to be able to enter the sidings via the new connection, an auxiliary token

Severn Beach track and signal diagram, showing the branch to ICI top right of the plan.

View from Severn Beach Down Sidings South (see also Severn Beach track and signal diagram, left) towards Severn Beach station and box in 1965. Did visitors really expect to find a holiday resort here? (R. Cuff)

machine was installed here; once a train was 'In Clear' of the single line, the driver could restore the Electric Train Token to this machine and the signalman could accept another train. Otherwise, the driver would have had to walk the quarter of a mile to the signal box to hand in the token. Another auxiliary token machine was installed at the Up Inner Home bracket signal, 130 yards from the signal box.

The new connection was equipped with points and facing point locks worked from the same lever, No.10. As the points were over a thousand yards away from the signal box, they were operated by point motors, with power supplied by a hand generator situated in the signal box. To move the points, the lever 10 was pulled halfway across in the frame. The generator handle was wound until an indicator showed 'reverse' then the lever was pulled right across.

As Severn Beach signal box had no night shift, the box was switched out of circuit for a number of hours. However, trains were still booked to run on the branch during the night-time, so the box needed

to switch out and clear the signals in both directions on the single line. Boxes with double tracks had a Block switch, but boxes with single lines had a switch lever. At Severn Beach this lever was No.11. It was used as follows:

To switch out…Pull Facing Point Lock Levers Nose 15, 19, 20 and 25 [15, 18, 20 and 25 after the alterations]. Pull signals 1, 2 and 5 to Clear for the Down road. Send 'Closing of Signal Box where Section Signal is Locked by the Block' bell signal to Pilning Low Level and Hallen Marsh boxes. When these signalmen have answered the bell and are 'holding down' the plunger on their respective token machines, the switch lever must be pulled over to position 2 in the frame. Pull signals 31 and 29 for the Up road [30, 31 and 32 after the alterations], then pull lever 11 right over. Check with Hallen Marsh and Pilning low Level boxes by phone to ensure they are connected.

Switching in was the reverse: First, the signalman checked by phone with Low Level and Hallen

The ICI branch as it entered the factory complex in 1965. Compare this to the 2017 view (see later).

Four box vans (used as barrier wagons) and a couple of ammonias keep an ICI 'Janus' loco company. Even at ICI, the surroundings did not seem to reflect a huge industrial area

BELOW: Possibly the biggest loco to enter the ICI sidings: 40150 waits to return to Severn Beach sidings from the works in 1980.

Marsh to see if the line was clear of trains. If so, he replaced all signals to Danger, and put the switch lever to the 1st position. He then sent the '5-5-5 Opening of Signal Box' bell signal to Low Level and Hallen Marsh. When they had replied and were holding down their respective plungers, the man at Severn Beach would replace the switch lever to Normal.

All Distant signals here were fixed at Caution.

The Severn Beach signalman was also required to give two rings on the selector phone to the station office when an Up train was approaching and three rings for a Down train. This alerted the station staff and the person responsible for closing the crossing gates at Ableton Lane during the daytime hours. The signalman also gave two rings for Up trains and three rings for Down trains to Green Lane crossing, allowing 3–4 minutes before an Up train was due to leave.

Known to have worked Severn Beach box over the years are Signalman Percy Lock, and Mrs Winnie Widdows, who worked the box during the Second World War. Mrs Widdows stayed on as signalwoman after the war but, by the end of November 1957, she had left the railway and moved with her husband to Newport, South Wales. Norman Humphries replaced Percy Lock. Johnny Horder came to Severn Beach from Henbury box. Mr Washbourne also worked Severn Beach, as did Tom Plant, Johnny Southall, Vic Oakhill, Wilf Stanley, Jim Barnes, Harry Rose, Ralph Thatcher, Gordon Holmes and Brian Chaney. Humphries and Horder were the regular men at the box, while the others were relief signalmen covering Rest Days and holidays.

As was the case for Hallen Marsh, the single line could be busy and at certain times any delay could have a knock-on effect. Signalman Ralph Thatcher opened Severn Beach box one morning at the right time and found that the 05.30 Avonmouth and Severn Tunnel goods was running late. After the first passenger train arrived at Severn Beach, Ralph had a chat on the phone with the Hallen signalman and they decided to give the 05.30 a run. However, the freight did not do well and by the

time it had arrived at Severn Beach, slowed to exchange tokens, and cleared the section, the 06.43 Severn Beach to Bristol, which was waiting in the Bay platform, was late. Passengers relied on this train to go to Avonmouth and there to change to the train for Filton. On this occasion, they missed their connection.

Pilning Branch (Low Level)

The only brick-built GWR box on the Pilning–Avonmouth–Clifton line, Pilning Branch Signal Box, to give it its correct title, was opened on 4 December 1917, replacing an earlier structure. It had a ten-lever frame, numbered 0–9. The acceptance lever for trains from Pilning junction was No.4; the crossing gates were worked by hand and released by lever 5. Lever 6 was the interlocking lever for the branch ground frame, working the Avonmouth end of the sidings. There was a passing loop and two loop sidings. The loop held sixty wagons, two brake vans and two 'average'-sized tender or tank locos. The first siding held fifty-two wagons and the third held forty-eight wagons.

Working between Pilning and Avonmouth was by single-line token for the section Pilning Branch to Hallen Marsh. After the opening of Severn Beach signal box, the section became 'Pilning Low Level to Severn Beach' and a train staff was used for the section to Hallen Marsh when Severn Beach was closed at night-time and on Sundays. In later years, the staff was replaced by another token.

Luckily, night shifts at Low Level were quiet affairs, usually with only two trains to deal with: the 01.10 Severn Tunnel junction to Avonmouth and its return as the 05.05 Avonmouth to Severn Tunnel junction. After the passage of the 01.10, the Low Level signalman would often walk up the station approach road to the station box for a cuppa with his main-line colleague.

It was between Pilning junction and Low Level that elaborate shunting moves known as 'Double Low Level' took place, in order to reverse goods trains travelling to and from the Severn Tunnel. It is worth reiterating how much work was involved.

Pilning Low Level box looks a little under-used in this 1968 photo. (R. Cuff)

In the case of freight trains for Avonmouth that had run via the Severn Tunnel, these would arrive at Pilning junction and reverse carefully on to the branch. The level-crossing gates at the bottom of the short incline would be closed against road traffic by the signalman at Low Level box. Once at a stand on the single line between Pilning junction and the level crossing, the brake van would be cut off and would run downhill under its own momentum, and under the guard's control, over the crossing and on to a loop. The points would be changed and the train minus brake van would be backed slowly into the platform road. The loco would be cut off and would run round its train – via the level crossing – and back into the second loop, running round the brake van as it did so. Backing into the first loop, the loco would collect the brake van and then shunt it on to the rear of the train. Next, the engine would run along the first loop again and set back on to the front of the train via the ground frame, accompanied by the signalman.

From there, when the train was ready to leave, the signalman had to walk all the way back to Low Level box to get the single-line token and then all the way back to the locomotive again to hand the token to the driver. If the road was clear, the train could now proceed on its way to Avonmouth.

In the event of Severn Beach (or Hallen Marsh junction if Severn Beach was switched out) being unable to accept the freight, or if priority had to be given to a train from that direction before the freight could be allowed to proceed, the procedure was slightly different. Once the freight had arrived at Low Level, the brake van was initially shunted into the platform line and the train into a loop before the

A marvellous inside night-time view of Pilning Low Level box, showing the two token machines (Low Level–Severn Beach and Low Level–Hallen Marsh). Great to work here on nights, but not on a day shift. (Wilf Stanley)

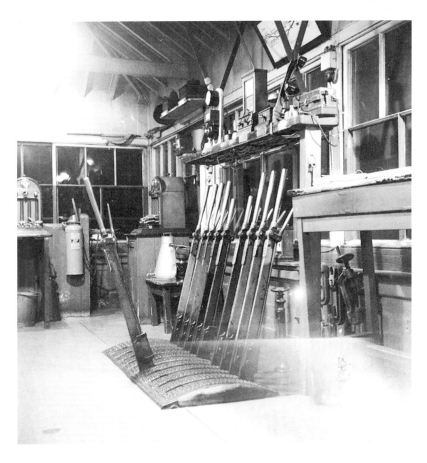

BELOW: *Layout plan of the facilities at Pilning Low Level.*

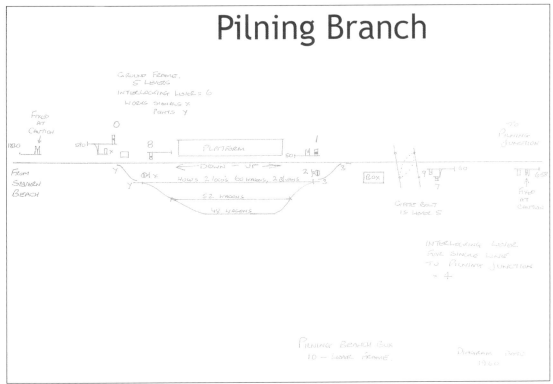

Pilning Branch

Track and signals diagram from Pilning Low Level ground frame.

brake van was shunted on to the end of the train in the loop and the loco run round to attach to the front. This left the platform clear for a train to arrive from Severn Beach.

Trains arriving from Avonmouth via Severn Beach would come to a stand at Low Level and the train engine would be detached and run round to the rear – via the level crossing – where it would back on to the train and attach to the guard's van. The guard's van would be shunted on to a loop and the engine would run round and attach to the other end of the van. The van would then be attached to what was now the rear of the train and the loco would run back to the other end and couple up.

Once the signalman had 'got the road' from Pilning junction and the latter signalman set the points for the Down refuge siding, and once the level-crossing gates had been closed to road traffic again, the train engine could propel its load up the short incline and into the refuge siding. From there, if the train was a 'double load', it could attach an assisting engine for the journey through to Severn Tunnel junction. A klaxon was installed at the west end of the loops at Low Level to enable the branch signalman to give the driver of a train the signal to commence the push up to the junction: five blasts on the klaxon was the signal to start.

In the case of a passenger train from the Severn Beach direction arriving at Low Level, the train engine had to run round as above and attach to the rear of the train, pushing it up to the junction. If there was a banker available, that had to be attached to the rear at Low Level and pull the train up to the junction. If assistance through the tunnel was needed, the banker would run round and attach to the front for this purpose. Three bankers were provided for assisting trains up to Patchway and beyond. The 'Double Low Level' banker turn entailed the banking loco going down to Low Level to attach to the rear of an ex-Severn Beach or Avonmouth freight. The train would then be pushed up to the main line and the train loco taken off the rear and run round to attach to the front. The train would then be double-headed through the tunnel.

Passenger trains for Avonmouth from the Severn Tunnel direction had to be run round at the junction before going on to the single line.

As Low Level box was at one end of the loops and the ground frame at the other, and as the latter could only be released and operated by the signalman, it

Class 42 'Warship' diesel D823 Hermes performing the Low Level shunting act. (Wilf Stanley)

meant a lot of walking for him. If he arrived at the ground frame and discovered that he had left the keys in the signal box, that was even worse, as he would have to walk back to the box for them; he would probably only do it once. It was certainly one way to keep fit!

Clearly, each shunt meant a move over the level crossing. Although this was released and locked from the signal box, the gates were manually operated, which meant that the signalman was frequently having to open and close the gates between each move. Cars would build up – even in those days of infrequent motor traffic – so the gates would be shut for the traffic to move off, then the gates would be closed across the road and the whole charade would begin again. Unfortunately, there were usually far more trains requiring shunts at Low Level during the day shifts; it did not pay for signalmen to be over-sensitive, as they were frequently subjected to the abuse of the frustrated motorists when working at Low Level box. The story has been told of a Bristol Special Class relief signalman who, on being allocated a rare shift at Low Level, thought he had got lucky and was looking forward to a nice quiet turn of duty. Such was the shunting nuisance that, after a rough shift of shunting trains in and out of the sidings and dashing in and out of the box to operate the gates or the ground frame, or both, this individual, who was used to very busy boxes such as that at Bristol

Temple Meads East, swore he would never again accept a shift at Low Level!

The alternative to all this work would have been to run the goods trains to Stoke Gifford and run round them there, proceeding afterwards to Avonmouth via Filton West junction and Henbury. The high capacity of the main lines at Stoke Gifford in later years would have made this almost impossible without incurring long delays to the goods traffic. Another alternative was to construct a loop line between Patchway junction and Filton West; this was eventually done in 1970 and the 'chord line', as it was known, came into use in 1971 with the advent of the Bristol Area Resignalling.

Another annoying factor at Pilning was the lack of a water column at Low Level, either in the platform or sidings. Locos requiring water had to be cut off and run up to High Level station for water; if the loco was on a passenger train, it had to leave its train in Low Level platform and run to High Level first, running round its train on its return from the water column.

It is obvious from the description of the *danse macabre* carried out at Pilning Low Level whenever a train from or to South Wales arrived that things were not very efficient. It was obvious, even in the early days of the branch, that there had to be a better way of doing things. Astonishingly, even though the GWR recognized the need for a better solution and was reaching out for Avonmouth in

A BR DMU in early green livery stands at Low Level platform. (Wilf Stanley)

another direction, and the railway was in private ownership, the charade carried on for a further thirty-eight years. It was only under the nationalized British Railways that the railway version of the hokey-cokey was finally curtailed, when the branch between Severn Beach and Pilning Low Level was closed, in 1968.

Pilning Branch box was graded a Class 5 box when new Signalman Pete Grimstead started there in 1949. In 1953, Low Level signal box was open between 06.00 Monday and 06.00 the following Sunday, and on Sundays between 14.00 and 22.00.

All Distant signals were fixed at Caution.

Signalmen known to have worked here include Peter Grimstead, Wilf Stanley, Vic Oakhill, Malcolm Eggleton, Bill Lifton and Charlie Pye.

Blaise

Although the 1917 wartime munitions factory at Chittening served for a while, the eastern end of the site, with its Henbury end rail connections, was never developed. However, the government kept the land and in the Second World War utilized some of it as a huge underground fuel storage facility. Most of the fuel stored here was for use by the Royal Air Force. It was not long after war was declared that work commenced on the line between Hallen Marsh and Henbury, to lay in a new crossover and a facing connection on the Down line, leading to a series of sidings and fuel-loading stages. A new GW-style brick-built signal box was built and opened on 13 June 1940. The box was equipped with a twenty-two-lever GW five-bar vertical tappet locking frame. The frame had sixteen working levers and spaces were Nos. 4, 5, 6, 16, 17, and 18. During the wartime years there were two regular turns required at Blaise: 06.00–14.00 and 14.00–22.00. During hot weather, between trains the signalmen used to go swimming in a nearby static water tank.

In the fuel depot at Blaise, there was not a lot of clearance between tank wagons and the filling apparatus, so locos were prohibited from passing alongside the apparatus. Needless to say, locomen were urged to 'take the utmost precaution to avoid the emission of sparks' while working in the sidings!

After the war there was no need for the box to be open on two shifts, so it became 'open as required' and the duty was covered by the Henbury signalman. When Blaise was required open, the Henbury signalman had to shut his box, then take a walk of over a quarter of a mile along the trackside path to Blaise and open that box. When the work was complete, he would close the Blaise box and walk back to Henbury again. The working of the 10.30am Stoke Gifford to Avonmouth goods illustrates this well. This train called at Henbury and shunted there. When its work at Henbury was complete, it would be asked forward to Hallen Marsh and go off to Blaise, there to wait for the Henbury signalman to close Henbury box and walk to Blaise. This usually took twenty minutes. On arrival, the signalman would then open Blaise and the train would shunt into the Ministry of Petrol (MOP) sidings. When the work there was done, the train would back out on to the main line, the points would be replaced to Normal and the train would afterwards proceed to Avonmouth. When it had cleared Hallen Marsh, Blaise was switched out and the signalman returned to Henbury and opened up again there. The goods, having completed its work at Avonmouth, became the 12.15 Avonmouth–Stoke Gifford, which was often required to make another shunt at Blaise on the way back to Stoke Gifford. Once the train was on its way back from Hallen Marsh, Henbury would be closed and off would trudge the poor signalman, back to Blaise. This time, once the shunt was completed, he could ride on the loco back to Henbury, there to regain the comfort of his signal box and open up once more.

On one occasion, on a 14.00–22.00 shift, a signalman let an oil train out on the Up road, but it had failed to clear Filton West before he was asked a further freight by Hallen, which he had to accept. The freight, used to 'having the road', was going full bore up the bank when the driver suddenly noticed Blaise Distant 'On'. He applied the brakes and brought his train to a stand at the Home signal, only to find that, when he did get the road, he could not move his train on the steep incline and had to ask for assistance.

Being open only 'as required', Blaise became dusty, dirty and full of flies – more, as various relief signalmen recalled, than even the large population of spiders could cope with! The levers became rusty and stiff. BR did notice the state of the box and one day, during the 1963 snows, a relief signalman was booked at Blaise on a Middle turn of duty 08.00–16.00. Arriving at the box, he discovered that the painters were waiting to be let in! In spite of the freezing cold and the snow that lay all around, the box was duly painted, including the window frames.

When the line was singled on 22 May 1966, Blaise signal box was closed. As the sidings continued to be used, in place of the signal box was a ground frame of two levers. This frame was released by the single-line electric key token now in use. The ground frame was eventually taken out of use on 22 June 1980.

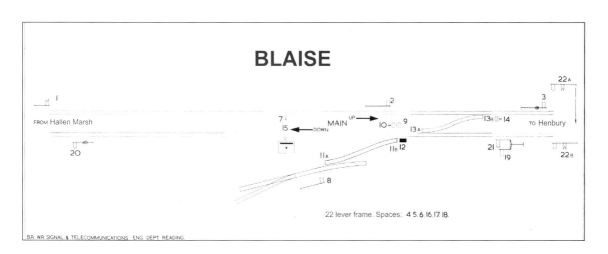

Track and signals diagram of Blaise sidings.

Stanier 8F 48110 climbs past Blaise sidings with a heavy freight from Old Yard in 1963. (Wilf Stanley)

Henbury

Henbury signal box stood at the Filton end of the Up platform. It was a small, pleasing, brick-built box to the 'standard' GWR design. Opened on 18 April 1917, Henbury controlled a 'typical' country station layout. There was a station, with a crossover at the Avonmouth end of the platforms, and a slip connection trailing from the Up main line into the Down sidings at the Filton end, where there were two sidings and a cattle dock. The line, which had climbed up from Hallen Marsh at a gradient of 1 in 100, eased through Henbury to become 1 in 186.

A 9F 2-10-0 blasts up to Blaise with the Avonmouth to Bromford Bridge tanks in 1963. (Wilf Stanley)

The box had a GWR lever frame of twenty-seven levers, of which Nos. 5, 6, 7, 21, 22 and 23 were spaces. Ex-GWR railcars were forbidden from being stabled on the cattle dock siding owing to the lack of clearance.

Almost to the end, Henbury signal box was lit by two ancient oil lamps, which had tall glass chimneys and were kept highly polished. One was kept on the booking desk and one on the signalmen's lockers.

The box closed on Sunday nights, so, on Monday mornings, if the early 06.00–14.00 shift was to be covered by a relief signalman, that individual would be booked to 'travel by 06.05 Bristol'. A lodging turn was not authorized for this turn of duty so the signalman travelled to the box by the 06.05 Bristol to Avonmouth via Henbury passenger train, arriving at Henbury at approximately 06.30.

Henbury was one of those boxes where the regular men had their own arrangements for relieving each other on shift change. This was fine amongst themselves but, when reliefmen were about, it could cause problems, especially when the reliefman was not familiar with the arrangements. This often resulted in a reliefman being stuck at a box for an hour or more beyond his turn of duty because the regular men habitually changed shifts

---

DETAILS OF BLAISE GROUND FRAME

Frame is 5in centres stud locking.
Levers pull above fulcrum.
(1) Facing Point Lock for 2. Key 'B'.
(2) Down Main Facing/M.O.P.sidings. (1)

---

later and the man relieving the reliefman failed to turn up at the booked time. The reliefman would then miss his bus home and, by the time he finally got there, his dinner would be spoilt!

Signalmen who worked here over the years include Brian Chaney, who moved in October 1955 from signalman at Henbury to Avonmouth relief, a job he held for the next 30 years; Morris Munster also spent a short while here as signalman. In September 1955, M.J. Jackson gained promotion from signalman at Henbury to signalman at Gloucester Central. Other signalmen here were Tom Lawler, Ray Wright and Ern Roberts. In May 1956, Roberts was appointed to the vacancy at Chipping Sodbury but there is little or no evidence that he ever took the post. The application for the post at Sodbury may have been a strategic move to get to a higher-class box nearer to home. Ray Wright applied for, and got, a Hallen Marsh vacancy without first visiting Hallen Marsh box; not long after starting there, he resigned from the railway. Stan Horn also spent a while at Hallen before moving on in 1949. Mick

Munden became signalman here in January 1958, later moving to Avonmouth Dock junction. Johnny Horder worked Henbury, then Severn Beach box. Brian Chaney started his railway career as Booking Boy at Pilning junction before getting a signalman's job at Henbury. From Henbury he got the job of Avonmouth relief signalman and held that job until he retired.

Shift working could certainly disrupt family life. The wife of one unnamed signalman was of a somewhat nervous disposition, and was afraid to be left at home on her own during the night whilst her husband worked in the box. He solved the problem initially by taking her to work with him on night turns, and having her stay in the box during his shift. This was not a good arrangement – if caught, he would have been dismissed. In the end, he applied for, and got, a job at a two-turn box and all was well on the domestic front.

Filton West

Filton West junction was the 'end of the line' from Avonmouth. It was the junction where the line divided and ran to Stoke Gifford West and Filton junction. The signal box here, which opened on 26 April 1910, was another GWR brick structure, with a frame of thirty levers, No.25 being a space. The layout then was double-track from Filton and Stoke Gifford West junctions through Filton

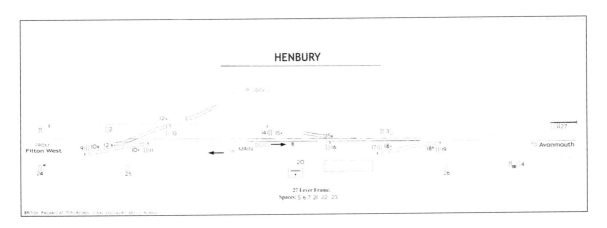

Track and signals diagram of Henbury.

In the snows of 1963, a GWR 2-6-0 No.5336 climbs through Henbury station with a coal train from Avonmouth. (Wilf Stanley)

West junction; it then became single just over 200 yards towards Avonmouth. In May 1917, the lines to Avonmouth were doubled. The station of North Filton Platform opened to the west of the junction in 1926 and the layout then stayed unchanged until the advent of the Second World War. In 1942, a block of three carriage sidings and a headshunt were installed on the west side of the line to Stoke

An unidentified 'Warship' diesel passes Henbury with a banana train. In the background is Rudrum's coal yard. Nobody appears to be shovelling coal. (Wilf Stanley)

Gifford, just beyond the junction to Filton. These sidings were still in use in the early 1950s and a carriage cleaner was booked to go there regularly to sort out the interiors of the carriages. One of these found that he would rather spend his time in the signal box, leering out of the window at any women passing on the path opposite. After two such incidents, the signalman closed the window and gave the man a lecture on propriety. The man went back to cleaning carriages.

The next development at Filton West came in 1948 when the aircraft level crossing was installed at a distance of just over a quarter of a mile further west. This was officially called the Bristol Aeroplane Company crossing, but was always known as the 'Brabazon' crossing (see 'Level Crossings'). There was a small lever frame housed in a brick and glass cabin, with levers that were released by Filton West signal box when it was possible to grant a request for an aircraft to cross. The interlocking lever in Filton West was No.24.

There was also a 'crash alarm', which was operated by the airfield control tower. This rang a bell in Filton West box whenever an aircraft was approaching 'in a damaged condition'. On receipt of the crash alarm, the signalman would place all signals to Danger and send the 'Obstruction Danger' bell signal to the signal boxes either side of Filton West. The crash alarm was tested daily. When Filton West box closed in 1971, under the

Bristol Resignalling scheme, the crash alarm was transferred to Bristol Panel box.

In June 1966, when the lines between Filton West and Hallen Marsh were singled, the single- to double-line junction was located at the Avonmouth end of North Filton platforms. It was operated by motor points worked from lever 12 (previously the west end crossover), which were powered by a hand generator in the signal box. In the alterations, levers 11, 13, 20 and 26 became disused and were removed, leaving spaces in the frame. The far end crossover, No.12, was always a bit 'dodgy' and sometimes failed to show reverse. In this case, a visit from the signalman was deemed necessary, to check it – it was a long walk.

Both before and after the singling of the line, North Filton platform was signalled for trains to start towards Bristol or Stoke Gifford from either platform.

On the resignalling of the Stoke Gifford area in 1971, Filton West was provided with a facility that it had always needed, which should have been built in 1910: a chord line between Filton West and Patchway junctions, enabling trains to and from South Wales to run direct to Avonmouth. This chord line was single. In the years after the Bristol Resignalling, the junctions at Filton West were all singled, but in the 1990s the line to Avonmouth was once again doubled in connection with the opening of a new bulk-handling terminal at Avonmouth.

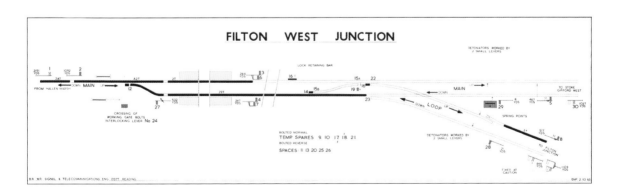

Track and signals diagram of Filton West Junction after the 1966 singling of the line to Avonmouth. Note the motor points 12 and the aircraft crossing.

9F No.92248 brings the return Bromford Bridge to Avonmouth (11.40 ex-Stoke Gifford) down past Filton West box. (Wilf Stanley)

The job of signalman at Filton West box was always thought to be relatively easy; passenger trains ran mornings and evenings, but the rest of the day involved passing freight trains or the odd loco from Stoke Gifford wishing to 'turn', by means of running to Filton junction and reversing down to Filton West, after which it would run chimney-first back to Stoke Gifford. As many test trains from Swindon works ran to Stoke Gifford, numerous important locos could be seen turning in this manner, including the BR Class 8P *Duke of Gloucester*.

Signalmen who worked here include Terry Dart, Ernie Old (who went there from Patchway Tunnel box), and Fred Hughes. Bert Howland, Don Harwood and Terry Dart were regular men there in 1948. Howland was there when the box closed in 1971, along with Fred Hughes and Ernie Old. Relief signalmen who worked here included Wilf Stanley and Chilston 'Chilly' Frampton.

CHAPTER 8

Bridges, Viaducts and Tunnels

Royate Hill (Greenbank) Viaduct

This magnificent 450-foot-long viaduct of seven arches still stands today, spanning the Coombe Brook valley and Royate Hill road/Rose Green road. It escaped demolition when most of the other disused bridges were being taken down, but was threatened again in the 1990s, when the site was earmarked for development. The disused bridge had become a haven for wildlife, and local people were keen for it to be saved as a nature reserve. Luckily, the County Council stepped in and compulsorily purchased the land, and the viaduct now stands protected thanks to the the efforts of those protestors. It runs adjacent to the Victorian Greenbank cemetery and is adorned in places with some interesting graffiti.

Thirteen Arches

Thirteen Arches was, as the name suggests, a 681-foot-long viaduct of thirteen arches, which carried the railway some 58 feet above, first, Stapleton Road and then the River Frome. It was a

The splendid viaduct at Royate Hill, seen here looking towards Greenbank cemetery in 2017.

well-known local landmark, adjacent to the home ground of Bristol Rovers Football Club, where the stand nearest the railway became known as the 'Thirteen Arches End'. The disused viaduct was demolished in May 1968, to make way for the construction of the M32 'Parkway' motorway. During the 1980s, the remains of the embankment were also removed and a row of houses known as Fremantle Road was built on the site. Today, nothing remains to show where the viaduct once stood, and the Bristol Rovers sports ground has gone too, replaced by an Ikea store and car park.

Bridge over Stapleton Road

This steel bridge over the road, just to the Eastville side of the junction with Muller Road, became well known as a landmark in later years as it had the symbol and name of Symonds, a Bristol brewery,

on it. The bridge stood for many years after the closure of the line and remained notable for the advertising of the Courage brewery (Symonds' successors) on it. The bridge was eventually removed, along with the embankments on either side, to allow for the widening of the road. The embankment all the way to where Thirteen Arches had stood was also removed, to make way for housing.

Bridge over GWR at Narroways

The Clifton Extension line crossed the Bristol and South Wales Union line at Narroways Hill. Originally, there was an iron bridge to carry the Midland line across the two GWR tracks. In the 1930s, when the Great Western widened the two tracks to four, the bridge was rebuilt to span the extra width. It stood for a while after the closure of

An 8F takes an Up Midland banana train over the GWR at Narroways Hill.

Cheltenham Road bridge, photographed in 2017. It was carefully repainted a few years ago, but it seems that no one has done any weeding.

the line between Kingswood junction and Ashley Hill junction, and remained a landmark for railway travellers on their journey up or down Filton bank. It was removed in the late 1960s. The abutments remained for many more years and are still in situ, although they are almost hidden by foliage in the summer months. They are sprayed with the inevitable graffiti.

Montpelier Tunnel

Built as a double-track tunnel of 289 yards in length, Montpelier tunnel takes the Clifton Extension under Ashley Hill. The tunnel curves to the right between its eastern and western portals. It is unventilated and now only has one track through it.

Cheltenham Road Overbridge

This bridge consisted of firstly one brick arch, and then the main span that crossed Cheltenham Road was a magnificent iron bridge, adorned with ornate ironwork in diamond patterns. There then followed a further four brick arches, the last one of which crossed the minor suburban street called Kingsley Road.

Clifton Down Tunnel

This tunnel was a major undertaking, running from Clifton Down station and under Durdham Downs for 1,738 yards on a falling gradient of 1 in 64, before emerging in the Avon Gorge. It has one ventilation shaft. It was built to take two tracks but now only has one.

Sea Mills Bridge

The Clifton Extension line crosses the River Trym inlet and old harbour entrance by means of a four-span steel bridge supported by cast-iron columns. This structure is in effect two bridges side by side, as one was built for each track. Today, only the inland span of the two is used.

Sea Mills viaduct 2017. It could do with a lick of paint…

M5 Bridge

When the M5 motorway between Birmingham and Exeter was built, it lacked one crucial link: a bridge across the River Avon just south of Avonmouth. The bridge was eventually planned and work started in 1969. It needed to be able to carry the motorway over houses, the Portway road, the Clifton Extension and the river and had to be high enough to allow tall ships visiting the city docks to pass underneath. The main span of the bridge is 538 feet (164m), with the total length being 4,554 feet (1388m). It is 98.4 feet (30m) above the high-water level of the Avon. It was built by Fairfield-Mabey and Tarmac Civil Engineering.

During the building of the bridge, the level crossing at Dock junction was realigned, along with the road.

The M5 conquers all: the view from Avonmouth towards Dock junction. 1982.

The bridge passed directly over Avonmouth Dock Junction signal box and as such was the bane of signalmen's lives, from the time it opened in May 1974 until the signal box closed, in 1988. There were several expansion joints in the road surface in the near vicinity to Dock junction and all day long there was the constant noise of vehicles passing over these joints. In heavy rain, another problem was caused by surface water tending to pour over the bridge on to the railway lines.

Rockingham Road Overbridge

Rockingham Road bridge started life as a stone-built hump-backed bridge over the Henbury lines near the end of Hallen Marsh spurs. By 1955 it became obvious that the bridge needed replacing.

To achieve this without interfering too much with railway traffic, the Up and Down Henbury lines were interlaced from the beginning of May 1955. The bridge was demolished and rebuilt during May, the lines being restored to their normal formation by the 22nd of that month.

Charlton Tunnel

This tunnel, 302 yards in length and unventilated, took the Filton West–Hallen Marsh line under the ground just to the south of Chariton village near Filton Airfield. Built for two tracks but opened with only one line of rails, it had two tracks from 1915 until 1966, when the line was again singled. It was restored to double-line use in 1994, when the line was once more doubled.

CHAPTER 9

Level Crossings

As can be expected, a railway line that served a commercial docks, industrial areas and rural needs, and was also built on flat, coastal land, had places where the road and the railway came into contact with each other: level crossings.

According to the law, there are two categories of level crossing: one has a public road crossing the railway tracks, and the other is a private crossing. The latter category is sub-divided into two types: 'occupation crossings', where, for example, a farmer needs to cross the line to gain access to his fields, and 'accommodation crossings', where, for example, a farmer may need to cross the line to gain access to his farmhouse and buildings.

The use of public roads crossing railway tracks was governed by the 1835 Highways Consolidation Act. This stipulated that gates were required at crossings on any highways used by road vehicles and that these crossing gates had to have a person to work them. The 1842 regulation of the Railways Act required that the gates be kept closed against the road and not the railway (although in later years there were local exceptions to this). The 1845 Railway Clauses Regulation Act reaffirmed the provision of the gates against the road traffic, but granted authority to the Board of Trade to empower railway companies to keep the gates closed against railway traffic where this would be a safer method. This Act also laid down that new

railways were required to cross over or under public roads, 'unless specifically authorized to do otherwise'. Last, the 1863 Railway Clauses Act prohibited railway companies from shunting trains over crossings, or allowing trains to stand on them. In addition, they were required to provide a 'lodge' at every level crossing – this meant a crossing keeper's hut, a ground frame cabin or a signal box.

Taking all the above into account, the Clifton Extension and the lines from Avonmouth to Pilning and Filton eventually had some ten level crossings, the various usages of which frequently defied all the relevant Acts and sometimes flouted the law of the land. The main crossings were as follows: Sea Mills station; Crown Brickyard level crossing (later renamed Avonmouth Dock junction); Gloucester Road (on the Corporation lines); Avonmouth Dock station; St Andrews Road; Smoke Lane (where the lines from Hallen Marsh ran into the National Smelting Works); Ableton Lane crossing (at Severn Beach station); Green Lane crossing (between Severn Beach and Pilning); and Pilning Low Level crossing. Sea Mills, Avonmouth Dock station, Ableton Lane and Green Lane were controlled by station staff; Smoke Lane was controlled by a member of the smelting works railway staff; and the remaining crossings were controlled from signal boxes.

In the late 1940s, another crossing was added, this time near Filton. The post-war relaxation of travel had given a boost to the aircraft industry, for which Bristol was renowned, and work had commenced on the Brabazon, a revolutionary new airliner of enormous proportions. So big was this marvel that it required what was the longest runway in the country in order to take off. It also needed a giant hangar to be built to house the plane. The village of Charlton was demolished in order to build the runway and the huge hangar was duly constructed.

However, between hangar and runway stood the Filton–Avonmouth railway line, and a new crossing had to be built. It became known as the 'Brabazon' crossing, after the aircraft, and was controlled from a cabin at the site, with the controls in turn being released from Filton West signal box.

Further crossings were added when the area of land near Hallen Marsh, previously occupied by the abandoned munitions factory, became the site of a new post-war trading estate. Many industrial units and factories set up home here and were rail-served – initially not by the main railway, but by Port of Bristol Authority locos and staff. Several sets of warehouses and a carbon black manufacturing factory (Philblack, later Sevalco) were served by rails that twice crossed the main A403 Chittening Road between Avonmouth and Severn Beach. The same road was crossed by rails serving the South Western Gas Board's Seabank works.

Sea Mills

The Sea Mills crossing stood at the Avonmouth end of the platforms and the gates were kept locked across the road. The keys for the gates were kept in the Booking Office. Before allowing the crossing to be used, the station staff at Sea Mills had to telephone the signalmen at both Clifton Down and Shirehampton signal boxes (or Avonmouth Dock junction should Shirehampton box be closed) to ask both for permission. If there were no trains in the section between these signal boxes and the respective signals were at Danger, this permission was given, and the station staff would unlock the gates and swing them across the railway.

Once the crossing was clear and the gates closed across the road and locked in position, the station staff would again phone the signalmen each side of Sea Mills and inform them that the crossing was clear and the gates were locked across the road.

Sea Mills level crossing in 2017.

Avonmouth Dock Junction

The normal position of the gates at this junction was across the railway lines, as the road over the tracks here was one of the gates into the docks complex.

When the signalman wished to close the level-crossing gates across the road, he had first to ascertain that the road was clear. Next, he replaced lever 27 to lower the gate stops and pulled lever 28 to raise the road gate stops. The gate wheel could then be wound until the four gates had swung across the road. Small levers were then pulled to lock the 'wicket' gates, to prevent people walking through them and across the lines. The necessary signal could now be cleared for the train.

By 1970, the gates had been replaced by four lifting barriers controlled from the signal box. The main line had also been singled and resignalled and the lever frame altered (*see* below).

Avonmouth Station

The gates for this level crossing, which crossed the Joint lines at Gloucester Road, were normally closed against the railway and opened for the passage of trains. A bell operated from the signal box would be rung three times to warn station staff that a train wanted to pass over the level crossing. On hearing the bell code, a designated member of station staff would hasten to the crossing. The gates were controlled by a level-crossing ground frame, which was sited just off the Pilning end of the Down (later redesignated Up) platform. The ground frame could be operated only when released from Avonmouth Dock Station signal box. The signal box instructions in respect of the level crossing were as follows:

> When it is necessary to shunt a vehicle from the Down line to the Up line or vice-versa, by means of the crossover near the level crossing gates, the gates must in all cases be opened before such a shunt is made and only in the case of an engine running round its train may the crossover road be used without opening the level crossing gates.

It is quite understandable that the railway officials who compiled the instruction would wish to ensure that no vehicle 'ran away' across the road, damaging the gates and possibly causing accident and injury to the public, but they obviously had complete faith that no engineman would fail to stop his locomotive in time.

Gloucester Road Crossing

Gloucester Road was the second level crossing on the road of the same name. The distance between Dock Station level crossing and Gloucester Road crossing was not much more than 100 yards. Gloucester Road crossing was controlled directly

Dock Junction level crossing with an Up freight.

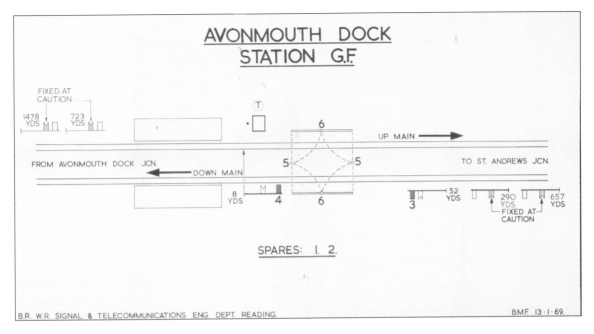

Track and signals diagram of Avonmouth Dock station level-crossing ground frame.

RIGHT: Dock Station level crossing seen from the Down (later Up)
platform. SA7 belongs to St Andrews box.

BELOW: Avonmouth Dock Station ground frame box. (Author's collection)

1948 BRITISH RAIL INSTRUCTIONS FOR DOCK STATION WORKING OF LEVEL CROSSING

British Railways (Western Region), Clifton Extension Line, Transfer from London Midland Region to Western Region Rules and Regulations

Commencing with the first train on Monday November 1st 1948, Western Region Rules and Regulations will be operative on the Clifton Extension Line (from Ashley Hill junction to Avonmouth Dock station inclusive.

AVONMOUTH DOCK STATION
WORKING OF LEVEL CROSSING GATES

The normal position of the gates is across the railway, and they must be kept in this position until it is necessary to close them against the roadway for the passage of trains.

The level crossing gates are operated by a wheel from the Gateman's Box at the level crossing.

An indicator is provided in the Gateman's Box worded "Gates unbolted" and "Gates bolted" and is worked from Avonmouth Dock Station signal box. The normal position of the indicator is "Gates unbolted".

When it is necessary for the gates to be closed against the roadway for the passage of a train, the Signalman at Avonmouth Dock Station signal box must give three rings on the bell fixed at the station.

On receipt of this bell signal, the person at the station appointed by the Station Master to do so, must first place lever No1 halfway from Reverse to Normal, which will release the gate stop in the roadway and he must then operate the wheel to place the gates across the roadway. When the gates are open across the roadway, Lever No1 must be placed fully to Normal which action will lock the gates in position against the roadway. Lever No2 must then be placed from the Reverse position to Normal which will cause an indicator in the signal box to shew "Gates Closed". The Signalman at Avonmouth Dock station box must then operate his bolt Lever No1 which will cause the indicator in the gateman's box to shew "Gates Bolted" After the train (or trains) have passed clear of the level crossing, Lever No1 at the Gateman's Box must be placed in the reverse position which will return the indication in the Signal Box to "Gates Open". The Signalman must then release the bolt by placing his Lever No1 to Normal causing the indicator at the Gateman's Box to return to "Gates Unbolted". Lever No2 at the Gateman's Box must then be placed fully to the reverse position and the gates closed across the railway by the operating wheel.

A gong is provided to intimate to the public that the level crossing is about to be used by a train, and the gong must be sounded four times immediately before the gates are closed across the roadway.

R.G. POLE
Superintendent of the Bristol Division
Temple Meads Station,
Bristol.
October, 1948

Gloucester Road level crossing, with its long gates. Yard offices can be seen to the left. The Corporation lines do not look well used. (R. Cuff)

from the GWR signal box there and after 1910 the crossing spanned the Up and Down GW lines and the Up and Down Corporation lines. This entailed the installation of four very long crossing gates. The instructions for the crossing were as follows:

> The level crossing gates at Gloucester Road must be kept normally across the rails of both the WR and Corporation lines and only be operated for the passage of trains.

The gates met end to end when across the road, but overlapped when across the railway. The road was very busy during the day as it was one of the main entrance roads into the docks. When the gates were closed, a large amount of both foot and road traffic would be held up. The general public and dock workers would, on hearing the warning bell, start to run in order to get across before the gates closed. If they did not make it, they would lean impatiently on the gates, waiting for them to open again. To add to the fun, the gates often needed to be closed against the road to enable shunting moves to take place. This would annoy the waiting foot passengers, who would often shout very derogatory remarks at the signalman. There was a footbridge provided next to the crossing, but members of the public usually ignored this!

GW 2-6-0 No.6364 looks as if it has recently been in the works for a small overhaul as it passes over Gloucester Road crossing. The tall white building in the background stands opposite St Andrews box, showing how tight a curve the four lines made going there.

Much the same view today: the two brick pillars carried the footbridge over the Main and Corporation lines.

St Andrews Junction Crossing

St Andrews Junction crossing was the next crossing after Gloucester Road and was the junction where the two lines from Dock station joined the two GW lines and the Corporation lines. There was another docks entrance here, King Road, and the site was very busy during the day. The dock gate was closed at night and the instructions were modified accordingly, as follows:

> The Level Crossing gates at St Andrews junction must be kept normally across the rails of both the WR and Corporation lines and only opened for the passage of trains between the hours of 5.30am and 10.30pm.
>
> Between the hours of 10.30pm and 5.30am, when the signal box is open, the gates are normally kept across the roadway.

Obviously, with no road traffic, the movement of trains was easier at night.

It was not unusual for impatient members of the public to cause problems at level crossings. One day at St Andrews a man rode his motorbike and sidecar over the crossing as the gates were closing. He failed to get across in time and his sidecar was caught by a gate. Once he had been freed and was clear of the crossing, he stormed up into the signal box and demanded to know who was going to pay for the damage. The signalman replied that it was

the man's own fault but, if he wished, he could write to the Area Manager at Temple Meads. As nothing more was heard of the incident, it was assumed that the man either could not be bothered, or had perhaps come to see the error of his ways!

On another occasion at St Andrews crossing, the signalman closed the gates as instructed to do so at 10.30pm. Having done so, he became aware of muffled cries from outside and slid the box window open to investigate further. To his amusement, two constables of the docks police were stuck between the gates, having committed the sin of trying to beat the deadline!

After the crossing at Dock station had been added to the equipment at St Andrews and supervised by CCTV, there was another notable incident here. A passenger train had been signalled on the Up line and was seen to arrive at Dock station. The signalman lowered the barriers and cleared his signals. The signalman's attention was drawn away for a moment and, when he looked again at his track circuit indicators, they showed Clear. He raised the barriers and was horrified to see the train suddenly appear and move over the crossing. Luckily, there was no road traffic and nobody was hurt. The signalman quite rightly reported this as a 'wrong side failure' meaning that the equipment had shown false indications. However, at the subsequent local inquiry, he was found to be at fault and was threatened with disciplinary action. A signalling supervisor stood up for him and pointed out that the

St Andrews Junction level crossing: a two-car DMU rattles over the crossing on its way to Severn Beach.

BRITISH RAIL ADDITIONAL INSTRUCTIONS FOR USING THE CCTV LEVEL CROSSING AT AVONMOUTH ST ANDREWS JUNCTION

Passing at Danger a signal protecting the crossing: In such instance the 'Crossing Clear' button is NOT to be operated.

When the train has come to a stand at the protecting signal:

- Lower the barriers (where possible)
- Confirm that the crossing is clear (where possible)
- Advise the driver of the circumstances and instruct him to pass the signal at Danger.

If there is no picture on the CCTV screen and:

- No attendant is at the crossing
- The red road signals have failed
- The barriers have failed in the UP position

– the driver must be instructed to proceed cautiously toward the crossing and sound the warning horn before crossing.

An attendant at the crossing MUST be sent for when:

- The signalman is unable to obtain a satisfactory picture
- The barriers fail to respond to the controls
- There is a failure of the track circuits between the protecting signals and the crossing, or a failed train occupying the track circuits causing the barriers to be held down.
- Failure of the track circuits between the protecting signals and the crossing with barriers raised.

Royal Train: The attendant NOT to take local control unless there occurs a failure of equipment.

If the Civil Engineer is to take Absolute Possession of one or more lines and the site of work is within 200 yards of the crossing (or within the protecting signals if those signals are further than 200 yards from the crossing) and movements in connection with the work require to occupy blocked lines within that distance. When the Civil Engineer takes Absolute Possession of the lines and an attendant is required, the possession must not be granted until the attendant has arrived.

Failure of equipment:

- Send for the Signal and Telecommunications lineman

If a barrier is displaced or does not rise within the prescribed time, an alarm will sound and the 'FAILURE' light will flash until the switch is put to the 'FAILED' position.

Power Failure: The standby will operate but if the failure is likely to last for some time, an attendant must be sent for.

Picture Failure: The signalman will advise the attendant on each occasion the barriers require to be lowered. When the barriers are down, the attendant will advise the signalman that the 'Crossing is Clear'. On recipt of this information, the 'Crossing Clear' button must be operated and the signals cleared as normal.

Failure of Red Traffic Signals in any direction: When the lights fail to illuminate after 5 seconds, the sequence must be stopped. The barriers must be lowered sufficiently to indicate to road users that the barriers are about to be lowered. After a short pause, the barriers must be completely lowered. The signals are to be maintained at Danger and the driver advised to pass the signal in accordance with the previous instruction.

Failure of Barriers in the Lowered position: During the period of failure, trains are allowed to proceed normally over the crossing, provided the red traffic lights are working. The civil police are to be informed.

Failure of Barriers in the Raised position (with the road traffic lights working): If the road lights are working, then each time the crossing is used the signalman must press the Lower button until the road lights are flashing. The driver to sound the horn and pass the signal at Danger after satisfying himself that the crossing is clear. When the movement is clear of the crossing, the Raise button is to be pressed to extinguish the road traffic lights.

If the road traffic signals have failed, trains must NOT be allowed to pass over the crossing unless an attendant is on duty. When the attendant arrives, the signalman must tell him whether or not a movement is approaching the crossing and, at the appropriate time, tell the attendant to take local control. Should a failure of track circuits between the protecting signal and the crossing occur, the barriers must be lowered and treated as failed (see previous instruction) until the fault has been rectified.

Wrong Direction Movements (other than Single Line Working)

The driver must be instructed to stop opposite the signal protecting the crossing and phone for instructions. The barriers must be lowered and when the movement is seen to have passed over the crossing, the barriers must be raised.

Single Line Working

A Handsignalman is to be on duty at the signals protecting the crossing.

For trains in the RIGHT direction: Barriers are to be lowered and signals operated in accordance with Section N of the *Rule Book*.

For Trains in the WRONG direction: Barriers are to be lowered at the appropriate time and whe the crossing is clear, the Handsignalman is to be told to authorise the driver to proceed. The barriers are to be raised as soon as possible.

The controls for St Andrews level crossing.

CCTV was only to *supervise* the crossing; it was not the fault of the signalman if the train had failed to operate the track circuits. In the end, the signalman was not held responsible.

The rails were found to be covered with a light layer of rust. A Class 08 shunter was sent to Avonmouth and coupled to a box van. The brakes of the van were locked down and the van was dragged over the crossing several times to clear the rust. Simple but effective! The problem was very much a 'one-off' owing to the line having been lightly used prior to a rainstorm.

The crossing gates at St Andrews were replaced by full lifting barriers in 1972.

Life at both Gloucester Road and St Andrews was made more complicated in conditions of fog and/or wind.

Poor visibility was a common problem at Avonmouth, as the line was on the riverbank and the River Severn was notorious for its thick fogs. On occasions when shunts from the Town Goods yard siding exit at St Andrews to the Corporation lines were necessary, while the Dock gate was open, the signalman had to take extra care. Before allowing the move to take place, he would make sure that guard, shunters and trainmen knew that they must not move without the signals being cleared and that, once the move commenced, they must complete the move and report to the signalman that they had done so and were 'In clear' on the Corporation line.

The signalman had to set the route up, close the crossing gates against the road traffic, and clear the signals. Often, once the train had passed over the crossing, it was lost to sight in the fog. The route then had to be set from Main to Corporation line and the signals cleared. If the train did not reappear, there was nothing the signalman could do but wait. If he thought the train had some problem and was not going to complete the move, he was not in a position to replace the signals and open the gates in response to the demands of the increasingly agitated motorists, as the train might suddenly appear and a collision take place. Likewise, if the train moved successfully on to the Corporation line but failed to report 'In Clear', then the poor signalman had to wait until he could ascertain that the train was indeed safely on the 'Corp' before opening the gates for the road traffic.

Windy conditions also presented an extra challenge to the signalmen at St both Andrews and Gloucester Road. Strong winds were another feature of the coastal Severn and closing the great long gates, at both crossings, could be at best

CCTV picture of Dock Station level crossing as displayed on the screen in St Andrews box. The barriers are raised. The building in the background is the old Seaman's Mission.

amusing and at worst, potentially dangerous. On many occasions, the signalman would start to open the gates for road traffic, and cars and pedestrians would start to hurry across. A sudden gust of wind would hit the crossing and catch the gates, overcoming the efforts of the signalman and pushing them shut again. Members of the public could be seen to stop suddenly and run backwards, chased by the gates! Funny as this was to the observer, many a signalman suffered bruises and sprains as the gate wheel was torn from his grip and spun in the opposite direction.

To prevent this happening, 'windmen' could be summoned when the gusts began. These were usually from the station staff or Permanent Way department and their job was to hold on to the gates as they were being opened or closed to assist the signalman. Often, the wind still proved to be too strong and the poor windman could be seen hanging on to the gate for dear life as it swung wildly about.

Should the gates get out of control, there was the chance they would 'overshoot' the gate stops and this would cause damage to the operating rodding. In this case, two men with red flags would have to stop traffic and handsignalmen would be called upon to operate the protecting signals until the gate mechanism was repaired and normal working could resume.

Smoke Lane Crossing

St Andrews Road runs almost dead straight northwards from Avonmouth town towards Severn Beach. After nearly one and a half miles, the road makes a sharp kink inland to the right and then left again, becoming known as Smoke Lane from this point. Smoke Lane crossing was located right on this 'kink' in the road. This was the level crossing where the two tracks, the Inwards and Outwards sidings, ran from Hallen Marsh junction into the smelting works, crossing the road in the process. Originally, the crossing was equipped with wooden gates, which were manually closed across the road by the National Smelting Works gateman. In the 1960s, they were replaced by lifting barriers controlled from the gateman's cabin. George Morley was the Imperial Smelting Company's gateman at Smoke Lane in the 1950s. Every morning he would take the tally of wagons in the smelter yard and collect the wagon labels. Don Williams, who previously worked as a shunter in the Royal Edward Yard, was gateman in the 1980s.

Being on a double bend in the road, Smoke Lane crossing was particularly vulnerable. There were a few incidents over the years in which road vehicles failed to take notice of the road warning signs and collided with a train moving over the crossing. Luckily, the trains were slow-moving so it was

Smoke Lane level crossing, looking north from Avonmouth.

usually only the road vehicle that was damaged, rather than the occupants.

There was one incident in the 1980s that could have been potentially fatal. A Class 46 diesel had moved from the main line at Hallen Marsh on to the Inwards sidings. Shortly afterwards, the shunters phoned the signalman and asked to go to Town Goods 'urgently'. The loco was brought back on to the main line and then away over the crossover and off to Town Goods *very* fast.

The signalman thought it odd to make such a move but thought no more about it until Don Williams rang up from the smelter sidings, wanting to know why a ferrywagon had suddenly appeared and banged into some stationary wagons. All became clear. The shunters had failed to properly secure the ferrywagon after an earlier shunt and now the loco had come up hard against the ferry-wagon on the Inwards and knocked it over Smoke Lane crossing, where it had run down into the smelter. Luckily, there had been no road traffic in the way at the time when the wagon ran across the road.

It was not the first time such an event had happened. Years before, George Morley had been going about his business checking wagons in the smelter when he came across a coke wagon with a set of crossing gates hooked over its buffers. Thinking it had been a joke, he rang the signal box to complain, and found out what had really happened. Apparently, a heavy shunt had sent the wagon rolling slowly down the sidings until it came to the wooden gates. Owing to the track being far from level, the wagon buffers had locked under the gate, lifted it off its hinges and carried it across the road, where it demolished the other gate and carried on into the factory.

There were wheel stops on both the Outwards and Inwards sidings and they ought to have been used on both occasions.

Ableton Lane Crossing

Ableton Lane level crossing was located at the point where the lane of that name (known latterly as 'Station Road') crossed the single line between Severn Beach and Pilning Low Level. The crossing was too far away for the signal box at Severn Beach to be able to work the gates, so a crossing ground frame and hut were provided. The normal position of the gates was across the railway instead of the road between the hours of 06.15–22.15 daily

View from Smoke Lane crossing into the ISC grid.

and from 08.00 Sunday to 06.15 Monday. During the times when the signal box was switched in, the signalman would telephone the station staff when a train required to cross the road and a member of station staff would operate the ground frame and gates as needed. When the station was open but the signal box was not, the station staff would be advised of an approaching train by Hallen Marsh or Pilning Low Level boxes.

When both station and signal box were closed, then the crossing keeper – who had a cottage near by – would operate the gates.

The ground frame had three levers, one for releasing the gates and one each working a stop signal and 'slotted' with Severn Beach box. In other words, they could be cleared only if both the ground frame and signal box levers were reversed.

Green Lane Crossing

Green Lane crossing was sited at the point where the track near Severn Beach, known as Green Lane, was crossed by the railway. The crossing was mainly used by agricultural vehicles and consisted of a small cabin, just large enough to contain the three-lever ground frame, a chair and a telephone. It was operated by a crossing keeper who had a fair-sized cottage built opposite the cabin. In later years and until closure of that section of the line in 1968, the crossing keeper was Mrs Michel, whose husband 'Hank' Michel' was a shunter at Severn Beach.

Instructions stated that the gates at Green Lane were to be 'left across the line free of the roadway' between the hours of 08.00 Sundays and 06.00 Mondays when Severn Beach signal box was in circuit, unless other arrangements were made by the station master at Severn Beach. At all other times, the gates were to be left across the roadway.

The signalling equipment here was basic. As Green Lane was not a Block Post, it involved just the operation of the gates and the signals. The procedure was that Severn Beach box would give three buzzes on the phone to Green Lane when a train for Pilning was leaving Severn Beach. The crossing

Ableton Lane crossing. On the left, behind the telegraph pole, is the crossing ground frame hut. To the right is the crossing keeper's house. (R. Cuff)

keeper would then operate lever No.2 to unlock the gates, and then move the gates by hand across the lane. The gates were then locked in position by lever No.2. There was a Distant signal in each direction (levers 1 and 3) and the appropriate one would be cleared when the gates were closed. In the Down direction towards Severn Beach, there was an Inner Distant, which was fixed at Caution and acted as the Down Distant signal for Severn Beach. The Up Distant signal was situated below the stop signal at Ableton Lane.

On occasions when a relief signalman was rostered to Green Lane to deputize for the regular crossing keeper, it often meant a 04.15 start from home to enable him to be at the crossing by 05.00 in order to close the gates for the passage of the 05.30 Royal Edward Yard to Severn Tunnel Junction goods.

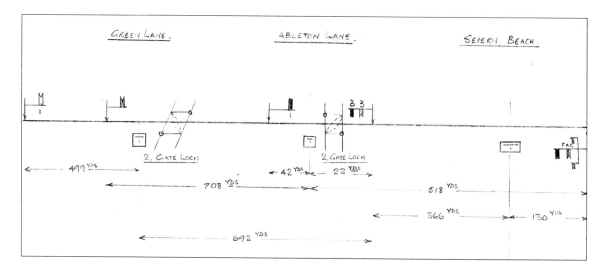

A signalling inspector's 1950 drawing showing the relationship between Severn Beach signal box, Ableton Lane crossing and Green Lane crossing.

BELOW: *View from Green Lane crossing towards Pilning. 1964. (R. Cuff)*

BELOW TOP: *Green Lane crossing keeper's house in 2017.* BOTTOM: *At Green Lane in 2017 the gateposts are still standing.*

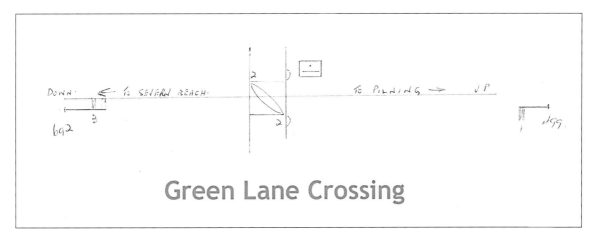

DOWN. ← To SEVERN BEACH. TO PILNING → J P

692 499.

Green Lane Crossing

Track and signals drawing of Green Lane crossing.

Pilning Low Level Crossing

Pilning Low Level crossing was located where the single line between Pilning junction and Low Level crossed Pilning Street, the track that ran between Station Road and the cluster of properties that made up Awkley. It was a busy road, with people coming from both directions to get to Pilning station GW where, in later years, they could park their cars. The farcical shunting moves that took place here caused no end of delays to road traffic, whether horses and carts or motor vehicles. The crossing

Pilning Low Level crossing: a large GWR 2-8-2 tank performs the Low Level shunt. Note the railway sign by the smokebox. (Wilf Stanley)

gates were worked by hand, which meant that the signalman at Low Level had to leave the box and walk the short distance to the gates in order to open or close them, thus exposing himself to the wrath of road users who had been held up by the shunts. Throughout the life of the signal box here, the gates were always worked by hand.

In their working books, drivers were given due warning:

> The Public Level Crossing at Pilning Low Level is at the bottom of a gradient falling towards the level crossing. Drivers must therefore approach the crossing cautiously and under no circumstances must the Signal, which works in connection with the Level Crossing Gates, be passed at Danger.

The normal position of the crossing gates was across the roadway and, having closed the box and before leaving duty, the signalman was to secure them in that position.

Brabazon Aircraft Crossing

The Brabazon level crossing was unique in the area as it was not a road that crossed the railway here, but an aircraft taxiway. It was created in 1948 during the post-war aviation boom. Bristol Aeroplane Company was at the forefront of this and was busy building a giant trans-Atlantic airliner. This machine was huge and was to snatch the trans-Atlantic trade from the Americans. There was a snag in as much as the aircraft – known as the 'Brabazon' – was powered by piston engines with contra-rotating propellers, whilst the rest of the west's aviation industry was turning to the jet engine.

The Brabazon was so big that it required the construction of a giant new hangar on the south side of the railway line. As the runway was built on the north side, a new level crossing needed to be built as well. This crossing was 90 yards wide, to accommodate the new plane, and was controlled by a ground frame in a new brick and glass cabin. The crossing

The crossing 'gates' at Filton's 'Brabazon' crossing.

'gates' were actually barriers on wheels, powered by electric motors. When the Bristol staff wanted to take an aircraft over the crossing, they phoned Filton West signal box and asked for permission. If there were no trains about, the Filton West signalman released the ground frame and the Bristol staff operated the 'gates' by means of electric motors and release levers (ex-GWR) in the gatehouse.

Once the aircraft was clear of the crossing and the 'gates' moved back across the taxiway and the ground frame restored, the signalman was again contacted and the release cancelled.

Unfortunately, the Brabazon proved to be a giant failure; only one ever flew and the project was duly cancelled. The hangars and the crossing remained in use until the closure of the airfield in 2014. (The crossing ground frame was a good place for a BR handsignalman to be stationed when there were air displays on!)

There were many other level crossings in and around Avonmouth serving small factories and warehouses, but, as these were all used by the docks locos, they are outside the scope of this book. (For the purist, yes, BR Class 08 locos did venture into the Chittening trading estate on lines previously

The reason why the aircraft crossing was built: the as yet uncompleted prototype Brabazon airliner at roll-out time. (Author's collection)

only used by PBA docks locos, but they only went as far as McGregor-Cory's warehouse and did not cross any roads. In any case, all the other small crossings were long out of use by the time the Class 08 was used on Chittening trips.) On rare occasions during the 1980s, a Class 31 or 47 diesel crossed into Chittening.

Inside the ground frame cabin. 1994.

Nobody other than a BRITISH RAILWAYS OFFICIAL may touch this equipment! Photo taken in 1994 after privatization.

CHAPTER 10

Goods Yards and Sidings

There were two main marshalling yards in Avonmouth: the Old Yard, which was situated between Avonmouth Dock junction and Gloucester Road signal boxes, and was mostly controlled by Avonmouth Sidings box, and the Royal Edward Yard, which was situated between Avonmouth Goods Yard box and Holesmouth junction.

Old Yard

The Old Yard was the original Midland Railway yard, which later became a mixture of MR and GWR sidings. The Great Western yard was predominantly the sidings between the Corporation lines and Dock station, with the MR sidings being closer to the docks themselves. Avonmouth Dock Sidings signal box controlled the MR sidings and the entrance and exit to and from the docks via the East gate. The dead end shunting line here was known as a 'shunting neck' in MR parlance; the same type of siding on the GW was always known as a 'spur'. Docks locos would rattle their way out of the docks sidings to pick up or drop off wagons.

Old Yard and sidings box. (R. Cuff)

The Gloucester Road (north) end of Old Yard. GW sidings to the left, MR sidings to the right. (Wilf Stanley)

Goods trains for the yard from the Clifton direction would enter the goods lines at Avonmouth Dock junction and proceed slowly until halting at a stop signal or on the instructions of a shunter. Goods trains from the Severn Beach or Henbury direction would be brought to a stand by the Home signal at Gloucester Road crossing. When the Yard Inspector or the shunter had ensured that all was clear for the train to enter the yard, he would give the signalman permission to lower his signals and the train could proceed into the sidings. All shunting moves taking place by PBA locos would be stopped before LMSR/GWR/BR trains could enter the yard.

After the Second World War, the yard foreman at Old Yard was Reg Towles. In October 1959, F.H. Young left Temple Meads Goods to become working foreman at Avonmouth.

In July 1955, P.H. Worner moved from Bristol Temple Meads Goods to Avonmouth Docks as yard inspector. In a reverse move, D.G. Grimes, checker at Avonmouth Docks, moved to Bristol East Depot yard as goods shunter in August 1955. R.C. Payne, a goods checker at Temple Meads Goods, moved to Avonmouth Docks around the same time. V.A. Hurley was assistant yard master in 1958. In October 1959, B. Cambell moved from Bristol East Depot yard to Avonmouth as yard inspector. One of the shunters was Mr Garland.

The northern end of Old Yard was controlled by the GW signal box at Gloucester Road junction.

Trains or locos for the MR arriving at Gloucester Road from the Hallen Marsh end would be routed across from the Down Corporation Line into the yard where the MR siding was always known as 'No.8 Road'.

As might be expected, a large variety of goods arrived and departed by rail and ship here, most notably bananas. As the ship offloaded and the banana trains were made up, so they would leave as soon as they were ready. With several banana trains leaving per shift, shunters and signalmen were kept active. Gloucester Road Junction box, at the northern end of Old Yard, was not particularly busy as a rule; a typical shift comprised several light engines arriving at different times for either the GW or LMR yards and freight trains arriving, departing or stabling on the Corporation lines. However, when a banana ship was in dock, all that changed and the box became a hive of activity. Records show that the afternoon shift at Gloucester Road on Monday 31 December 1956 saw signalman Jack Davies booking seventeen train moves, of which eight were light engine moves. In contrast, on Wednesday 2 January 1957, Signalman Malcolm Eggleton booked over twenty-seven moves on the same 14.00–22.00 shift. Nine of these were light engine moves, mostly locos arriving to collect banana trains. On this day, the 14.25 Avonmouth to Acton bananas left at 14.15, loaded to thirty-three vans; the 15.40 Avonmouth to

The same view today as photo on previous page: the tall building can be seen in both photos.

Great Western Railway.

Telephone Circuit between _____

and _____

STATIONS.	CODE-CALLS. (RINGS)
P.B.A. ASSISTANT SUPT.	1
" " RAILWAY SEC. OFFICE.	2
" " CHIEF FOREMAN SHUNTERS.	1 2
DOCKS NUMBER TAKERS (INWARDS).	4 1
" " " (OUTWARDS)	1 4
RAILWAY GOODS OFFICE.	4
" " STAFF OFFICE.	1 3
DEPOT MASTER'S OFFICE.	3
OLD YARD SHUNTERS.	2 3
G.W. LABELLERS.	4 2
R.E. SHUNTERS.	2 4
" " (SOUTH).	3 2
L.M.S. WEIGHBRIDGE.	3 1
GLOUCESTER ROAD BOX.	2 1
" " DOCK GATES.	5

2,500-L.C.-1945

Signal box telephone card for the Old Yard end of Avonmouth.

Tonbridge bananas left at 15.35, loaded fifty vans; the 18.10 Avonmouth to Acton bananas left at 18.35, loaded forty-five vans; and the 19.35 Avonmouth to Tavistock bananas left at 21.47, loaded thirty-four vans. The 20.45 Avonmouth to Llandilo bananas did not run. After 22.00, one more banana train left the yard, this time the 22.00 Avonmouth to Nottingham, which left at 22.40. This train ran under a 'D' headcode as it was fully fitted throughout with the vacuum brake. The others were all 'E' headcode as they were partially fitted with the vacuum brake on some vans.

Banana trains ran to Control orders from Old Yard, with a notice giving details of the destination of each individual wagon. When empty banana vans arrived back at Old Yard, staff would search the straw left on the floor of the vans for any ripe fruit left behind. Bananas were a luxury post-war!

Not all banana trains ran via Henbury or Clifton; owing to busy traffic on either line, banana trains occasionally ran via Severn Beach, Pilning Low Level, Pilning junction and then to Stoke Gifford and onwards to Westerleigh West junction.

As a rule, Midland locos were used on banana trains bound for Derby, Birmingham or Carlisle, while GW locos were used on banana trains bound for Weymouth.

The train engine on a banana train bound for the north was often an ex-LMSR Horwich 'Crabs', which, like most LMR locos, burnt Midland coal. When a train started off from Old Yard, it was easily identifiable from Holesmouth or Town Goods before it came into view, because of the clouds of dirty black smoke coming from its chimney. GW locos used Welsh steam coal and were much cleaner burners.

```
                    WEDNESDAY 22ND SEPTEMBER.

              Owing to the nature of the traffic conveyed, which is subject
      to quick deterioration, IT IS ESSENTIAL THAT SPECIAL ATTENTION BE GIVEN
      BY ALL CONCERNED TO THE TRAINS SET OUT BELOW.

      18.10 Avonmouth to Water Orton, via Gloucester & Barnt Green,(4.M.38.)
            Conveys 29 wagons.  Engine off shed 16.55.

      18.25 Avonmouth to Lawley St. (diverted to Bescot via Cutnall Green (4.X.75).
            Conveys 11 Bananas ex Avonmouth.  To detach normal traffic at Gloucester Barnwood
      Sidings and make up load with Barry Bananas.

      ─────────────────────────────────────────────────────────────────────────

      ARRANGE AND ADVISE ALL CONCERNED.

                                          for D. S. Hart.
```

Banana traffic notice.

The LMR train crews who worked to Avonmouth from the Midlands via Westerleigh junction and Henbury needed to get used to one particular operating issue, in the shape of GW 'fixed' Distant signals. The Midland had working Distants for almost everything, including running into terminal stations such as Bath Green Park. The Western abhorred this practice, which had dead ends or speed restrictions in place, and instead used 'fixed' Distant signals in such circumstances where a permanent Caution was required. Hallen Marsh Up Distant signal was fixed below Holesmouth's Up Starting signal and of course remained at Caution even when the junction was set and all Hallen

Thought to be empty banana vans returning from the Midland. LMS 5XP 'Jubilee' No.45726 Vindictive trundles past Holesmouth, en route for Old Yard. (Wilf Stanley)

BRITISH RAIL NOTICE: EXAMPLES OF GOODS
TRAIN DEPARTURES FROM AVONMOUTH OLD
YARD 1964

7T63: 03.30 Old Yard to Royal Edward Yard, thence to
   Severn Tunnel Junction.

7T81: 05.05 (MX) Old Yard to Severn Tunnel Junction.

5C23: 04.55 Old Yard to Penzance (MO) or Tavistock
   Junction (FO).

5C29: 06.00 (SO) Old Yard to Tavistock Junction – runs
   20th June to 5th September inclusive.

5F09: 06.52 Old Yard to Llandilo Junction.

6C42: 20.45 (SO) Old Yard to Tavistock Junction – runs
   20th June to 5th September.

6C49: 20.55 (SX) Old Yard to Tavistock Junction – will
   NOT run on Fridays 19th June to 4th September.

6O08: 10.10 (SX) Old Yard to Salisbury.

signals were Clear for the Henbury line. Midland crews, when seeing a Distant at Caution, would bring their trains almost to a stand before realizing that they actually had a clear road ahead.

Royal Edward Yard

The Royal Edward Yard consisted of sidings for the LMSR and GWR. The LMS sidings were at the Town Goods end and known as the 'Inwards' sidings; the 'Outwards' were the GW sidings. There were also exchange sidings with the PBA (Port of Bristol Authority). The Corporation lines ran through the yard.

No.10 siding on the Outwards side was dedicated to use by the carriage and wagon staff for repairs to wagons. Trainloads were usually examined on the Inwards sidings but from April 1970 this practice ceased and wagons were examined on the Outwards sidings.

The yard being spread over a large area, there were separate facilities for staff at each end and the shunters were dispersed between 'South End' and 'North End' of the yard; each end having its own pilot engine. Shunting locos here used shunters' trucks, popularly known as 'backers'. In steam days the yard 'pilot' engines were normally the immensely strong GW 57XX pannier tanks. To enable shunting to take place in such a large yard as the Royal Edward, a klaxon horn was fitted to a post adjacent to the North End shunting spur. This klaxon was worked by means of a plunger fitted to another post opposite the shunters' cabins and was operated by a shunter.

After nationalization in 1948, yardmaster at Royal Edward Yard was Dan Stokes, later succeeded by Fred Tuckett (senior) who had previously been working foreman. Head shunters at

An ex-GWR 'Prairie' tank pulls a string of box vans along the Up Corporation line towards the Royal Edward Yard. (Wilf Stanley)

Royal Edward in the 1950s were A. Beavis, Arthur Greenway and Bert Washbourne, whilst shunters included W. Pearce, C. Rosewell, Roy Moore, Don Drew, Arthur Greening, C. Lewis, Tom Gallop, John Duffy, J. Sample, Dai Baker, Vic Probert, Bert Ball (brother of Signalman Cliff Ball), Les Grant and Don Williams.

Also employed at Royal Edward were W. Cottrell (telegraphist), S. Harrison (checker), A.J. Manning and Tom Hillberg. The four numbertakers were Mrs Jenkins, Mrs Morrison, Mrs Hooper and Mrs Steventon.

After the closure of the Old Yard in 1967 an undertaking had been given that, in order to ease the extra workload now imposed upon the Royal Edward staff, trip workings from Stoke Gifford would be formed as follows:

Loco: Hallen Marsh traffic/BOCM (British Oil and Cake Mills) traffic/United Molasses/Crosfield & Bodey/Silcocks/R.W. Paul/Hosegood industries/Spillers/Empty vanfits/Severn Beach traffic/Blaise traffic/Cold Stores/Town Goods/Light Railway sidings/Shirehampton/Brake van.

(BOCM, Crosfield & Bodey, R.W. Paul and Spillers were all connected with the grain and/or animal feed industries.)

Of course, all these companies or destinations were not represented on every trip and sometimes there were not enough shunting staff available at Stoke Gifford yard to ensure that the above formation was strictly adhered to. On such occasions, the PBA would make representation to BR, BR would draw the attention of yard staff to the agreed formation, and things would revert to the agreed formation for a while – until the next time.

In the early 1970s, the Bristol area came under the BR-wide computer system known as TOPS (Total Operations Processing System). With this, every locomotive, carriage and wagon was allocated a TOPS number, which had to be entered into the computer at terminals set up at every loco

At the other end of the Royal Edward, a pannier tank No.9619 pulls a train of 'conflats' out of the yard at Holesmouth junction. (Wilf Stanley)

A mixed train of freight wagons passes Town Goods box on the Up GW line, bound for Hallen Marsh. Note the four-wheeled acid tank wagon labelled 'Imperial Smelting Corporation Ltd'. (Wilf Stanley)

depot, carriage sidings and freight yard. By means of this system, every item of rolling stock could be tracked anywhere in the country and nothing could move without being reported on TOPS. The Royal Edward Yard had a TOPS terminal by 1974, when it swiftly became obvious that there was a conflict between the old method of taking the numbers of each wagon and the new way of doing things. The numbertakers at Royal Edward, of whom there were three by now, were unable to keep pace with the requirements of the new system, mainly because movements at the yard took place at both the North and South Ends at the same time.

In order to speed up operations, BR set out the duties of the numbertakers, so that TOPS reporting could be done accurately and efficiently. The female numbertakers at the North End of the yard would continue to cover the job 07.00–18.00 daily in two shifts, of 07.00–16.00 and 10.00–18.00. During these hours they were responsible for carrying out TOPS requirements at the North End in respect of all trains and trip workings entering or leaving the yard, with particular attention being paid to wagons passing to or from the PBA sidings or docks lines.

Henceforth, the male numbertakers would cover the work over a 24-hour period, 06.00–14.00, 14.00–22.00 and 22.00–06.00, but between 18.00 and 07.00 they were to be responsible for reporting to TOPS all movements at the South End of the yard. In addition, they were to carry out stocktaking at Rowntree's siding, Severnside Storage (a firm that had moved into the sidings at Town Goods yard) and Fisons tank farm.

A BR 9F starts out of the Royal Edward Yard on the Down Corporation line. (Wilf Stanley)

The TOPS terminal was situated in an office in the yard and operated by a TOPS clerk. The former yard supervisor's office was vacated and turned into an office for the numbertakers. The male numbertakers were to share mess-room accommodation with the shunters whilst the female numbertakers would take over the carriage and wagon examiner's office as a mess room; the examiner was moved to an office nearer his workshop. As their accommodation needed some modification, the female staff booked on duty at Avonmouth Dock station and cycled to work at the Royal Edward Yard.

As the 1970s followed the 1960s as an era in which railways were closed to save money, the Royal Edward Yard came under the scrutiny of the BR management team. Freight traffic to Avonmouth had declined since 1970, when 955,326 tons of goods had been moved through by rail in 57,567 wagons. By 1971, this had fallen to 834,190 tons in 49,686 wagons and fell further in 1972 to 637,950 tons in 35,367 wagons. A 1973 Work Study showed that more efficiency could be achieved by combining a number of yard jobs and as a result five posts were withdrawn, including leading railmen and one clerical officer.

Continuing the theme of saving money, it was proposed to withdraw from the Royal Edward Yard at the end of 1977, when the lease with the PBA ran out. The reason cited by BR was the fact that leasing the yard cost £31,000 per annum. In addition, maintaining the fixtures and fittings cost a further £500,000 spread over a ten-year period. It was claimed that, as the track and fittings had been 'installed during the last war by the US Army', they

The Royal Edward has been 'closed' for at least four years, so what is this Class 47 doing pulling a train out of the sidings?

DUTIES OF LEADING RAILWOMAN (NUMBERTAKER), ROYAL EDWARD YARD

Carry out a physical check of all unlabelled wagons waiting movement in Royal Edward Yard.

Supply list of such wagons to the Chargeman.

On instructions from Chargeman, prepare labels for and attach to wagons from consignment holder.

Take details of all sheets, ropes and containers in Royal Edward Yard.

Advise TOPS clerk of wagons labelled (released) giving full details of destination, consignee and commodity.

Visit sidings of BOCM (Bristol Oil and Cake Mills), Spillers, Crosfields and C.W.S. (Co-operative Wholesale Society) on PBA estate each day taking record of stock on hand showing whether loaded or empty.

Pass BOCM, Spillers and Silcocks information to Chargeman.

Collect consignment notes from BOCM and pass to Chargeman.

Assist as required.

September, 1953.   8946

W.R. TELEPHONE CIRCUIT NO. 1163

BRISTOL EXCHANGE – AVONMOUTH EXCHANGE.

STATION	SEL.CALL	
Bristol Exchange	3	1
Filton Jc. B.O.	2	4
" " S.M.O.	2	3
" " Box	2	1
" " West Box	2	2
North Filton Halt	6	4
Henbury Box	5	2
" B.O.	5	4
Blaise Box	5	3
Hallen Marsh Box	6	1
Holesmouth Box	6	2
Stoke Gifford West Box	5	1
" " Up Side Inspr.	1	2
" " Dn. " "	6	3
" " Depot Master	1	3
Avonmouth R.E. Shunters	8	1
" Depot Master	1	1
" Old Yard Shunters	4	1
" Exchange	7	1
Town Goods Box	*1*	*4*

Signal box telephone card for the north end of Avonmouth.

consisted of non-standard equipment, which was now in need of renewal.

The Royal Edward Yard being officially closed on 5 December 1977, all traffic in and out of the docks supposedly ceased, but as the PBA allocated some sidings for the purpose of exchanging wagon load traffic, trains were still stabled there and some sidings were used well into the 1980s. The wagon load traffic was now to be centred on Bristol's Kingsland Road sidings. Block trains and trip working would be recessed at Stoke Gifford and tripped to Avonmouth as required. It was rather odd that this money-saving closure should require traffic to be centred on two yards that had supposedly closed some years before, but such are the vagaries of economics.

With the yard mostly closed down and the remaining sidings handed over to the Port of Bristol Authority, Don Williams took a job as shunter in the smelting works, whilst Tom Gallop, Roy Moore and John Duffy moved to be shunters at Hallen Marsh. Bernard Reid took over from Tom Gallop when the latter retired. The old Royal Edward shunters' cabin was situated near St Andrews Road station; when the yard shut, a Portakabin previously used in the Royal Edward Yard was moved to Hallen Marsh and sited adjacent to the Column Road for use by the four shunters now based there. The TOPS terminal was installed here and used by the shunters.

Propelling

At any signal box, the area between the first stop signal of that box and the last stop signal on either track was designated as the 'station limits'. On single lines it applied in either direction between those points. Any activity was permissible within station limits, as long as it did not contravene any special instructions issued. However, in an area such as Avonmouth, where signal boxes, sidings and yards were close together and the transfer of traffic between these was essential, the station limits needed to be modified. The 'normal' place for a locomotive was generally at the head of its train but after shunting or forming of trains to run round the wagons each time, getting the engine to the head of the train would be very time-consuming. Because of this, 'propelling' of vehicles was permitted between certain places and with specified loads, governed by special instructions. The following instructions applied to Avonmouth:

Between Ashley Hill Junction, Stapleton Road Gas Sidings and Kingswood Junction: up to two brake vans.

Between Ashley Hill Junction and Hallen Marsh: up to two brake vans.

Between Avonmouth Dock Junction and Ashley Hill Junction: up to two brake vans.

Between Avonmouth Dock Junction and the Light Railway Sidings: up to sixty wagons.

Between Dock Sidings and the Light Railway: up to sixty wagons.

Between Avonmouth Dock Junction and the Earth Sidings: up to sixty wagons.

Between Avonmouth Dock Junction and St Andrews Junction: up to six wagons

Between Avonmouth Dock Station and Avonmouth Dock Junction: maximum of six empty passenger coaches with the brake working on all, or up to three with the brake not operative.

Between St Andrews Junction and Town Goods over the Corporation lines: up to six wagons.

Between Pilning Low Level and Pilning Junction: up to twelve wagons without a brake van.

Between Pilning Junction and Pilning Low Level: any goods train with the brake van leading.

Between Hallen Marsh and Holesmouth: up to thirty wagons without a brake van in daylight hours only. Maximum speed 10mph.

Between Filton West Junction and Stoke Gifford: up to fourteen coaches in daylight hours only.

Between Avonmouth Dock Junction and Hallen Marsh: up to twelve 'Standard Length Units' (SLU)

(This latter applied during the 1970s–1980s.)

A 'Standard Length Unit'.

The Rowntree's trip working propelling back to Hallen Marsh past Holesmouth box. Shunter McIlwain looks out of the van.

One interesting anecdote relating to propelling concerns a Rowntree's trip in the early 1980s: An old relief signalman was on duty one day at Holesmouth box. A freight train was asked forward on the Down GW line. It was the morning Rowntree's trip. All signals were duly cleared for this train and soon it appeared from under the bridge at Hallen Marsh. As the loco and wagons plus brake van passed Holesmouth, the reliefman saw that the train had five pallet wagons on. The limit for propelling back from Dock junction was twelve SLU and the formation here was thirteen and a half! (A 'Standard Length Unit' was roughly equivalent in length to a standard 10-ton mineral wagon.)

Seizing the opportunity to show the younger signalman at Town Goods a thing or two, the Holesmouth man duly sent the bell signal 'Stop and Examine Train' (seven bells) to Town Goods. The lad at Town Goods rushed to his levers on hearing the bell signal and put all his Down GW signals to Danger before acknowledging the bells. The telephone buzzed. 'That's the Rowntree's,' came the voice of the older man. 'They're over length for the propelling move!'

Luckily, the line between Holesmouth and Town Goods is more or less dead straight and the train crew saw the signals go back to Danger in good time to pull up at Town Goods' Home signal. As the train halted, a shunter scrambled down from the cab and hurried to the signal box. 'What's up, Signalman?' he called as he ran up the stairs.

'You're over length,' came the reply.

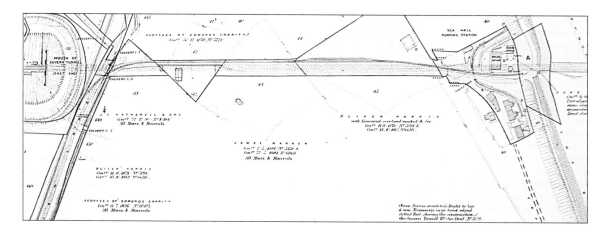

Plan of the short siding to Sea Walls pumping station. (Wiltshire History Centre)

The shunter's response is unprintable – and justifiably so. The train was *not* over length at all, at least, not until it reached Dock junction and wanted to propel back to Rowntree's siding. The signalman at Town Goods had no option but to let the train proceed on its way.

Once it had arrived at Dock junction, the experienced signalman there had two options. He could order the train to proceed to Clifton and Bristol, where it would need to go either into Temple Meads or Kingsland Road sidings in order to run round and return to Avonmouth via Henbury, which would cause delays to the Rowntree's and other traffic. The other option – the one that he took – was to turn a blind eye and let the Rowntree's run with one over length as far as the depot.

After serving the depot, the Rowntree's trip propelled four empties back to Hallen Marsh.

The whole thing had been a stunt by the shunters to wind up the man at Holesmouth, knowing he would over-react. They were right, of course. They knew the rules and that they were quite in order to haul as many wagons as they liked on the *Down* line, as long as they did not try to push them all back again.

One over length was, technically, wrong. Had any officialdom been in the area they would no doubt have given all concerned a 'rap over the knuckles' and told them not to do it again. As it happened, nobody found out.

Pumping Station Siding

This siding was situated on the single line between Severn Beach and Pilning Low Level, serving the Severn Tunnel pumping station at Sea Walls. It was operated by a ground frame at the 11 and a quarter milepost. The ground frame was released by the key on the single-line token or train staff. The siding was roughly a quarter of a mile in length and had a loop 225 yards from the entrance points, which was capable of holding ten wagons. Deliveries here were mostly coal for the pumping engines. Traffic could be put off or collected from either the Severn Beach or Pilning direction, as directed by the Pilning station master under whose control the siding fell.

Wagons could be propelled from Low Level but were not allowed to exceed thirty wagons and had to have a brake van at the Avonmouth end of the train. Speed was not to exceed 10mph. The guard, who had to travel in his brake van, was equipped with a horn, which could be used to attract the attention of any workmen on the line.

Propelling to the siding was not permitted after dark or in times of poor visibility, fog or falling snow.

CHAPTER 11

Avonmouth at War, 1939–45

Defence Measures

The threat of war loomed large in the late 1930s, although it was hoped that conflict could be avoided. With docks at Portishead, Bristol City and Avonmouth, plus important railway junctions, yards and other facilities, it was feared that this area would inevitably be targeted by the German air force, the Luftwaffe, aiming to destroy as much of the transport infrastructure as possible in order to restrict the movement of troops and goods. Sadly, 'peace in our time' was not to be, and by September 1938 the government had announced that barrage balloons were to be provided for a number of provincial towns and cities, including Bristol. Whilst it would have been preferable to have balloon cover over the entire area of the city and its ports at the City Docks and Avonmouth, the close proximity of Filton aerodrome did not allow this. It was decided, therefore, to protect the harbour installations at Avonmouth and City Docks by employing small independent balloon installations. The system involved raising a lethal cable barrage into the air around the potential target. This compelled enemy bombers to fly above the balloons and therefore at a height at which other anti-aircraft weapons could be brought to bear against them. It would also mean that the enemy planes would not be able to bomb very accurately.

The balloons were flown from a mobile winch and were designed to be deployed at a maximum altitude of 5,000 feet. When there was no threat of an air raid, the balloons were grounded or kept at 500 feet, to pose as little potential danger as possible to 'friendly' aircraft.

Light anti-aircraft guns were provided to give protection from attacks carried out at altitudes of less than 3,000 feet against certain important installations, including the National Smelting Works at Avonmouth.

Around the time of the declaration of war, in September 1939, newly formed balloon squadrons took up their positions around the vital port facilities at Avonmouth and Bristol. Heavy anti-aircraft guns had also moved to their war stations by early September 1939, and, although initially operating from temporary sites, by late November 1939 they were on their permanent positions. Those immediately protecting the Avonmouth area were sited at Rockingham near Hallen Marsh, just to the north side of Avonmouth Docks. The heavy anti-aircraft battery at Rockingham Farm was sited approximately a mile and a half north of Avonmouth. This gun site comprised a command post, four gunpits and an ammunition magazine, and it is thought that some light anti-aircraft guns may also have been located there. The site was operational from February 1940 until the end of the war. To aid in the

DEPLOYMENT OF ANTI-AIRCRAFT SMOKE GENERATORS

'In the autumn of 1940 the Ministry of Home Security decided that smoke screens should be provided to cover vital targets such as munitions factories, dams and ports. June 25th 1941 saw the arrival at Avonmouth of No.810 (SM) Company, whose purpose was to operate a screen around Docks in the event of an enemy air attack. Two types of smoke generator were used in the defence of Avonmouth Docks and railway installations; the old No.24 Mark II and the newly introduced Haslar. The Mark II, known as the 'smoke pot', was a small and entirely static piece of equipment fitted with tall chimneys and operated by hand. It used Pool Diesel Oil and had a burn time of 5 hours, hence the fact that they were arranged in pairs to cover up to 10 hours of operation. By contrast, the Haslar was mounted on a trailer and towed by a lorry, the complete installation being sent each night to the required location. Haslars produced biscuit-coloured smoke by means of partly burnt oil enclosed in a film of water which was comparable in colour, nature and consistency to a London fog and were able to produce some 50 times the quantity of smoke generated by the Mark IIs. 45 Haslars were arranged on a radius of about 1500 yards around the target and an Inner Circuit formed by 2510 Mark II generators installed about 1000 yards out from the target, notably along the Portway, Portview Road and St Andrews Road, with the individual generators spaced in pairs at intervals of around 5 to 10 yards. This Inner, or "quick cover", Circuit was lit instantaneously by exploders and provided a satisfactory screen during the interim period whilst the smoke from the Haslars joined up and covered the target. The Avonmouth Smoke Screen was first used early on the morning of July 5th 1940.'

Extract from humanities.uwe.ac.uk

forewarning of incoming raids, the Observer corps also had a post near Avonmouth.

Anti-aircraft guns sited at Cribbs Causeway were mainly there to protect Filton airfield but could also assist with cover for the Avonmouth area. On 26 June 1940, the Cribbs Causeway site became the first in the Bristol Area to fire in anger, during the course of a nuisance attack aimed at Avonmouth and Portishead Docks. By July 1940 an additional five heavy gun positions were built, although it was to be some time before the majority of them, including those located at Avonmouth and Henbury, received any weapons. During the period March to April 1941, eight more 3-in semi-mobile and twenty 3.7-in mobile guns were added to the existing sites at Avonmouth, and Henbury, amongst others.

In addition, anti-aircraft machine guns were sited around the local docks. In Avonmouth, they were set up at the smelting works, but they were to prove to be short-term deployments and were all removed by early 1940 when balloon barrages effectively covered these locations. By this time, the barrage layout around the Bristol area was complete, with thirty-two balloons flying at Avonmouth, twenty-four at Filton and forty around Bristol itself.

Further defences were located at Severn Beach. In 1941, the Petroleum Board constructed a bombing decoy site at a location near to the modern warehouses north-east of the village. It was one of series of 'oil decoys', which were designed to simulate an industrial or residential area on fire. On the approach of enemy aircraft, a group of controlled, oil-fed fires would be ignited. The idea was that the German pilots would see these fires from above, assume they had been started by other raiders and then drop their own bombs on the flames. The site at Severn Beach was to simulate both an industrial site on fire, as a distraction from Avonmouth, and also a residential area, as a distraction from Bristol. This type of site was code-named 'QF'.

There was another Avonmouth oil decoy site located at Sheepway, near Portbury, on the other side of the Avon estuary, and a further site was built on the banks of the Severn between Clevedon and Weston-super-Mare. The latter was made to resemble a railway yard; rather cleverly, from above, the geographical details look just like the Avonmouth area, including the mouth of the River Avon.

Preparations

The railway companies had also been preparing for war. In June 1940, the Great Western Railway issued a booklet to staff, entitled 'BRISTOL DIVISION Notice shewing the arrangements for Diversion of THROUGH trains to Alternative Routes in cases of EMERGENCY'. It went on to state that, in the event of 'any special emergency' (the words 'enemy action'

Diversion of Trains to Alternative Routes in cases of Emergency—*continued*.

B.D. 41.—*continued*.

ENGINE RESTRICTIONS.

CLIFTON EXTENSION JOINT LINE: See Code B.D. 7, page 14.

OFFICIALS AND STATIONS TO BE ADVISED.

The Avonmouth Yard Master to make the necessary arrangements and also advise the following by telephone, viz. :

Divisional Superintendent ..	Bristol.
Divisional Engineer	Bristol.
Divisional Inspector	Bristol.
District Traffic Inspector ..	Bristol.
Loco. Running Superintendent.	Swindon.
Divisional Locomotive } Superintendent }	Bristol.
Control	Bristol.
Joint Station Master	Bristol (Temple Meads).
G.W. Guards' Inspector ..	Bristol (Temple Meads).
Station Masters	Pilning, Severn Beach, Henbury, Filton Junction, Ashley Hill, Bristol (Stapleton Road), Lawrence Hill, Montpelier, Clifton Down, Sea Mills and Shirehampton.
Yard Master	Stoke Gifford.
District Controller	L M S Gloucester.

Obstruction between Holesmouth Junction Exclusive and Avonmouth Town Goods Yard Junction Exclusive.

CODE B.D. 42

ALTERNATIVE ROUTE.

Bristol Corporation Railway.

Trains usually running over the G.W. line via St. Andrew's Road Passenger Station must run over the Bristol Corporation Lines between Holesmouth Junction and Goods Yard Junction.

Passenger traffic usually dealt with at St. Andrew's Road Station must be dealt with at Avonmouth Dock Station.

SPECIAL INSTRUCTIONS FOR WORKING PASSENGER TRAINS OVER BRISTOL CORPORATION LINES.

All trains running over the Bristol Corporation Lines must run at a slow speed and the enginemen must be prepared to stop short of any obstruction between signals..

While this working is in operation no engine or vehicle must be shunted or moved from one running line to the other, or from the running line into a siding, or from a siding to the running line. Before passenger trains are allowed to pass, the Avonmouth Yard Master must, in addition to arranging for Facing Points in the running lines to be clipped (or clipped and padlocked) as shewn in this notice, see that Hand Points in adjoining lines which lead in one direction to lines converging with, fouling, or crossing the running lines, are set for the other direction and securely wedged. He must also see that the wheels of vehicles standing on lines converging with the running lines, where there is no protection by points, are properly scotched to prevent the possibility of vehicles running foul.

Trains must be signalled on the G.W. Block instruments between adjacent signal boxes or B.T. Reg. 25 (a iii) and absolute block working must be maintained.

Wartime notice for diversion of Avomouth traffic in case of lines blocked by enemy action.

were never mentioned), when certain routes were not available, arrangements needed to be made to divert up and down through passenger and freight services as set out in the booklet. Each route had a route code, so the Clifton Extension route between Stapleton Road GWR (exclusive) and Avonmouth Dock junction (inclusive) was coded BD37; Stoke Gifford (exclusive) to Filton West (exclusive) was BD38; Filton junction (exclusive) to Hallen Marsh junction (exclusive) was BD39; from Pilning junction (exclusive) to Hallen Marsh (exclusive) via Severn Beach was BD40; Hallen Marsh (inclusive) to Holesmouth junction (inclusive) was BD41 (the latter distance was less than a quarter of a mile); Holesmouth (exclusive) to Avonmouth Town Goods Yard junction (exclusive) was BD42; from Town Goods (inclusive) to St Andrews junction (exclusive) was BD43; at St Andrews junction was BD44.

Obstruction of the GW lines between St Andrews junction (exclusive) and Gloucester Road (exclusive) was coded BD45; between Gloucester Road (inclusive) and Avonmouth Dock junction was BD46. Obstruction of the Clifton Extension (Joint) lines between Avonmouth Dock junction (exclusive) and St Andrews junction (exclusive) was BD47.

In the event of LMSR lines being obstructed, diversions were listed; if the lines between Avonmouth and Kingswood junction were blocked (as was the case several times), then the following applied:

LMS freight trains were permitted to run over the GWR lines between Yate South junction on the Bristol–Gloucester line, and via Stoke Gifford, Henbury and Hallen Marsh, to reach Avonmouth. LMS locos and crews worked throughout, with pilot drivers and guards from the GWR to accompany them where required between Yate and Avonmouth and vice versa. These latter were provided by the GWR Divisional and Locomotive superintendents. The following locos were permitted to use this route: 5XP (Jubilee) class, 5P/5F (Black 5), Midland Compound, 3P 4-4-0, 2P 4-4-0, 5P/4F 2-6-0 (with taper or parallel boiler), 4F 0-6-0, 8F Stanier 2-8-0, 7F 0-8-0 and MR 3F 0-6-0.

Enemy Attacks

Major air raids began over the Severnside area in 1940. During the night of 1 September 1940, thirty-one German bombers carried out a raid on the area between Bristol and Portishead. In all, 23 tons of high explosives and 9 tons of oil bombs were dropped during the raid, but, although four people were killed and five injured in the Portishead area, overall damage was slight. The next night, the Luftwaffe returned with forty-seven aircraft but, whilst Bristol was hit, the Avonmouth line remained untouched. Overnight on 24 September 1940, a small attack on Avonmouth resulted in the shell-filling factory at the Royal Edward Dock being hit and set on fire. On 4 January 1941, the Germans returned with a large fleet of aircraft. Between the hours of 18.35 and 06.15 the next day, 103 aircraft attacked Avonmouth and other places north and west of Bristol, dropping 106 tons of high explosives, 1.5 tons of oil bombs and more than 27 tons of incendiaries. The raid failed to hit the right targets and the bombs were mostly scattered along the Severn coast between Clevedon and Weston-super-Mare. In Weston, thirty-four people died and eighty-five were injured.

On 16–17 January 1941, in a night raid between 19.30 and 05.10, 158 tons of explosives and 54,000 incendiaries were dropped over Avonmouth town and the northern part of the docks. On the same night, another wave of 164 bombers dropped 164 tons of explosives and 33,840 incendiary bombs over Bristol and Avonmouth. Although rising mist and poor visibility meant that the raids were not as successful as they were planned to be, such was the damage and disruption caused by fires that the docks complex was stopped from working during 17 January. This was to prove to be the only occasion during the conflict when work was stopped.

Elsewhere during this raid, Stapleton Road gasworks was hit and bombs also caused damage in a line between Fishponds and Clifton. Montpelier station, which had escaped early bombing raids, was badly hit in this one, with the main station building destroyed and the station master's house flattened. The signal box also suffered some bomb damage. Buildings were also damaged and destroyed in nearby Bath Buildings, Cheltenham Road, Ashley Road, Wellington Avenue, York Road, Richmond Road and Fairlawn Road, as well as in the Eastville, St Paul's, Kingsdown and Cotham areas of Bristol. Railway traffic to and from Avonmouth via Bristol was disrupted when bombs fell near Stapleton Road (GWR) and damaged the signal box, and further bombs fell on the GWR lines at Lawrence Hill. Traffic was resumed on 18 March, but Avonmouth passenger trains were diverted via Henbury until 19 March, in accordance with the instructions of Code BD37.

It was, in fact, an unexploded bomb, which had fallen during the raid on the gasworks, that caused the biggest problem to the Avonmouth railway that night. The bomb went off around 10.00 on the morning of 18 March and damaged the brick bridge that carried the Clifton Extension over Glenfrome Road. The line was blocked and two people were injured. Workmen got the Up line clear by 14.00. As soon as possible, a temporary crossover, not connected to the signal box, was laid in at Ashley Hill junction and single-line working between Kingswood junction and Ashley Hill junction commenced. Freight traffic was both heavy and important so, in order to avoid delays, the Mangotsfield–Avonmouth passenger service over the line was suspended. In the event, although the Down line was restored for normal running by September 1941, the passenger service never returned.

A near miss on the single line between Hallen Marsh and Severn Beach caused the track to be misaligned and communication cables were cut, but normal running was resumed by 16.30 on 17 March.

Overall, 257 people lost their lives in these raids and a further 391 were injured.

Avonmouth was attacked again on the night of 26 March 1941, when thirty-six planes dropped bombs on the area. The Germans claimed to have dropped a total of 33 tons of explosives and over 13,000 incendiaries between 21.05 and 22.00. A number of fires were started in the dock area and three oil storage tanks belonging to the Anglo-American oil company were set alight. Six people were killed and seventeen injured.

A raid on Avonmouth on 29–30 March 1941 saw thirty-five German planes drop bombs on the National Smelting Works and the docks. The smelting plant was badly damaged and several mills in the dock area were set alight. The Up platform at St Andrews Road station was hit and both lines were blocked, and the goods shed at Town Goods was damaged. Trains resumed running by 16.00 the following day.

April 1941 saw a raid on Avonmouth Docks by seventy-six Luftwaffe planes. Between 21.16 on 3 April and 00.45 on 4 April, the Germans claimed to have dropped 80 tons of explosives and over 8,000 incendiary bombs. However, the weather closed in and only forty-nine aircraft actually bombed Avonmouth, with the others attacking sites along the River Avon. Thanks to the rain, the fires started at Avonmouth were largely prevented from spreading and little overall damage was caused, although the National Smelting plant was hit.

The following evening, 4 April 1941, brought an eighty-five-bomber raid to Avonmouth. It was a clear night and 80 tons of explosives and 19,675 incendiaries were dropped. Most of the bombs were reported as falling in fields around Shirehampton and at Sea Mills, and near misses by explosive bombs caused the tracks to be moved out of alignment by blast. Passenger services were diverted via Filton and Henbury again until the tracks at Sea Mills could be restored for normal running, which was achieved by 16.00 on 5 April.

It was during this raid that Holesmouth Junction signal box was badly damaged. Bombs falling near the tracks at St Andrews Road also caused wagons to be damaged and derailed in the Royal Edward Yard. This damage led to the suspension of the services that ran via Henbury, although a minimal shuttle service ran between Pilning Low Level and

Severn Beach for any passengers who wished to travel between these two places. GWR rail access to the docks was only possible via St Andrews junction and Gloucester Road, using the Corporation lines.

The railway was restored between St Andrews Road and Holesmouth by the afternoon of 7 April. Passenger services were restored via Henbury and Severn Beach by means of trains running round at Hallen Marsh. Holesmouth signal box was rebuilt a short distance nearer to Hallen Marsh, using the same lever frame and much of the original wooden structure. The lever brasses bore the evidence of that night in the shape of scratches and dents, until the box closed in 1988.

On the night of 7–8 April 1941, the Luftwaffe again returned to Bristol, with twenty-two aircraft attacking the city as part of a main raid on Liverpool. Despite nine planes dropping bombs on Avonmouth, there was little damage to the railway.

Development of the Docks Area

After the 'phoney war' period of 1939, the Second World War began in earnest. The government recognized that, in the event of enemy action crippling the country's major ports, food and material supplies could be seriously affected, as any enemy bombing of a port would be likely to destroy its distribution depot as well. The Ministry of Transport took the decision to construct several large sorting depots at a safe distance away from the major ports, but also within a fairly short distance by rail. The main objective of the Ministry in choosing where to site a newly built depot was to increase the amount of goods that could pass through the port by clearing the goods as quickly as possible from the port and sorting them for distribution at a safe, distant location. This would serve another objective in that it would remove the goods from the danger of being destroyed by enemy air raids. Once sorted

at the distribution depot, the goods could then be transported to their destinations by less congested routes, by both rail and road.

Avonmouth Docks was one of the ports affected. The decision was taken to site a new depot near Chipping Sodbury, on the South Wales Direct route from Swindon. Known as 'Wapley Common', after a nearby open space, it would consist of four large sheds, each measuring 500×100 feet (150×30m). It was designed to receive five trains per day of mixed loads totalling 250 5-ton wagons, which would represent the discharge of eight ships simultaneously. A similar figure of outward trains of sorted goods was expected to leave the depot daily.

The new depot would cost £300,000 and would be operated by the Ministry of War Transport on behalf of the PBA (Port of Bristol Authority). The PBA would be responsible both for supplying the labour force and for the policing of the premises.

As with the previous world conflict, Avonmouth Docks saw a huge amount of military traffic as well as imports of food and military supplies from the USA. Railway locomotives, in the shape of the 0-6-0 docks shunting engines designed for the US Transportation Corps, were brought in from across the Atlantic. Some of these stayed at Avonmouth on loan to the PBA.

Sadly, hospital ships and trains would also have to pay frequent return visits to the docks again, with injured soldiers, sailors and airmen from many countries.

The Avonmouth docks were enlarged from 1941, with more facilities added for unloading oil and petrol. A new oil products supply pipeline was established to London via the 'Government Pipelines and Storage System', an underground line better known by the acronym 'AVGAS', reflecting the fact that it carried aviation fuel as well.

On 27 December 1948, workmen recovered one alarming legacy of the conflict from No.2 Depot of the Regent Oil Company Ltd – an unexploded 500-pound bomb.

CHAPTER 12

The Passenger Service

The passenger train service was initially operated between Mangotsfield and Avonmouth Dock
station by the Midland Railway company, then,
after the Grouping, by the LMSR. There were
thirteen trains a day from Mangotsfield, where
the trains arrived and departed from the bay line
behind Platform 4. Trains more often ran between
Mangotsfield and Fishponds and Clifton Down as
the demand was greater. There were no Sunday
services, which was a gift to the Great Western,
which initially ran ten trains to Avonmouth from
Temple Meads during the week and seven on
Sundays. The GWR gained more of a monopoly
on the Avonmouth services in this fashion. The
Midland services continued until 1917 when the
First World War caused them to cease. Passenger
trains resumed in 1919 and ran – although they
were sparsely used – until enemy action in the
Second World War closed the line between
Kingswood junction and Ashley Hill junction.
They never resumed.

By 1923, there were some twenty-four daily
trains from Temple Meads to Clifton Down and
twelve from Mangotsfield or Fishponds to Clifton
Down. With the increase in popular travel after the
Second World War, a total of thirty-three trains ran
each way between Temple Meads and Avonmouth

TRAIN SERVICES AND CHEAP
DAY RETURN FACILITIES

between

BATH SPA, BRISTOL,
WESTON-SUPER-MARE and
CLEVEDON

BRISTOL, AVONMOUTH DOCK,
SEVERN BEACH, PILNING and
PORTISHEAD

13th JUNE to 18th SEPTEMBER, 1955

inclusive

Cover of the summer 1955 timetable.

PILNING (Low Level), SEVERN BEACH and AVONMOUTH DOCK

Week Days

Mile	Station	am	am	am	am	am	am	am S	am E③	am V	am	am E⓪	noon E	pm	pm S	pm	pm S	pm	pm	pm S	pm	pm E	pm	pm E
1	Bristol ┌ T. Meads dep	..	..	7 30	..	825	..	9 10	..	..	..	1050	..	..	..	1K 7	..	2F 0	..	..	..	..		
1¼	├ Law. Hill	..	..	7 35	..	828	..	9 16	..	..	..	1054	..	..	..	1 12	..	2 13	..	..	..	..		
1½	└ Stapleton Rd.	..	..	7 39	..	831	..	9 20	..	..	..	1057	..	..	..	1 16	..	2 16	..	..	..	..		
2¼	Ashley Hill	..	..	7 43	..	835	..	9 24	..	..	..	11 1	..	..	..	1 19	..	2 18	..	..	..	..		
3¾	Horfield	..	..	7 47	..	839	..	9 29	..	..	..	11 5	..	..	..	1 23	..	2 22	..	..	..	..		
4¼	Filton Junction	..	..	7 51	..	844	..	9 33	..	..	..	11 9	..	..	..	1 27	..	2 26	..	..	..	..		
6	Patchway	..	..	7 56	..	849	..	9 37	..	..	..	1113	..	..	..	1 31	..	2 30	..	..	..	..		
9¾	Pilning (High Level) arr	..	..	8 2	..	857	..	..	..	..	..	..	..	..	..	..	..	..	..	..	..	..		
9½	Pilning (Low Level) dep	..	..	..	8 10	..	..	9 45	9 50	..	..	1123	..	..	..	1 40	..	2 38	..	..	..	..		
10½	Cross Hands Halt	..	..	..	8 12	..	..	9 47	9 52	..	..	1125	..	..	..	1 42	..	2 40	..	..	..	..		
10¾	New Passage Halt	..	..	..	8 14	..	..	9 49	9 55	..	..	1127	..	..	..	1 44	..	2 42	..	..	..	..		
11¾	Severn Beach { arr	..	..	..	8 17	..	..	9 52	9 57	..	..	1130	..	..	..	1 47	..	2 45	..	..	..	..		
	Severn Beach { dep	6 43	7 35	..	8 23	..	9 0	..	..	10 0	11 0	12 0	1223	0 25	..	2 0	..	..	3 0	3 35	4 0	4 20		
15¼	St. Andrew's Road	6 51	7 44	..	8 30	..	9 8	..	..	10 8	11 8	12 8	1230	8 33	..	2 12	..	..	3 8	3 43	4 8	4 27		
16½	Avonmouth Dock arr	6 54	7 47	..	8 34	..	9 11	..	..	10 11	1111	1213	1233	1 11	1 36	..	2 15	..	3 11	3 46	4 11	4 30		
—	Avonmouth Dock dep	7 20	7 52	..	8 35	..	9 15	..	..	10 15	1115	1215	1235	15 1	40	..	2 16	..	3 15	3 50	4 15	4 32		
17¾	Shirehampton	7 24	7 56	..	8 40	..	9 19	..	..	10 19	1119	1219	1239	1 19	1 45	..	2 20	..	3 19	3 54	4 19	4 36		
19¼	Sea Mills	7 28	8 1	..	8 45	..	9 23	..	..	10 23	1123	1223	1243	1 23	1 49	..	2 24	..	3 23	3 58	4 23	4 40		
21¼	Clifton Down	7 36	8 8	..	8 52	..	9 30	..	..	10 30	1130	1230	1250	1 30	1 58	..	2 31	..	3 30	4 5	4 30	4 47		
22	Redland	7 38	8 10	..	8 54	..	9 32	..	..	10 32	1132	1232	1252	1 32	2 0	..	2 33	..	3 32	4 7	4 32	4 49		
22½	Montpelier	7 40	8 12	..	8 57	..	9 34	..	..	10 34	1134	1234	1255	1 34	2 2	..	2 35	..	3 34	4 9	4 34	4 51		
23¾	Bristol ┌ Stapleton Rd.	7 45	8 16	..	9 1	..	9 38	..	..	10 38	1138	1238	1259	1 38	2 5	..	2 39	..	3 38	4 13	4 38	4 56		
24¼	├ Law. Hill	7 48	8 19	..	9 3	..	9 41	..	..	10 41	1141	1241	1 2	1 41	2 11	..	2 42	..	3 44	4 16	4 41	5 0		
25¼	└ T. Meads arr	7 52	8 23	..	9F16	..	9 45	..	..	10E45	1145	1245	1D45	..	..	..	2 46	..	3E45	4 20	4E48	5 5		

D Arr 1 48 pm on Saturdays
E or E Except Saturdays
F Change at Stapleton Road
G On Saturdays dep Bristol (Temple Meads) 5 0 pm and change at Stapleton Road

H Saturdays only; also runs Mondays to Fridays, 25th July to 26th August inclusive
K On Saturdays dep Bristol (Temple Meads) 1 0 pm and change at Stapleton Road
H Third class only

S or **S** Saturdays only
V Third class only on Mondays to Fridays. First and Third class on Saturdays
Z 8 minutes later Mondays to Fridays

③ Third class only

ABOVE: The 1955 summer timetable.

RIGHT: Summer visitors to Clifton Down! Elephants from a circus train head for the exit on their way to the nearby Durdham Downs. I hope they all had tickets. (Wilf Stanley)

Two morning services pass at Holesmouth. Note the two different front-end liveries. (Wilf Stanley)

Snow did not stop the railways in the 1950s. (Wilf Stanley)

Dock. After the war, the ex-GW railcars were used on some services, along with three-car DMUs – commencing on 3 January 1955 – and steam-hauled services also continued.

Trains ran to various destinations and via different routes. For example, the 06.02 Bristol Temple Meads ran to Avonmouth Dock station via Henbury; the 06.10 ran via Clifton and terminated at Dock station, thereafter forming the

In steam days, 2-6-2 3MT tank pauses at Shirehampton with a local passenger service. (Wilf Stanley)

06.50 Avonmouth Dock station to Bristol Temple Meads via Henbury. In another example, a train of empty coaches departed from Filton West carriage sidings at 16.25 and ran to St Andrews Road station, where it became the evening workmen's train to Bristol.

Avonmouth trains to and from Bristol Temple Meads arrived and departed from Temple Meads 'Old Station' platforms 12–15. After the closure of Old Station and the renumbering of the platforms, trains to and from Avonmouth normally used the short stub of track left on the approaches to Old Station, numbered platform 1.

Boat Trains

Boat trains were an irregular feature of the docks. Those for passengers or troops ran via either Henbury or Clifton, worked in and out by a particular method (see 'Gloucester Road Crossing'). It was not just holidaymakers who arrived or departed Avonmouth by ship. It was also the point of entry for many foreign immigrants, who were transported onwards from the docks by train to their destinations. People are familiar with the West Indian immigrants, some of whom arrived at Avonmouth, but before then, in 1948, it was not unusual for emigrants (that is, people leaving the country to live abroad) to pass through here. Some of these were children or young adults from Dr Barnardo's orphanages, most from a poor background, and Special Instructions were issued for railway staff dealing with such people.

Any carriages that had carried emigrants were to be disinfected after use, so it was mandatory for the station from which the train was starting to telegraph the yardmaster at Avonmouth, to advise him of the relevant coach numbers. The yardmaster would then advise the carriage and wagon examiner which coaches had carried emigrants and these vehicles would be locked out of use once the train had unloaded at Avonmouth Docks. They were then sent to either Bristol's Dr Day's or Barton Hill workshops, where they would be thoroughly disinfected before being returned to traffic.

> **EXTRACT FROM BRITISH RAILWAYS APPENDIX TO THE SERVICE TIMETABLE, DECEMBER 1948**
>
> Foreign Emigrants, Temple Meads to Avonmouth.
> The Guards Inspector at Bristol T.M. will be responsible for ascertaining the number of the coach in which Foreign Emigrants are loaded in Ordinary or Special trains from Temple Meads and he must advise the carriage and wagon Foreman at Barton Hill as soon as possible after he has obtained particulars, giving number of each coach, and the Locomotive Department will take the necessary steps to ensure the coaches being properly disinfected. He must also instruct each Guard before leaving Bristol what coaches conveying Foreign Emigrants are on the train and after the passengers have been dealt with at Avonmouth, the Guard must lock up each compartment and hand the number of each coach to the Western Region representative at Royal Edward Dock, or the Station Master at Avonmouth as the case may be, who will be responsible for seeing that they are not used before they are disinfected.

There were special instructions too, for passengers travelling to either Cross Hands or New Passage halt; both of these halts had a short platform of 150 feet (around 48 metres) in length. This meant that neither platform could accommodate a train of more than two carriages. Passengers travelling from Pilning towards Severn Beach who wished to alight at Cross Hands or New Passage were told to sit in the rear two coaches of the train and the driver would ensure that these two vehicles were drawn up alongside the platform. Anyone travelling from the Severn Beach direction would be advised to sit in the front two coaches, which would also be stopped alongside the platform.

Guards on these trains had to collect the tickets from passengers alighting at either halt and hand them to the person in charge at Pilning Low Level or Severn Beach stations, as the case may be. It was the duty of the guard of a passenger train calling at either halt to take notice of any passenger who joined the train there who had with him or her a 'bicycle, mail cart or dog', and report this to staff at the next station in order that the 'necessary charges' might be collected.

The very last 'Ghost Train' creeps over Filton West Junction heading for North Filton platform.

Guards on the last train of the day to stop at either halt were also responsible for extinguishing the Tilley lamps used to light the platforms. He then had to collect them and take them to the signalman on duty at Pilning Low Level or Severn Beach. (It was the duty of the station master at either Severn Beach or Pilning as necessary to arrange for the trimming and lighting of the lamps at Cross Hands and New Passage.)

The 'Ghost Train'

Every line ought to have a ghost train, but this one was never seen at Avonmouth, except on rare occasions. Headcode 2B03, it was the workers' train, which ran from Parson Street station

through Bristol Temple Meads every morning and returned each evening, carrying workers to and from the British Aerospace and Rolls-Royce aircraft factories at Filton airfield. The train was usually a three-car DMU and ran into and departed from Filton North platform. This station was not open for public use by the 1970s and the train did not appear in any public time-table, hence its nickname. BR, in the spirit of the 1980s, decided that the service was not paying its way, claiming that only around three passengers at a time used the service. Although protestors disputed the passenger figures, asserting that the train provided a valuable service for Rolls-Royce and British Aerospace workers, BR disagreed and, in May 1986, discontinued the service. Labour

Contrary to BR statements, there were passengers for the 'Ghost Train'; but what a state the platforms are in! No wonder people took the bus.

A 'Warship' Class 42 pulls a 'Monkey Special' round the curve from St Andrews junction towards Dock station in the 1960s. (Wilf Stanley)

Party supporters in the Bedminster (Windmill Hill) ward of Councillor Claire Warren commemorated the passing of the 'Ghost Train' by delivering a wreath to the councillor.

For operational reasons, the 'Ghost Train' did run back to Bristol via Henbury once or twice more, and thus haunted the Avonmouth and Clifton line again before being 'exorcised' by BR.

Excursions

'Edex' (educational excursion) trains ran from South Wales and the Southern Region to Clifton Down for Bristol Zoo and were commonly called 'Monkey Specials'. The ones from the Southern ran via Westbury and Bathampton to Dr Day's, Stapleton Road and Narroways junction, and thence via the Clifton Extension to Clifton Down, where the passengers would disembark. The empty coaching stock then ran via Avonmouth and Henbury to Filton West, where it took the spur line up to Filton junction, then down the bank to Bristol and Malago Vale carriage sidings. The return working would start as ECS from Malago sidings and run via Stapleton Road again to Clifton, where it would pick up its passengers. The train then ran via Avonmouth and Henbury to Filton West and Filton junction, then down Filton bank once more to Dr Day's and round the 'Rhubarb Loop' to North Somerset junction and the line to Bathampton.

A Class 37 hauls a 'Monkey Special' past Town Goods box, summer 1980.

The 'Monkey Special' passing St Andrews crossing, heading back to South Wales.

These SR specials brought 'West Country' and 'Battle of Britain' locos to the line, running from Malago carriage sidings to Bristol St Philips Marsh shed for servicing. On 30 June 1961, an excursion from the Southern Region brought unrebuilt 'Battle of Britain' Class loco No.34057 *Biggin Hill* to the Avonmouth line. As usual, the loco was serviced at St Philips Marsh shed.

Edex trains from South Wales would run to Stoke Gifford, where they would reverse and take the Avonmouth line at Stoke Gifford West junction. The train would run via Avonmouth to Clifton where the ECS would run to Malago via Stapleton Road. The return working ran ECS from Malago Vale to Clifton to pick up its passengers, and then the train ran via Avonmouth to Filton West and Stoke Gifford West, where it would reverse and set off to South Wales via Patchway. These trains were more often than not headed by an ex-GW 'Hall' Class loco.

When Stage 7(b) of the Bristol Resignalling came in over the weekend of 20–22 February 1971, a new chord line was opened between Patchway

Seen from St Andrews junction, an excursion to Bristol's Eastville market passes Town Goods box. It looks like Town Goods is switched out as all the signals are Clear.

Seen here at Bath Green Park shed on the last day of the S & D, 34057 Biggin Hill. (Wilf Stanley)

and Filton West, obviating the need for South Wales–Avonmouth trains to run to Stoke Gifford for reversing.

On diesel days, 'Monkey Specials' were frequently headed by a Welsh-based Class 37.

During the 1980s, the Avonmouth line became a popular venue for rail tours. With the ever-present threats of closure and the fact that, although colour-light signalling had encroached on the line from both the Bristol and Filton ends, it was a haven of semaphore signals and goods working. On one occasion even a 'Hastings' DMU was used. Several of these excursions would call at Severn Beach where, if loco-hauled, they could run round in the sidings. These trains brought a variety of motive power to the line, including Class 20 and 40 locomotives. One such excursion on 24 November 1984 was run from Euston station, then on to the Western region at Barnt Green, and then to Bristol Parkway from where it ran to Avonmouth via Henbury. The train would pause at Shirehampton for a photographic stop. Presumably, the subject of the photos was the diesels – 40086 and 40118 – rather than

Shirehampton station, which was, sadly, by this time not very photogenic.

During the 1980s, a local pressure group, which had been formed to call attention to the lack of BR interest in the line, organized excursions from stations in Avonmouth and Severn Beach to places all over the country. As they were advertised to the public, these were known as 'Advertised Excursions' or 'Adex'.

Class 20 No.20022 heads the 'Severncider' excursion past Hallen Marsh box on Sunday 30 June 1985. A Class 31 was on the rear to head the train back from Severn Beach.

CHAPTER 13

Goods Traffic

As can be expected of a busy docks, there was an enormous amount of goods traffic for the majority of the twentieth century. The docks internal railway was far more extensive than the main railway system that served it – and that was extensive enough. All sorts of goods (or freight, to use the later-adopted American term) passed through Avonmouth Docks over the years. To list every train and cargo would be a volume in itself, but a number were particularly interesting.

Fuel

Fuel as a product to be transported has been a feature of Avonmouth almost since the opening of the first dock. The Anglo-American oil company, Regent Fuels, Texaco, Shell and Esso were among the companies who made use of the docks area. One regular oil train was the Avonmouth to Bromford Bridge, in Birmingham. This was a company oil train run on behalf of the Esso oil company and comprised four-wheel rail tankers hauled by a steam loco. After the Second World War, this was normally a 9F 2-10-0 working. After Beeching and the end of steam, the working was allocated to a Class 47 diesel loco hauling 100-ton bogie tanks. The 4V50 was the 11.00 (Saturdays excepted) Bromford Bridge to Avonmouth Royal Edward, with empty fuel tanks, a company block train on behalf of Esso. Another arrival from Bromford Bridge was 4V36, again con-

92244 pulls the Avonmouth to Bromford Bridge tanks out of the Royal Edward Yard at Holesmouth. (Wilf Stanley)

A 9F thunders up the bank towards Blaise. (Wilf Stanley)

veying empty fuel tank cars and this time arriving at Royal Edward at 23.40.

The Esso company block trains 5M12 and 5M20, from Avonmouth to Bromford Bridge, left the Royal Edward Yard at 00.20 and 08.40, respectively. The fuel was conveyed in four-wheel tank cars leaving the yard and ran via Henbury, Filton West, Stoke Gifford and Westerleigh West junction, where it took the branch to Yate and the LMR, thence via Gloucester to Birmingham. The train was booked to pass Henbury 17 minutes after departure and Filton West junction at 09.13, where it

RIGHT: The Down Bromford Bridge to Avonmouth passes Charfield on the LMR main line from Gloucester. (Wilf Stanley)

BELOW: An April 1968 notice amending the Bromford workings.

ESSO TRAINS - AVONMOUTH TO BROMFORD BRIDGE AND RETURN
W/C 8TH APRIL.

5.M.12 00.10 MX Avonmouth to Bromford Bridge
4.V.59 11.00 MX Bromford Bridge to Avonmouth

    Will run Tuesday and Wednesday only.
    Will not run Thursday - amending Easter Notice 1427.

5.M.20 09.00 SX Avonmouth to Bromford Bridge
4.V.36 20.00 SX Bromford Bridge to Avonmouth

    Will not run Monday and Wednesday. Run Tuesday and Thursday only.

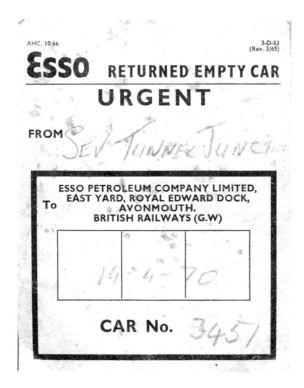

Wagon label for Esso tanks.

The ubiquitous ICI plastic fertilizer bag! Every railwayman and -woman in Avonmouth had several of these…

would be regulated for other traffic to precede it from Stoke Gifford. By 1970 this traffic was reduced to one loaded train per day as the fuel was by then carried in 100-ton bogie tankers, leaving Royal Edward as 6M35 at 23.55 and returning the empty tanks as 6V50, leaving Bromford Bridge at 11.15. Later still, it was retimed, with the Bromford tanks leaving Avonmouth at 09.00. The return working left Bromford Bridge at 11.00, arriving at the Royal Edward Yard at 14.30.

By the 1980s, this train had ceased to run, as the transfer of fuel was taken over by pipeline.

Another fuel train was the Avonmouth to Exeter train, run for Texaco fuels.

Chemicals

By the 1960s the main freight, after bananas, was fertilizer. In 1957 planning consent was given to ICI

(Imperial Chemical Industries) for the construction of a chemical and fertilizer plant near Severn Beach. The plant was to be rail-served, with the new rail connections running from an extension of the Severn Beach carriage sidings southwards on a short new branch, which turned westwards into the works. New signals and points were installed and brought into use over the weekend of 15–16 June 1963. In the works was a grid of some nine sidings together with a loco shed and 'cripple' sidings for wagons awaiting repair.

The fertilizer plant was opened in 1964. The main traffic outwards from the plant was bagged fertilizer, which was on pallets and loaded into BR standard box vans. These vans were never really

A DMU stands in the bay platform at Severn Beach and the sidings are full of four-wheel vans for fertilizer traffic. 1979.

BRITISH RAIL METHOD OF WORKING FOR I.C.I. WORKS, SEVERNSIDE

On and from Monday 19th May 1969, a revised method of working will be introduced for traffic working between Severn Beach and I.C.I. Severnside Works. The following procedures will apply:

The signalman at Severn Beach will inform the I.C.I. Transport office of the approach of all incoming trains.

The I.C.I. Transport office will allocate a reception line on the I.C.I. Rail Grid for the receipt of trains and will inform the Leading Railman (Shunter) which line is available for use by British Rail. This will be done in advance of any information concerning the receipt of a particular train. I.C.I. will ensure that after giving this information that the line is clear and no conflicting movements with their own locomotives will take place unless a clear understanding has been reached with the Leading Railman. Trains will then be berthed without any further involvement of I.C.I. staff.

On completion of the arrival of a particular train the Leading Railman will inform the I.C.I. Transport office of the fact and the number of the Reception Line on the Rail Grid.

A line will be kept clear for the release of the BR train engine and this will return to the Severn Beach end of the Rail Grid under the control of the Leading Railman. I.C.I. will not allow this road to be fouled by their own locomotive without a clear understanding being reached with the Leading Railman.

As soon as possible after the arrival of a train the Leading Railman will prepare a Train Sheet showing the detailed information of the vehicles which have arrived and a copy of this document will be made available to the I.C.I. Transport office.

I.C.I. will allocate two sidings on their Rail Grid for Departure purposes. Traffic will be placed on these sidings by I.C.I. locomotives and shunters. One will be allocated for 'general' traffic and the other for special lots. Should it be necessary for Block loads to be formed or a greater amount of outwards traffic is available than can be accommodated on the two sidings, this will be done in accordance with a pre-arranged programme which I.C.I. will agree with BR.

Traffic will be cleared from these allocated Departure sidings by British Rail locomotive and men under the direction of the Leading Railman without the involvement of I.C.I. staff. When it is necessary for I.C.I. locomotives to place wagons on these roads or carry out a conflicting movement between these sidings and Severn Beach when it is known a BR locomotive is within the Rail Grids at Severnside this will not take place unless a clear understanding has been reached with the Leading Railman as to what is to take place.

The Middle Turn Leading Railman will prepare a Train Sheet giving wagon details for all departures during the time he is on duty. A copy will be made available to the I.C.I. Transport office.

When the Leading Railman (Middle Turn) is not on duty (i.e.: first thing in the morning and last thing at night) the train sheets for Inwards and Outwards trains will be prepared by the Leading Railman Early or Late Turn as appropriate.

The Leading Railman (Middle Turn) will prepare by 09.00 hours each day the Rolling Stock details for Severnside. These figures will also include the private owner wagons (i.e.: not BR stock). This data will be made available to the I.C.I. Transport office as well as being telephoned to the Rolling Stock clerk at Avonmouth.

The consignment notes for I.C.I. traffic will be sent to Severn Beach and, before despatch to Bristol must be marked off against the appropriate Train Sheet by the Leading Railman (Middle Turn).

[Signed] W.R. Holmes, Freight Manager 15th May 1969.

designed for this type of loading as the maximum capacity could not be attained. Some vans were converted to take pallets but the problem was never successfully resolved until BR introduced purpose-built pallet vans, by which time the pallet traffic was mostly on the roads.

The ICI rail system had its own shunting and locomotive staff. The actual method of working was as follows: BR shunting staff phoned the ICI shunters from the Stop Board at Severn Beach sidings and asked which roads were clear. If they were unable to contact the ICI shunters, the BR staff had to phone the Transport office and get them to contact the ICI staff via two-way radio to ask the question. This led to delays. According to the proper method, the ICI staff were supposed to inform their Severnside Transport office which reception sidings were available. This was because there was restricted room in the sidings as ICI staff often broke up an incoming train and placed it on two sidings.

Inwards traffic was in the form of anhydrous ammonia from Immingham and potash. For many years, the ammonia traffic was, like the oil traffic, handled in four-wheel short-wheelbase tanks, but the advent of the 100-ton 'Jumbo' tankers made the job much easier. Speeds were increased and larger block loads could be moved. For rail staff it meant that a train of ten 100-ton tankers arriving at Hallen Marsh via Henbury needed to run round not between Hallen Marsh and Holesmouth, but between Hallen Marsh and Town Goods boxes, owing to the length of the trains.

Similar methods applied when the bulk potash trains from Tees yard to ICI Severnside were introduced in the 1980s. These trains, which comprised bogie container flats, were usually described as '7V66' or '6V66', but on some occasions they ran to Stoke Gifford sidings, where they would be forwarded to Avonmouth by the trip loco and described as '6B51'. The containers of this working were manufactured by Cobra Containers Ltd and painted a pale browny-yellow colour, with 'Cobra' on the side; as a result, rail staff sometimes described the trains themselves as 'cobras'.

BRITISH RAIL LOCAL INSTRUCTIONS FOR SEVERN BEACH

The Person in Charge must reach a clear understanding with the Guard of the train concerned, regarding the movement from the Down Sidings South to the I.C.I. sidings and vice-versa.

The Person in Charge of shunting must accompany all non-fully-fitted movements from the I.C.I. sidings.

I.C.I. locomotives are authorised to work over all BRB sidings at Severn Beach.

All movements from the I.C.I. sidings must be brought to a stand at the stop board provided at the converging point with the connection from the single line to the Down Sidings South and must not proceed until the Person in Charge has satisfied himself that it is safe to do so.

Ableton Lane Siding

Wagons may be stabled on the siding between the stop blocks and Ableton Lane level crossing.

All movements to and from the siding must be under the control of the Person in Charge and must be made with caution.

No propelling moves towards the siding must be commenced until the gates at Ableton Lane crossing have been secured across the roadway.

Before the locomotive is detached from the wagons positioned on the siding, sufficient brakes must be applied on wagons at the station end to prevent any movement towards the level crossing.

7th December 1969, Bristol Divisional Movements Manager

Carbon dioxide came from Bow depot in London in four-wheel rail tankers and anhydrous ammonia came from Severnside to and from that company's Haverton Hill works at Teeside. There was also an 'exchange' of ammonia between the ICI Severnside plant and the Fisons plant at St Andrews Road. Fisons was a long-established fertilizer company, which had a wider range of products than ICI. In the early 1960s, a decision was made by Fisons not to continue with basic ammonia production and to buy ammonia from other suppliers instead. ICI had an ammonia plant built at Severnside dedicated to supplying Fisons' main site at Immingham, near Grimsby, Humberside. This was the plant that sported the 'landmark' 400-foot high stack from

The ICI Severnside to Tees yard potash train thumps over Hallen Marsh junction, hauled by a pair of Class 20s. It will run round between Hallen and Town Goods boxes and then take the right-hand tracks up the bank to Stoke Gifford and beyond. Manufactured by Cobra Containers especially for this potash traffic, the containers carry 27 tonnes of potash each and each flat carries two containers.

which a stream of yellow smoke was emitted. Fisons at Avonmouth had a similar, but shorter, stack, again with a plume of yellow smoke. Rather than reflecting a by-product that was being exhausted from the plants, the smoke was yellow because of a dye that had been added to the exhaust gase, to indicate which way they were being taken by the wind.

Technology moves on and by 1990, after making a loss over four years, ICI had taken the decision to sell off its fertilizer division. After being taken over by Terra Nitrogen, the former ICI Severnside works was closed in January 2008 and the plants there demolished on 16 November 2008. The familiar 300-foot nitram tower and the nitric acid stack

were both felled. The rail branch into the works, which had been out of use for some years, was lifted. However, new life has been breathed into the old ICI site. Part of it was used for the construction of the new Seabank natural gas-fired power station, and in November 2009 waste management company Sita UK (now known as Suez) made a planning application to South Gloucestershire Council to build an energy recovery centre on another part. It would once again be rail-linked and would provide new treatment and recovery facilities to manage commercial and industrial waste from the region, along with household waste from west London. The new plant would be capable of

Anhydrous ammonia traffic was a regular working to ICI and Fisons. Here it is carried in 100-tonne 'Jumbo' tanks.

A general view from St Andrews Road station footbridge, showing Town Goods box, Fisons tank farm and the cold store.

Class 25 No.7507 leaves the sidings at Town Goods and heads for Hallen Marsh. (Brian Dyson/author's collection)

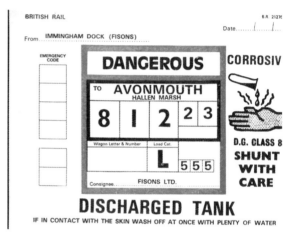

Ammonia tank wagon label.

processing up to 400,000 tonnes of non-recycled waste and would have the capacity to generate up to 32 megawatts of electricity – enough to power approximately 50,000 homes, equivalent to half the homes in South Gloucestershire. The application was refused by South Gloucestershire Council but, after a public enquiry, the case was passed to the Secretary of State, who upheld the appeal on 16 September 2011. The works went ahead and the rail link from Severn Beach sidings was reinstated. The movements of domestic refuse from west London

for incineration in the Severnside Energy Recovery Centre commenced in 2016.

Operationally, the single line between Hallen Marsh and Severn Beach could, until the mid-1960s, be a bottleneck, with freight and passenger trains all vying for the single line of metals. Often it took the signalmen at Hallen Marsh, Severn Beach and Pilning Low Level to get together on the telephone to arrange the moves. For example, the Hallen Marsh signalman would suggest that freight was released to run from Low Level while he let

In April 1979, Rowntree's ground frame became accessed from the Dock Junction end only.

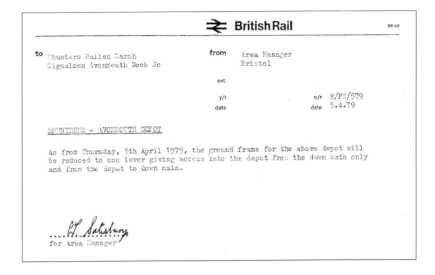

the passenger train run to Severn Beach. When the passenger train arrived in Severn Beach bay platform, then the freight could be given a clear road through to Hallen Marsh. The Hallen Marsh signalman would wait for the 'Train Out of Section' signal from Severn Beach for the passenger train and then release the token instrument his end, which released a token at Severn Beach. He could then watch from the North End windows of the box to see the well-spaced puffs of smoke climb into the air as the freight loco got hold of its load. If he saw the puffs were rapid, he would know it was being driven by 'Jack the Rat', who always kept the regulator wide open; he was known as the signalman's friend, never letting them down.

Rowntree's Trips

Chocolate and sweet manufacturer Rowntree-Mackintosh opened a distribution depot in 1971 on the site of the Avonmouth Dock station bay lines. The depot was served by a siding, which in turn was accessed from the Down main line via a single slip connection in the Up main. These were operated by a ground frame released by Avonmouth Dock Junction signal box.

Rowntree's traffic came from the company's factory at Foss Island, in York. Trains would be hauled from Hallen Marsh or Town Goods by the area trip engine as far as the ground frame, where the shunters (who travelled with the train) would phone Dock junction and ask for a release for the ground frame. Once their work was complete, they would place the train on the Up line, close the ground frame and tell the Dock Junction signalman, after which the train would be able to proceed on its way back to Hallen Marsh, or wherever it was going.

After an incident in April 1979, when a Rowntree's trip ended up following a passenger train in the same section, the slip connection was taken out of use and a particular working applied. Comprising not more than twelve standard-length units plus brake van, the working would run to Avonmouth Dock junction as an unfitted freight. Dock junction would describe the train to Bristol Panel box, advise the signalman there that this was 'a shunt' and, when a release was given by the Panel, the train would proceed on to the single line under Clear signals as far as the Dock Junction Up Main Home signal, where it would come to a stand. The points would be reversed and the train asked to St Andrews junction as a 'Freight Train Stopping in Section' 2-2-3 bell code. Once accepted by St Andrews under the 'Warning Arrangement' (necessary because of the Dock Station level crossing), Dock junction would slowly clear the Up

The Rowntree's warehouse at Dock station seen in 1982. It has been gone a long time.

Home signal and lean out of the window, holding a green flag steadily in full view of the driver, who would now begin to propel the train back over the crossing. Once the driver sounded his loco horn in acknowledgement, the Dock Junction signalman cleared his Up Main Starting signal.

On arrival at the Rowntree's Siding ground frame, the shunter phoned Dock Junction box for a release and things proceeded as usual.

Banana Trains

The banana trade first came to Avonmouth as long ago as 1901, when Elders & Fyffes commenced a service from Costa Rica. Every two weeks, the Elders & Fyffes shipping line brought the fruit in to Avonmouth, where it was offloaded manually from ships into railway box vans using casual docks labour. The railway vans were four-wheeled and strewn with straw, brought in from outlying stations such as Badminton, Coalpit Heath and Little Somerford, to protect the bananas. The perishable tropical fruit had to be kept at a constant temperature, especially in cold weather, so the box vans were steam-heated. Following the privations of the Second World War and enemy attacks on convoys, bananas had become increasingly scarce and they were considered a luxury both during and after the conflict. After the war, when shipping was reinstated and able to move freely, Avonmouth Docks once again became well known for its banana trains.

Since their freight was classed as 'perishable', the banana trains were given priority from the start of their journey to their destination. When a banana train was loaded, weighed and ready to leave, a siren mounted on a post at the Docks East gate, opposite Avonmouth Sidings signal box, would be sounded to alert all staff that it was about to be propelled from the weighbridge into Old Yard. Most other movements would cease until the train had got 'Right Away' and left the yard.

A 'box to box' message ('boxer') would be sent up the line from signal box to signal box giving the starting time and load of the train. A message from February 1966 – 'Boxer: 18.10 Avonmouth–Water Orton Bananas @ 18.10. Load 31' – told the signalmen along the route that the 18.10 banana train left Avonmouth on time and carried thirty-one vans.

Being classed as 'perishable', banana traffic was timetabled to run to various destinations from Avonmouth Old Yard. Some examples of these timings are below.

Banana traffic was lost in 1968 when Elders & Fyffes pulled their trade out of Avonmouth in favour of Southampton docks.

Other Freight Trains

5C50: Old Yard to Tavistock junction service. Departing Old Yard at 13.15 (Saturdays only), it ran via the Corporation lines to Royal Edward Yard 13.21–13.50 to attach more traffic. Then it ran via Hallen Marsh, Henbury, Filton West and Filton junction to Bristol and the west of England. The Wednesdays-only service started from Old Yard at 13.45 and took the same route, calling at Royal Edward 13.51–14.30.

7T63: departed Avonmouth Royal Edward Yard at 16.00 for Severn Tunnel junction via Hallen Marsh, Severn Beach and Pilning Low Level-Pilning junction.

5C23: 16.55 (Wednesdays and Saturdays excepted) Old Yard to Penzance via Hallen Marsh, Henbury, Filton West and Stoke Gifford.

4E22: a 17.40 Royal Edward Yard to Immingham service consisting of rail tank cars. Ran via Severn Beach and Pilning Low Level-Pilning junction.

5E04: (Mondays and Wednesdays only) 17.55 Royal Edward Yard to Thames Haven via Henbury, Filton West and Stoke Gifford.

6M12: 18.20 Royal Edward to Lawley Street via Henbury, Filton West and Stoke Gifford.

5C29: (Saturdays only) Royal Edward to Tavistock junction via Henbury, Filton West and Stoke Gifford.

5F09: 18.52 Old Yard to Llandilo junction (Saturdays excepted) ran via the Corporation lines to Royal Edward Yard calling to attach traffic 18.59–19.20 then running via Severn Beach and Pilning Low Level–Pilning junction. This service ran under the same headcode Saturdays only, but started from Royal Edward Yard at 19.20 and ran via Severn Beach and Pilning Low Level–Pilning junction.

4M31: ran from Royal Edward Yard to Hartlebury or Nuneaton as required, starting at 20.00; a company block train still booked for steam haulage as late as 1965.

5N12: started at 19.55 from ICI/Severn Beach sidings to York Tees yard running via Pilning Low Level.

6C49: 20.40 (Saturdays excepted) Old Yard to Hackney.

6O02: 21.10 Old Yard to Eastleigh.

6C36: a mixed freight train which was booked to run from Swindon late morning, calling at Bristol East Depot Down yard and the running via Clifton to Hallen Marsh, where it would arrive early afternoon and pick up traffic before proceeding to Severn Tunnel junction via Henbury, Filton and Patchway. This train ceased to run after 1982.

6B10: the Margam sorting sidings to Avonmouth service which ran Monday to Friday, conveying coke for the smelting works. On arrival at Hallen Marsh, after running via Patchway, Filton West and Henbury, the train would be shunted into the forward section then backed on to the spur. The loco would detach and run via the Up GW line on to the Inwards to pick up the return empty coke wagons placed there earlier by the smelting works loco. On occasions there would be a full load of empties and these were placed on both the Outwards and the Inwards sidings, necessitating collection first from the Outwards, then running on to the Up GW and backing on to the rest of the train on the Inwards. The return working ran as 6C09.

7T81: the 05.05 Avonmouth and Severn Tunnel junction freight usually ran with fifty-plus wagons and a brake van on. It started from Old Yard and ran via the Corporation lines to Royal Edward Yard where it called to attach traffic 05.15–05.40 and then ran via Severn Beach and Pilning Low Level, where it would perform the shunting rigmarole to reverse the train and propel it up the short incline to Pilning junction and thereafter 'Right Away' to Severn Tunnel junction. This train could never be relied upon to start on time and frequently left the Royal Edward around 06.00. It was best to wait until the 06.43 ex-Severn Beach had passed Hallen Marsh on its return run before allowing the 05.05 to leave Holesmouth for Pilning.

6B62: the 10.10 Severn Tunnel junction to Old Yard arrived at 12.45.

The 05.10 Avonmouth to Weymouth carried animal feed trains to the coastal town during the day in the 1950s, returning as 6B68, the 23.35 Weymouth to Avonmouth empty vans, which arrived at the Royal Edward Yard via Henbury. There used to be up to five trains a day to Weymouth from Avonmouth but by 1965 this was down to one.

Other freight services included the 01.35 Avonmouth to Barnwood (Gloucester), which ran from Old Yard via Henbury, Stoke Gifford and Westerleigh West, where it took the branch line to the LMR at Yate South; the 09.20 Avonmouth to Salisbury, which ran via Henbury and Filton West to Filton junction, thence down Filton Bank to Dr Day's junction, where it took the loop for the Bath lines; the 04.00 Royal Edward Yard to Bristol West Depot conveyed traffic for the west of England to be sorted and marshalled into trains at that yard.

Fertilizer was big business for the area and among the trains that carried the product was 6M32, the 20.00 Avonmouth to Ince and Elton (UK Fertilisers-UKF). This returned empty as 6V87, the 17.24 Ince and Elton to Avonmouth. The train ran both ways via Severn Tunnel junction, reversing at Stoke Gifford yard. It was classed as a company block train.

Because of the exchange of ammonia between Fisons at Avonmouth Town Goods and the ICI plant at Severnside, Fisons had a tank farm and sidings behind St Andrews Road Down platform. The trip loco was used several times a week to run trips between Severnside sidings at Severn Beach and the tank farm.

Other Traffic

In 1953 or 1954, a set of coaches was built at Swindon for possible export to Canada. Nicknamed 'Toronto' coaches, these were out of gauge and had to be moved at night to avoid delaying other trains. Signal and telegraph staff were required to be at various signal boxes en route as ground signals had to be removed at some stations and boxes to enable

the coaches to pass safely. Arriving at Holesmouth junction one Sunday night, the coaches were shunted on to the UP Corporation line, then carefully taken on to the docks, to be loaded on-board ship for export.

Another famous export through the docks was ex-GWR 'Castle' Class loco No.4079 *Pendennis Castle*. The loco, privately owned and preserved initially at the Great Western Society depot at Southall and later at Didcot railway centre, had been sold to the Australian Hamersley Iron Co., one of the largest iron-ore producers in Australia. On 29 May 1977, *Pendennis Castle* made what was then thought to be her last run in the UK, at the head of the 'Great Western Envoy' special from Birmingham to Didcot and back. The following day, 30 May 1977, she headed to Avonmouth, where she was uncoupled from her tender and loaded by crane aboard the cargo vessel *Mishref*, which sailed for Sydney on 2 June 1977.

After 23 years in Australia, the *Castle* came home in 2000, again via Avonmouth Docks.

Blaise fuel sidings, when the signal box was in place and before the line was singled, could be serviced from either direction. After the closure of Blaise and Henbury boxes and the singling of the line, it was normal practice for trains calling at Blaise to travel from the Hallen Marsh direction and call at Blaise en route to Stoke Gifford, gaining entry to the sidings via the ground frame, which was released by the single-line token. After Hallen Marsh became a fringe box to Bristol Panel, this practice changed. The single line being worked under the Track Circuit Block regulations, a train calling at Blaise stopped short of the ground frame and the guard phoned Hallen Marsh. Hallen Marsh released the ground frame and the train shunted as required. Once the work was done, the ground frame was restored to Normal, the guard again phoned Hallen Marsh and the release was 'cancelled', and the train could then proceed on its way.

CHAPTER 14

Motive Power

Locos

A popular morning commuter train, the 06.50 Avonmouth to Bristol Temple Meads service was usually loaded to six carriages and headed by a GW 'Grange' tender loco. Most other passenger services outside peak times were usually three coaches headed by a GW 61XX 2-6-2 'Prairie' tank loco. GW diesel railcars also ran on off-peak services. In the late 1950s, most services were taken over by three-car DMUs and the single power units known as 'Bubble Cars'. The 1980s saw the trials of the next-to-useless Leyland experimental R3 railbus, which caused no end of operational problems and delays for staff and did not help to encourage passengers to travel on the line at all. Later still, the uncomfortable Class 142 'Pacer' two-car units were used for some years; not for nothing did these units acquire their nicknames of 'Nodding Donkeys' or 'Burgervans'.

Robinson ex-Great Central ROD 2-8-0 locos were often employed on Stoke Gifford to Avonmouth freights, in particular the 10.30 Stoke Gifford–Avonmouth and 12.15 Avonmouth–Stoke Gifford. This latter service often had seventy-two wagons plus a banker in the Up direction. The ROD locos

92248 trickles off the Down Corporation line on to the Down GW line at St Andrews junction. In the right middle distance is Town Goods station, which at the time of this photograph, still had its access on to the main line here. (Wilf Stanley)

are remembered as having a distinctive hollow 'whoof' exhaust.

LMS 4F 0-6-0 tender engines were often employed on the banana trains. If they were running via Henbury where, between Blaise and Henbury, the incline was 1 in 400, they found it hard going. They would pound their way out of the yard and set off for Hallen Marsh where the driver would open up the loco for the start of the climb up to Filton. The engine would sway from side to side as each piston took steam and the valve gear between the frames could be seen clearly from the light of the fire.

Ex-LMSR 'Jinty' 0-6-0 tank engines often shunted Clifton Down coal yard. Ex-LMSR Horwich 'Crabs' were also used on banana trains and other traffic for the Midlands and ex-S&DJR 2-8-0 locos were often seen in the yards as well as working the Westerleigh yard to Stapleton Road gas sidings coal traffic. The usual working here was for the 2-8-0 to run from Bath Green Park to Westerleigh sidings with freight. It would then work the 07.40 Westerleigh to Bristol St Philips yard goods. After detaching the wagons at St Philips yard, the 2-8-0 with a brake van would run back up the Midland line as far as Kingswood junction, where it would reverse on to

Ivatt 2-6-0 No.46510 has no problems on Henbury bank.

Clun Castle did not always pull passenger trains! Hallen Marsh, late 1950s. (Wilf Stanley)

Fowler 'Crabs' were frequent visitors to Avonmouth. 42756 is crossing from Up to Down main lines at Rangeworthy near Bristol during single-line working. (Wilf Stanley)

4F 43979 passes through Henbury. Are those men on the platform shovelling snow or coal? (Wilf Stanley)

the Clifton Extension and propel the brake van to Old Yard, where it would work an Avonmouth to Westerleigh goods back up the Clifton Extension. Both LMSR and GW 2-8-0 engines were common. Ex-GW 2818 was preserved by Bristol City Museum and was stored in a shed in the docks complex for some years before being removed and restored to preservation traffic. Other fairly frequent visitors to the docks yards included the 'Austerity' 2-8-0 class, which often worked down from Stoke Gifford.

Otherwise, Great Western locos were in abundance. Almost every GW class could be seen in Avonmouth at some time or other, on goods trains or passenger traffic, from the humble but ubiquitous pannier tanks and 0-6-2 tanks to the 'Castles'. Even a 'Saint' was seen during the 1950s. 'King' Class engines, however, were banned from the Avonmouth lines owing to their axle loading. Nonetheless, mistakes do happen. One Sunday in the 1950s, the Hallen Marsh signalman had signalled the 4.30pm Avonmouth to Bristol (via Henbury) service as Normal, but, when the train approached Hallen, he could see that it had a 'big blue engine' on the front. It was a 'King'. The signalman was so surprised that he failed to note which particular 'King' it was.

47XX 2-8-0 locos were also banned from Avonmouth but this did not stop one turning up at Old Yard one day. It was swiftly sent to Dock station, where signalman Cliff Ball put it on the turntable whilst the local 'powers that be' decided what to do with it. It was eventually sent back to Bristol light engine via Henbury.

'Halls', 'Manors', 'Granges' were all seen there, as were the 2-6-2 tanks locos of various classes. The late 1940s saw occasional 'Saint' and 'Star' Class locos in Avonmouth: one old railwayman recalls *Clevedon Court* appearing on a freight train at Royal Edward Yard.

The 10.40 Stoke Gifford to Avonmouth via Henbury goods was usually hauled by a 66XX 0-6-2 tank loco.

Southern 'West Country' Class locos – both unrebuilt and rebuilt – often brought the 'Monkey Specials' to Clifton from South Wales, while it was not unknown to see Eastern Region B1s and the odd K1.

Most British Railways standard classes of steam loco were seen at Avonmouth and the 9F 2-10-0 locos (both the standard and Franco-Crosti versions) were to be seen on heavy coal and oil traffic.

Banking of freight trains was allowed between Hallen Marsh and Stoke Gifford or Filton junction. During the 1950s, on night shifts, the banker was stationed at Hallen Marsh and took water from the water column there. According to the instructions laid down, the banker had to be coupled to the rear of the train at Avonmouth and assist to Filton West where the train had to stop and detach the banker. Then, should the train be proceeding via Filton junction, the banker continued to assist up to the junction, but not coupled to the train. If the train was going to Stoke Gifford or beyond, then the banker had to stay coupled to the train and come off at Stoke Gifford.

In steam days, the Royal Edward pilot engine would come to Hallen Marsh at around 05.00 to take water.

Diesel shunting locos were stationed at Old Yard and Royal Edward Yard, taking over the duties at the latter from the 57XX pannier tanks. The ubiquitous 350-horsepower 0-6-0 shunting locos – later to become Class 08 – were used as North and South End pilots in the Royal Edward Yard and others would occasionally would come to Avonmouth on trip workings. It has to be said that their use on local trip workings was hardly a good replacement for the pannier tanks. Although the 08 was a powerful loco, it was limited to a top speed of 15mph; the following is a list of local workings allowed for these locos:

Avonmouth Dock to Stoke Gifford (via Henbury): forty 'Basic Wagon Units' (BWUs, each unit equivalent to a 10-ton mineral wagon; later superseded by 'Standard Length Unit', or SLU);

Avonmouth Dock to Stoke Gifford (via Pilning): twenty-five BWU;

Avonmouth Dock to Bristol West Depot (via Henbury): forty BWU;

Avonmouth Dock to Bristol West Depot (via Clifton): twenty-eight BWU;

West Depot to Avonmouth Dock (via Henbury): thirty BWU;

West Depot to Avonmouth Dock (via Clifton): thirty BWU;

Stoke Gifford to Avonmouth Dock (via Henbury): sixty BWU;

Stoke Gifford to Avonmouth Dock (via Pilning): sixty BWU.

20075 stands at Hallen Marsh in 1985.

D134/45076 stands on the Column Road at Hallen Marsh.

31143 at Hallen Marsh on a crisp snowy day in 1983.

25309 was the trip engine one day.

A Class 37 runs into Town Goods sidings, on its way to Fisons to collect the 'Jumbo' tanks seen in the tank farm.

A variety of lengths of train were permitted on a variety of routes to and from Avonmouth, but all at a published maximum speed of 5–10mph. This information was published in April 1968, 5 years after Dr Beeching's plans were implemented and a few months before the end of steam traction in the UK; he must have wept!

Main-line diesel locos included most classes, and the diesel-hydraulics were used extensively. The none-too-successful Class 22 diesel-hydraulics were used on freights. Class 45/46/47 Brush and Sulzer locos took over from the 'Westerns', 'Warships' and 'Hymeks'. Class 14 Paxman 0-6-0 diesels – nick-named 'Teddy Bears' – were often seen on freights to and from Avonmouth via Clifton or Henbury.

Class 20s, usually working in pairs, were not an uncommon sight on fertilizer trains. Classes 31 and 37 became common in the 1980s; December 1983 was notable for an unusually high number of Class 37 visits: 37101, 37158, 37171, 37176, 37242, 37274, 37275, 37279, 37280, 37281, 37283, 37292, 37295, 37297, 37300, 37307, 37609, 37684, plus a couple of others whose numbers were not noted, all visited Avonmouth during that month.

On one occasion, on 14 April 1982, a Class 40 arrived on a train for ICI. This loco took the train to Severn Beach and into the ICI works, then returned north on 6Z12, the 08.30 Severn Beach to Heysham tanks.

Class 25 also came to Avonmouth, sometimes in tandem, frequently on the Bow carbon dioxide tanks for ICI. On 20 October 1982, 25236 was seen on the

Class 42 'Warship' D813 Diadem standing at Hallen Marsh in 1973.

A Class 31 waits for the road at Dock junction with three condemned box vans and three brake vans for Bristol's Kingsland Road yard in 1982.

Class 08 shunters still appeared in Avonmouth after the yards had closed. This one has been deputized to do the Fisons to ICI ammonium nitrate trip to Severnside one Sunday.

A silver-roofed 47478 in excellent condition has a rest at Hallen Marsh.

Before its type was banned from the smelting works sidings, a Class 45 No.45050 heads over Smoke Lane crossing and into the works. 1982.

Fisons to Immingham working; on 29 October 1982, 25060 and 25120 were noted on the Severn Beach to Heysham 'Jumbo' anhydrous ammonia tanks. On 19 January 1983, 25176 arrived at Avonmouth with the Severn Beach ICI to Tees yard potash working. Even the Class 50 *Sir Edward Elgar* put in an appearance one day on a track-testing special.

Owing to the condition of the track and their weight, Class 45 diesels were banned from the smelting works sidings from 18 October 1985.

The 'Dockys'

The 'Docky' locos did not normally run over the main lines, except at Hallen Marsh, where they crossed the single line to Severn Beach to gain access to Chittening trading estate. The ISC loco did come

as far as the spur at Hallen, but on occasions these industrial workhorses did run on BR lines. PBA 41 ran from the docks at Holesmouth over BR metals via Henbury to Bristol, Ashton junction, where it went to work on the coal depot at Wapping Wharf.

The Port of Bristol Authority ran a variety of steam and diesel locos throughout its time. Peckett and Avonside were among the local builders, and Sentinel was the main supplier of 0-6-0 diesel locos until the end of the docks railway, which was announced on Wednesday 12 January 1983. The PBA railway finished on 21 March 1983. After PBA locos ceased to run, a BR Class 08 shunter was occasionally stabled on the old PBA sidings behind Hallen Marsh box and used for some local trip workings and to take wagons across to Chittening trading estate.

At the end of the PBA railway system, one of their Sentinels was loaned to the Western Fuel Company at Bristol Wapping Wharf. PBA 41 heads out of the yard at Holesmouth and on to pastures new.

PBA 41 in its new role at Wapping Wharf.

Fisons trialled this little shunter for a week or two. It proved fairly hopeless and soon went elsewhere.

Refusing to be defeated, Fisons had another go with this loco: it, too, proved underpowered for the task and soon followed its predecessor out of Avonmouth.

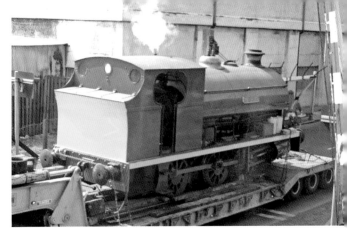

The sound of a steam loco whistle and there was 'Henbury' – on a low loader!

Another two industrial locos were trialled 'on loan' to Fisons at Town Goods for a while in the 1980s, shunting the ammonia tank farm. As usual, each of these locos arrived via Henbury and Hallen Marsh. Neither was a success and both left shortly after their trial period.

A most surprising move took place one day at St Andrews. I was on duty when the unmistakeable sound of a steam loco whistle was heard coming from the docks. It came closer and, when I looked out of the box window, there was one of the PBA steam locos *Henbury* coming out of the docks on the back of a low-loader – still in steam! Luckily I had my camera with me.

During the works leading up to the removal, in 1984, of two of the four main lines on Filton Bank, between Bristol Dr Day's junction and Filton junction, trains were diverted through Avonmouth. This brought a variety of traffic to the line, including for the first time, HST sets.

In steam and still whistling, Henbury steams away from the docks. On the following low loader was a PBA box van.

Labelled up for duty with Western Fuel Co., Henbury rests at the Bristol Industrial Museum. Nameplates have been removed for safe-keeping.

During the work to remove two of the four lines between Bristol and Filton in 1984, HSTs were diverted via Avonmouth.

CHAPTER 15

Accidents and Incidents

Collisions and Derailments

Inevitably, a major railway complex such as Avonmouth will have its fair share of minor incidents over the years. There were frequent derailments, of course, with the Corporation–main-line junctions at both Holesmouth and Dock junction bringing about the inevitable collisions. At Dock junction in the 1950s a notable incident occurred when a loco was in the process of running round via the Corporation line spur and another freight was allowed into the yard. The two locos collided side to side and the signalman who had hand-signalled the loco into the spur was disciplined. A similar collision occurred at Holesmouth junction, again in the 1950s, when a freight was let into Royal Edward Yard while the yard North End pilot, a 57XX pannier tank loco, was hand-signalled into the spur. The freight train, headed by a GW tender engine, collided with the pilot and both locos fell over. Again, the signalman was disciplined. Fortunately, no injuries were sustained in either accident.

Back at Dock junction, a move was required to propel back from the Corporation lines to Earth Sidings. The signalman closed the crossing gates and tried to clear the ground signal. When it would not clear, he hand-signalled the train to move back. It did – and piled the wagons over the stop blocks at the dead end. It transpired that the signalman had forgotten to set the points for the move, which was why the signal would not clear.

In 1994, just after the Avonmouth bulk-handling terminal was commissioned, a merry-go-round wagon managed to become derailed right inside the plant, causing a few problems.

Another derailment incident, this time at Hallen Marsh junction, involved a 28XX locomotive. A man who had been a porter at St Anne's Park station on the Bath line applied for and got a signalman's post at Hallen Marsh box. After a few weeks' training in the box he passed the rules and took the job on with enthusiasm. Sadly, on his very first shift he was too quick to replace the points on the Inwards sidings and was off the road with the loco. He soon went back to platform duties.

In a further incident at Hallen Marsh, a freight train was stopped at Hallen's Up Filton Starting signal. This train would normally pick up a banker from Hallen and a 'Hall' Class was waiting on the Outwards road for this purpose. However, the train had failed to pull right up to the signal, and the brake van was standing on the points, so the banker could not be signalled on to the rear of the train. The signalman was trying to get hold of Henbury box on the phone, to ascertain how long the freight would be stopped at Hallen, when he heard a 'chuff-chuff' and saw to his horror that the

Hall on the siding was moving slowly forward. He ran to the box window, yelled '*Stop!*' and waved a red flag. This alerted the guard of the freight train but not the crew of the banker. The points were open and the Hall derailed its front bogie. Luckily, it was not fouling the main line. Another banker was found in the shape of the Royal Edward North End yard pilot (a pannier tank), and the freight was able to proceed on its way without much delay. The errant Hall was re-railed using ramps from the Royal Edward Yard and waited on the sidings for examination by fitters.

In May 1955, repairs were needed to Rockingham Road bridge, which carried the road over the Hallen Marsh to Filton line at Chittening. The tracks between Henbury and Hallen Marsh were interlaced at Chittening and Electric Train Token working was put in between Hallen and Filton West for three weeks. A signalman who shall remain nameless was working at Hallen Marsh box and on the day in question had two trains imminent: Avonmouth for Filton and Avonmouth for Severn Beach. To save time, the man took two tokens out, one for each line. This was quite in order but what he did next was not. Without checking the token, the signalman gave the Severn Beach token to the driver of the first train, which was the Filton. This driver did not look at the token and proceeded on his way. The train for Severn Beach arrived and its driver was given the other token. This driver carried out his duties correctly and checked the token. Discovering that he had been given the wrong one, he refused it and the game was up. The Filton train arrived at Filton West and surrendered the incorrect token. In order to balance the token machines, it then had to be returned to Hallen by taxi and replaced in the machine. Disciplinary action followed.

During the 1970s and 1980s, the Bristol–Severn Beach off-peak service was usually operated by WR single power car units, nicknamed 'Bubble Cars'. These units distinguished themselves on several occasion by failing to stop at Severn Beach, instead demolishing the buffer stops and the railings and coming to a halt with the front bogie in the station yard. Nobody was hurt. Having attended one of

'Bubble Car' 55033 waits at Severn Beach for its return working.

Happy in his work: driver Pat Williams in charge of 55033 along the branch towards Hallen Marsh. He has not had time for his ciggy yet.

Another 'Bubble Car' passes Dock junction's home signal in snowy weather.

these derailments as a member of the Bath Road Depot breakdown gang, I was interested to know how this accident occurred, so I asked an old fitter at the depot.

'Ah,' he said, ''tis the loss of "Topside" vaccum what does it. The line to the Beach is dead straight, see. They drivers do start making small brake applications when they'm way out from the station. When they get to the platform and makes a full brake application, there's no vaccum left in the cylinder so the brakes don't work no more!' Having later studied the braking system, I understood what he was getting at.

Later on, when I was signalman at Town Goods box in the early 1980s, a 'Bubble Car' did it again. I think it was W55032 or 33, but stand to be corrected on that. The unit went straight through the blocks and railings as usual, and landed in the station yard. After the breakdown gang had attended and re-railed the unit, it was towed back to Bristol as an 'Out-of-Gauge' load; passing on adjoining lines by other trains was forbidden, as the cab was bent out of line. Again, no one was hurt in the incident, although the driver was shaken, as would be expected.

Behind Town Goods box was a dog-leg curve. One day, not long after a new, young, signalman had started work at the box, the local trip working went into the sidings and a wagon became derailed on this curve. Although it was not the fault of the signalman, he was quite embarrassed. The following day, the same trip working went into the

The long bay platform at Severn Beach. The 'sand drag' visible at the end of the line is to stop any more DMUs parking in the station yard.

31258 negotiates the Town Goods dog-leg with a very long train from the 'Town' shed.

'Town' again – and exactly the same happened again! Once more the poor signalman was full of apologies for the delay, even though it was not his fault. The Permanent Way department spent some time putting the trackwork in order and no further derailments occurred.

In all the line's history, there was only one major accident, on the morning of 18 February 1947. Signalman Jack Wheeler was on early shift duty at Hallen Marsh signal box. It was a cold, foggy morning and Jack had accepted the 01.30 Severn Tunnel junction to Avonmouth freight from Severn Beach. The freight was trundling along the single line between Severn Beach and Hallen Marsh and Jack was busy dealing with the 9.20pm Avonmouth–Salisbury freight, which was ready to leave for Filton via Henbury. Finding that he was unable to pull off his Up Main to Filton Starting signal, he leaned out of the window and shouted to the driver of the Salisbury train to pass the signal at Danger. The driver acknowledged the instruction with a toot of his whistle and set off. However, in a breach of the *Rule Book*, the driver had passed the signal without checking that the points were set for the right direction.

Unfortunately, Jack had not realized that the reason why he could not clear his signal was because the junction was still set towards the single line towards Severn Beach after the last move in that direction. The Salisbury train was heading off along the single line along which the Severn Tunnel to Avonmouth was travelling. Too late, Jack realized his mistake and shouted to the train crew to stop, but his warning was drowned out by the noise of the train. He rushed down the stairs and, grabbing his pushbike, pedalled frantically off along the trackside path in a vain attempt to catch up with the slow-moving train.

It was too late.

The Avonmouth–Salisbury train was hauled by an ex-GWR 69XX Hall Class 4-6-0 engine and comprised forty-four wagons and a brake van. Forty-three wagons were loaded and one was empty. The Severn Tunnel Junction–Avonmouth train was drawn by a 9XXX Class type 4-4-0 engine, running tender first, and comprised forty-eight empty wagons and brake van. Both trains were loose-coupled and unbraked, except for the normal handbrakes. The weight of the Avonmouth train was about 600 tons and the Cardiff train weighed

Headline in the Bristol Evening World *of 18 February 1947. (Jim Barnes/author's collection)*

about 350 tons. In the fog, neither driver nor fireman saw the other train, and the two trains collided head on near the 13th milepost, one and a half miles from the junction, at a combined speed of approximately 37mph.

The resulting collision was violent. Both engines and tender were derailed and damaged, whilst twenty-six wagons were also derailed and a number were completely destroyed. Prompt assistance was given by the police, national fire service, the local doctor and the ambulance services, and of the six members of the train crews who were injured, five were conveyed to hospital. Although all were discharged the same day, some were not fit for duty for over a month afterwards.

After the collision, the fireman of the 01.30 was in such shock that he refused to let go of the (correct) single-line token.

Jack Wheeler was reprimanded but, after a period of suspension, eventually went on to work at Bristol East Depot Main Line signal box and, when later made redundant by the resignalling, became a train announcer in the panel. In that role, he kept a close eye on the train service at Temple Meads station and on many occasions was of great help to younger signalmen at busy times.

Still on the single line to Severn Beach and Pilning Low Level, on the morning of 16 May 1958, Signalman Johnny Southall arrived at Severn Beach box at 06.00 to start the day shift. He was unable to switch the box into circuit. The extract from the signal box Train Register tells the tale:

> J. Southall on Duty 06.05. Unable to open at 06.05. Goods train stopped in section. Ableton Lane crossing gates destroyed by 05.05 Avonmouth freight. Hallen Marsh and Low Level advised.

Signal linemen arrived soon and the box was switched in at 06.29. The first two Up trains both terminated at Severn Beach before starting back to Bristol, so were signalled into the bay line. The locking was 'disarranged' by the lineman at 08.40 and signals 1 and 30, which protected the crossing, were also disconnected and maintained at Danger. District Signalling Inspector Alec Wade arrived at 10.38 and Station Master Mr Hankey called at the box at 11.05.

It has to be assumed that all necessary repairs and replacements were carried out very quickly, because there are no further entries about the incident in the Train Register. It must also be assumed that the 05.05 Avonmouth to Severn Tunnel junction freight had passed the signals protecting the crossing at Danger and wrecked the gates, which would have been closed across the rails.

One 'minor' incident at Hallen Marsh involved a long train of freight wagons, which had come down from Stoke Gifford in the evening. As it was late, the decision was taken to shunt the wagons back into the spur and deal with them the next morning. The engine duly pushed the wagons back onto the spur, uncoupled and left for shed. Nobody stopped to think that the spare brake van kept at Hallen Marsh was standing on the spur. Next morning, that brake van was found neatly balanced atop the buffer stops!

On 2 May 1985, a Class 47 diesel, 47214, ventured into Chittening trading estate with seven VDA wagons. By 10.26, it was in disgrace, having managed to derail both itself and one VDA. When the appropriate manager arrived, 47254 went to Chittening, returning a while later to Town Goods with six VDAs. The breakdown vans arrived at 12.31 and went into the Royal Edward Yard to gain access to the Chittening branch, crossing into the trading estate at 13.05. The errant 47 and the VDA were re-railed and, after inspection, came back during the afternoon.

In a much more tragic incident, a porter working at Dock station overslept and missed his usual train to work, a Bristol to Avonmouth via Clifton service. He was not worried about being too late for work, as another service left for Avonmouth half an hour later, this time running via Henbury. There was a third passenger service that ran via Clifton, but the porter caught this second train and duly alighted at Dock station. Being in somewhat of a hurry, he decided to cross the line not by the footbridge but round the back of the train. Sadly, he failed to look out for other traffic and ran straight into the path of the arriving third train. He could have saved himself by stepping backwards, but instead he threw himself to the ground between the platform and the train, where he curled himself into a ball.

It was to no avail; he was struck by the nearside cylinder of the locomotive – a 'Hall' Class – thrown into the side rods and killed.

Fire at the Depots

In a place such as Avonmouth Docks, where inflammable fuel oil was stored and pumped from ships into storage tanks and storage tanks into rail tank cars, it was inevitable that some sort of accident would occur over a long history. Whilst the following incident was not caused by any railway operations or staff, it certainly caused a significant amount of disruption to railway operations for a day or two.

At around 23.15pm on 5 September 1951, the tanker *Fort Christina* arrived and tied up at No.5 berth at the oil basin at Royal Edward Dock. Near by was the tank farm, which was the premises of the Regent Oil Company Limited. The *Fort Christina's* cargo consisted of about 13,000 tons of motor spirit and 2,050 tons of gas oil.

The Regent company's depot consisted of two sites, known as No.1 Depot and No.2 Depot. No.1 Depot covered an area of about seven acres on the bank of the River Severn and was licensed to store 12,000,000 gallons of petroleum spirit. No.2 Depot was licensed for the storage of 5,300,000 gallons of petroleum spirit, all in overground steel tanks.

Tankers were discharged from a jetty at the oil basin by means of a 10-inch diameter earthed pipeline, which ran from the jetty to the depot: a distance of about 3,250 feet. Separate pipelines were used for different products. Early in the morning of 6 September, it was concluded that the *Fort Christina's* cargo had been cross-contaminated by overflow between onboard tanks. The decision was taken to pump out the two contaminated tanks of motor spirit into No.3 onshore tank in the Regent depot. At the same time, No.9 starboard and port tanks on the ship were to be pumped out into No.1 shore tank in the Regent Company's Depot No.1. These operations would take place at the same time, but with the discharge from the contaminated tanks to be slightly ahead of the discharge from No.9 tanks, so as to keep the level of the motor spirit in No.8 tanks about two feet below the level of the gas oil in No.9 tanks, to prevent further contamination of the gas oil. During the operation, samples of motor spirit were taken by two Regent employees to test for contamination.

At 02.47 an explosion rocked the depot and fire broke out immediately. A witness saw one of the two men who had been checking samples on top of one of the shore storage tanks blown into the air towards the Royal Edward sidings. Other workers rushed to shut off the discharge valves and all pumping was stopped as the fire brigade was called.

The fire and explosion had started in No.13 tank and the flames spread rapidly owing to a northerly wind. Flames soon reached the roofs of tanks Nos. 5 and 6, which contained aviation spirit and motor spirit respectively. Within about 25 minutes, eight more horizontal tanks containing benzole aviation spirit and motor spirit were involved. The ends of these tanks were blown out and their contents added fuel to the fire, which spread towards a further three tanks and along irrigation ditches towards the river and down towards tank No.1. The flames came over the bund wall surrounding the tanks and set fire to the sleeper stop blocks on the siding, where three rail tank cars loaded with aviation spirit stood.

Three road tankers were in the process of being filled with spirit from the horizontal tanks and tank No.6. It took some heroic efforts by staff to move both road and rail tankers to safety. The Regent depot firefighters also went into action quickly, running two depot hoses to the fire and deploying foam before the fire brigade arrived and ordered them away from the site.

The massive inferno could be seen from miles away and the heat was such that all railway operations were suspended in the area. Signalman Wilf Stanley was on night duty at Hallen Marsh box and colleague Jim Barnes at Holesmouth. The 01.30 Severn Tunnel junction–Avonmouth freight was approaching when the fire started and this was swiftly stopped. Jim Barnes closed Holesmouth box as the fire was almost opposite and ran to Hallen Marsh to join his colleague. The 01.30 train had to be shunted into the spur and stabled at Hallen Marsh. The loco was sent 'light engine' back to Severn Tunnel junction.

In the Royal Edward Yard, the pilots moved to the South End away from the fire, as did shunter Les Grant. At Gloucester Road box, Signalman John Brazneill could do nothing more than look out of the north-facing window of his box and watch the light of the flames above the flour mill. It was only by talking on the phone to his colleagues further up the line that he was able to find out what was going on.

The fire lasted about 38 hours. When it was finally extinguished, it was discovered that vertical tanks Nos. 5, 6, 16 and 1, although damaged, were still standing, whilst tanks Nos. 13, 4 and 3 had collapsed and tank No.2 had partially collapsed. The horizontal tanks 7, 8, 9, 10, 11, 12, 27 and 28 all had their ends blown out. Two men died in the explosion.

An investigation was started into the many possible causes for the fire. Was it due to a lightning strike, an unexploded wartime bomb or staff smoking? Had it been started by sparks from static electricity or steam locomotives, or bacterial organisms producing iron sulphide, which might have ignited spontaneously on contact with air? It was swiftly established that there were no locomotives anywhere near the tanks at the time; the nearest locomotive was at least 300 feet away. The Regent staff involved were very trustworthy men, who were fully aware that smoking was forbidden, and meteorological records ruled out any thunderstorms in the area. It was concluded that the action of the men dipping the storage tanks to take samples must have caused a discharge of static electricity, which ignited motor spirit that had got into the gas oil.

All in all, despite the tragic loss of two men, it was considered to have been a lucky escape all round; the damage was extensive, but it had been contained within the Regent depot and there was little damage to the railway other than a few burnt sleepers in the yard.

Engine Drop-Outs!

If something went wrong on a moving train, it was always the practice for the driver or guard to write a note to a signalman and throw it out of the train window as they passed the signal box, after having attracted his attention. The signalman could then contact the necessary department and arrange for someone to meet the train at a convenient station. Usually it was fitters or police that were wanted.

One such note was thrown out of the cab window as the 18.24 Severn Beach to Bristol passed Avonmouth Dock Junction box one evening. It said:

> 18.24 Severn Beach–Bristol T.M. No.2 engine Power Car 51093. This engine keeps dropping out. Arrives Bristol T.M. 19.04, platform 1.

The gist of this was that No.2 engine kept stopping and had to be restarted. This slowed the train and time would be lost. The signalman phoned Bristol Temple Meads station manager and the latter arranged for fitters to meet the train on arrival.

In another incident, one Saturday afternoon an Up train was signalled between St Andrews junction and Town Goods boxes. After some time, the Town Goods signalman became aware that the train seemed to be a long time coming, so phoned his colleague at St Andrews to ask about the whereabouts of the DMU.

When the St Andrews man came to the phone, he was almost speechless. He explained that the DMU could be seen, at a stand, between Dock station and his box. Eventually, the guard came to the box and explained that the engine had dropped out. This time, though, the engine really *had* dropped out! The mountings on the underfloor-slung Leyland unit had broken and it had actually fallen off the train. Luckily, the DMU had been travelling slowly and had not been derailed.

Train services for the afternoon were suspended whilst breakdown staff and fitters managed to remove the fallen engine and make the power car safe for towing back to Bristol Bath Road depot. Once the Permanent Way Inspector had declared the lines safe to use again, normal service was resumed.

CHAPTER 16

Run-Down and Closures

Post-War Changes

By the time the railways were grouped into four main companies, it was inevitable that some closures and alterations would have taken place. On 30 June 1922, just before the Grouping took place, Hotwells station and branch closed. Although traffic during the First World War had increased to such an extent that a second platform had been constructed at Hotwells terminus, passenger traffic fell away after the war and the line was closed. Sneyd Park junction ceased to be a junction and the box was renamed 'Sneyd Park' in February 1925, by which time the track to Hotwells had been lifted and the new road between Bristol and Avonmouth – the 'Portway' – was being built on much of the trackbed of the old Port and Pier line.

In 1924, the loco shed at Avonmouth Dock station, which had been built by the joint committee in 1905 and had been disused for some years, was closed. In the same year, the same fate awaited the 'Break Section' signal box at Horseshoe Point. In 1938, the Light Railway, which had been taken over by the GWR and LMSR in 1926 and operated by the Great Western since 1928, was closed beyond Portview Road level crossing and stop blocks were erected just on the Dock Junction side of the crossing.

Britain's railways were in poor condition after the war. A lack of money and staff had led to years of neglect in terms of maintenance, and in many places speed restrictions had to be imposed because the track was not good enough. The Clifton Extension and other Avonmouth lines were no exception. On the section between Clifton Down and Avonmouth, the rails were seriously worn. Indeed, the ride on the Down line was so rough that many commuters would catch the train in the mornings to Clifton from Sea Mills, Shirehampton or Avonmouth, and take a bus back to Avonmouth in the evenings.

Redland signal box closed in 1950 and Montpelier signal box in May 1959, the functions of the latter being absorbed into a new box built at Ashley Hill junction and opened at the same time as Montpelier closed. At Avonmouth Dock junction, the sidings into Crown Brickyard closed in 1954 and were removed in July of the same year.

The Beeching Report

The year 1963 saw the publication of *The Reshaping of British Railways*, also known as the infamous 'Beeching Plan', proposed in a speech made in Parliament in 1960 by Prime Minister Harold Macmillan. The railway system envisaged by the infamous Dr Beeching and his team on behalf of the Transport Minister was to be a super-efficient, economical mode of transport. That, of course, was everyone's wish. To be fair to Beeching, he was only carrying out his government's brief. Not all his plans were bad and his 'Freightliner' service – where it was brought into use properly as he wished it to be – was a masterpiece. However, the brief was to cut out almost anything which did not make a profit. The problem lay in how to create such a system. How, for instance, did France and Germany manage their railways? How did they carry so many passengers and so much freight? The difference was that France and Germany believed in a 'social railway' that served the people, and was heavily subsidized by the state. Beeching's masters looked towards efficiency and profit, using what was arguably the typical economist's approach, summed up in a sentence: 'If it isn't used much and doesn't bring in lots of money, get rid of it.' And their calculations were not going to favour the railways if the Transport Minister concerned, in this instance Ernest Maples, had a vested interest in road transport and road-construction companies.

For the next couple of years following Macmillan's speech, officials (many of them young and very keen) went around the network gathering information as to its financial viability. At Shirehampton station, Station Master Harry Pike at first cooperated with the officials who were sent to Avonmouth by the BR Board in order to scrutinize the takings. It soon became clear that these officials were adding all the figures and receipts for passengers and goods on the line and then adding these figures to those of two local unprofitable lines. Then they took an average from this, which inevitably made *all* the lines appear unprofitable. Harry Pike was so angry about the fiddle that he thereafter refused to cooperate with the Beeching men. Such stories abounded at the time, so much so that there must have been an element of truth in them, even though various men employed by the BR Board to rationalize the railways under the Beeching-Marples regime still maintain that there was never any manipulation of passenger and goods receipts. A census taken in November 1962 had shown that 2,250 people used the line every weekday. An earlier census had recorded 425,000 tickets being issued on average for the stations on the line, but in 1962 this had fallen to 313,300. Surely the main

reason was because BR had increased fares and cut the service.

In due course, the Beeching Report was published and, sure enough, the Avonmouth line was in it. In a list of over 1,100 English stations to be closed, Clifton Down, Sea Mills, Shirehampton, Avonmouth Dock, St Andrews Road, Chittening Platform, Henbury, Filton West Platform, Severn Beach, New Passage, Cross Hands and Pilning Low Level stations were all deemed to be 'unprofitable'. This was despite the fact that hundreds of dockers and other workers used the railway every day and shift workers, especially, relied on it. With the various industries and the docks, the Avonmouth line was well used and there was no doubt that many stations were profitable. Shirehampton station in particular was well patronized in the 1940s and 1950s. The Western Region had even introduced an improved, more frequent service in 1955, using GWR diesel railcars in conjunction with steam-hauled services. BR diesel multiple units took over the services in October 1958, running to Avonmouth via Henbury, Clifton and Pilning.

BR locally made swift plans to withdraw the passenger service between Bristol and Avonmouth via Clifton Down. All freight traffic for Avonmouth would run via Filton and Hallen Marsh, and the line between Narroways Hill and Avonmouth Dock would be closed completely. A report was prepared for the Transport Users Consultative Committee (TUCC) and the local trade unions. It was supposed to be a confidential document but somehow it was 'leaked' (proving that such events are not a modern thing), which gave the unions and the Chamber of Commerce time to prepare their defence against the closures.

A meeting between BR managers and staff was organized, with a view to 'apprising' the staff of the proposed closures. Forewarned, the staff fought back with a well-reasoned case and, after a somewhat disruptive meeting, BR decided to withdraw and modify the plans. The Transport Minister had however, refused to give consent to the closure and BR had to look for other ways to reduce the apparent financial losses.

A new plan was put together, proposing that the service would continue with trains operated by conductor guards who would issue tickets on the trains and with some stations having their staff removed. Booking offices would also close. This was to happen from December 1963. Redland station had its staff withdrawn after 14.00 and was treated as an unstaffed halt between then and 06.00 the following morning, but little else happened for a further two years.

The March 1941 bombing which had seen the withdrawal of the Mangotsfield to Avonmouth passenger service had also seen the Kingswood junction to Ashley Hill junction of the line reduced in importance. Some freight traffic from Avonmouth still ran via Clifton, Kingswood junction and Mangotsfield to the North, but usually ran via Hallen Marsh, Henbury and Stoke Gifford to Westerleigh West junction on the WR South Wales main line where it took the branch to Yate South and regained LMR metals. Traffic to and from Stapleton Road gasworks ran via the ex-GWR lines. There was, in truth, little point in keeping open a little-used section of line with two major viaducts and a rail-over-rail bridge, along with two signal boxes. Accordingly, BR closed the Kingswood junction to Ashley Hill junction section on 14 June 1965, along with Kingswood junction and the little-used Stapleton Road Gas Sidings signal box.

Ashley Hill Junction box, opened in May 1959 as a replacement for the original box, lasted until 27 February 1966, when it was closed after a life of only just over six years.

New Attempts to Close the Line

In August 1966, BR began considering plans to close the line once again. Rumours abounded and local city councillors, traders and commuters voiced their protests. Nothing official had come from BR at that time but, on 2 February 1967, the early edition of the *Bristol Evening Post* carried an article entitled 'Bristol Passenger Line to be Axed'.

According to the article, British Rail had that day confirmed that they were to close the Bristol to Avonmouth railway. A BR spokesman was quoted as saying that it was 'a fact that the Minister of Transport has agreed to the publication of proposals that British Rail be relieved of the obligation of running this unremunerative passenger service'. John Ellis, Labour MP for the Bristol North West constituency, at once contacted BR. The response confirmed that not only was the line to be closed, but also that the last passenger trains were expected to run within three months. The proposals would be put before the local Transport Users Consultative Committee on 25 February, after which there would be a six-week period for any objections to be lodged.

City Councillor and loco driver Bill Graves, Chairman of the Bristol Joint Transport Committee, described BR's decision as a 'harsh blow'. He and John Ellis would meet with local railwaymen, trade union officials and constituents to decide what actions they could take to stop the closures.

Over the next day or two, letters were sent to the *Evening Post* in support of keeping the line open. One correspondent even proposed that BR electrify the line from Kingswood junction to Avonmouth! Another pointed out that BR had previously done little to attract passengers to the line; instead, they had reduced the train service and put up fares, making the railway unattractive to passengers and uncompetitive in comparison with the bus services. The same correspondent also asserted that the railway was an essential utility for workers travelling to the docks, mills and other industries in the Avonmouth area. Further letters asked that the paper use its influence to retain the line. 'It is clear that British Rail does not intend to run trains to suit potential passengers,' said another correspondent.

Labour councillor Jim O'Neill launched a petition to protest against the closures, with forms made available in local shops at Avonmouth, Shirehampton and Lawrence Weston. O'Neill pointed out via the pages of the *Evening Post* that the railway was popular for shoppers wishing to travel from Avonmouth to Clifton and Bristol centre. He also claimed that BR's 'reorganization' of the times of trains in 1964 had made it 'inconvenient' for shoppers to use trains. At that time, nineteen trains a day ran in both directions. The first early train left Bristol Temple Meads station for Severn Beach at 05.10 and the last at 21.13. The first train from Avonmouth to Bristol Temple Meads started at 06.15 and the last train from Severn Beach (calling at Avonmouth) left at 22.05. Sunday trains had been discontinued. There had been three timetable changes in six months. Others proposed at the time that BR should offer a realistic timetable to suit connections into London services at Bristol, and that the last departure from Severn Beach in the evenings should be retimed to leave after the closure of the local hostelry! A traffic census held over the winter of 1966–67 had shown that there had been an average of 2,156 passengers using the Bristol–Avonmouth services every weekday and 1,056 on Saturdays. It was hardly a little-used line.

The Reshaping of British Railways had said this about local stopping services:

> As a group, stopping trains serve the more local rural communities by linking small towns and villages with each other and, sometimes rather indirectly, with one or more major towns... railway stopping services developed as the predominant form of rural transport in the [nineteenth] century when the only alternative was the horse-drawn vehicle.

The report had gone on to say that, even in the past, such services had failed to pay their way and that by 1963 the stopping rail services and buses were serving the same purpose.

City Councillor Bill Graves was firm in his view: 'The closure is madness. This line is an integral part of the transport pattern of Bristol. With continuing development going on at Severnside the area is to require a lot of both private and public transport and with road traffic congestion in Avonmouth, the problem is going to get worse.'

On 8 February, Bill Graves and George Easton (Secretary of the Bristol Trades Council) announced that a deputation of Bristol railwaymen were to seek a meeting with Labour Transport Minister Barbara Castle. However, before this could happen, BR officials and MP John Ellis found themselves embroiled in a row.

Labour MP Ellis had written to BR's Western Region General Manager, Lance Ibbotson, explaining how local railwaymen were very critical of the way the closure of the Avonmouth line had been announced. Ibbotson's reply was that the railwaymen had not 'gone though the proper channels' to voice their complaints. Ellis and the railwaymen had indeed been through the correct procedure over the past couple of years, and they were angered by Ibbotson's response.

BR Western Region's closure procedures were causing problems all around the region. In Devizes, the line between Patney and Holt junction had been closed apparently without objection from the local populace, because it had been omitted from a statutory notice of closure. In the Devon holiday resort of Ilfracombe, hoteliers were having to reassure prospective customers that the town did still have (at that time) a railway station, as BR was giving the impression that it was already shut. Elsewhere in Devon, BR (WR) advertised a special cheap day return service for shoppers, then cut out the train service between 11.25 and 15.35! Likewise, in Chard, Somerset, local firms had been assured by BR that their goods station would remain open for another 'forty years'. It closed within a year and at least one firm went out of business. Labour MP for Exeter Gwyneth Dunwoody joined forces with Bristol's John Ellis to demand a meeting with Mr Ibbotson.

The meeting only brought about further anger and confusion, when it emerged that the railwaymen and the management had a different understanding of previous talks. Managers said that BR staff had not proceeded through the correct negotiating channels, while the railwaymen blamed management for failing to keep promises made in 1963 to try out conductor guards on trains. It was also claimed that trade unions had met with the BR managers in May 1966 and had been promised further negotiations over the future of the line. The sudden announcement of closures had been made, they said, without negotiation. Mr Ibbotson's explanation was apparently that the Western Region had been 'going through a bad time'.

John Ellis came away from the meeting dissatisfied with BR's answers. He went to London and that evening in Parliament he tabled a motion demanding an immediate enquiry into BR's Western Region management. The motion had four other West Country MP co-signatories: Gwyneth Dunwoody (Exeter), Dr John Dunwoody (Falmouth and Camborne), Ray Dobson (Bristol North East) and Dr David Owen (Plymouth Sutton).

A local meeting of members of Bristol Corporation and trade unions was called at Southmead for the following day, 10 February.

Meanwhile, the Transport and General Workers Union (TGWU), which had 11,000 members working in the Avonmouth area, joined the fight to save the line. They pledged to back John Ellis, support the campaign by Bristol City Council to save the line, seek the support of twenty TGWU MPs and support Bill Graves and George Easton in their call for a deputation to meet with Barbara Castle.

In an unprecedented move, Elders & Fyffes announced on 10 February that they were pulling out of Avonmouth. This was a severe blow both to local employment and to the plans to save the railway passenger service. Banana trains had been a feature of Avonmouth Docks since 1901 and much casual labour was employed in the unloading of ships and the loading of bananas into railway trucks. The withdrawal would have a serious effect on the railway; in 1966, thirty-three banana ships had docked at Avonmouth, each requiring 400 railway trucks to carry its cargo to destinations in the UK. Up to 300 dockers were usually involved in off-loading each ship. Work would be lost in many areas, including tug-boat crews, waterfront men and hopper operators, as well as railway shunters, checkers and despatchers in Old Yard. The Port of Bristol Authority stood to lose the rent paid by Elders & Fyffes for what was the largest dockside installation in the docks, and also the dues paid on 50,000 tons of bananas per year.

Elders & Fyffes said that the last banana ship to dock at Avonmouth, the 6,738-ton SS *Tilapa*, was in fact discharging its load at that moment. After the end of March, they would close all facilities at Avonmouth and concentrate on their main depot at Southampton Docks.

In a series of bizarre twists to the story, BR was now involved in discussions with Bristol City Council concerning land at Chittening. The Council was considering swapping 24 acres of land it owned at Chittening for 23 acres owned by BR next to St Andrews Road. A piece appeared in the local paper announcing that, if the deal went ahead, the Chittening site would become the site for a new Freightliner depot, which could be 'open and in service by the end of the year'. This was the site of the old wartime munitions depot and currently in use as a trading estate. It seemed odd that BR was intending to bring more employment to the area, while at the same time planning to withdraw the passenger rail service.

Stranger still was the article in the *Evening Post* on 16 February: 'Site to be sought for new £1,000 million Severnside "City"', shouted the headline. It went on to explain that Bristol, Bath and Gloucester councils had been asked to help plan a new city that would be 'bigger than Bristol and Cardiff combined', and that the government was considering building this city somewhere in an area defined as being between Gloucester and Bristol on the eastern bank of the River Severn, and Gloucester and Newport on the western bank.

Again, the question arises as to why BR was planning to close a line that had carried over 695,000 passengers during 1966 when the government was planning a new city in the area. This apparent lack of forward planning was all too common during the rail closures of the 1960s and did nothing to suppress stories that the railways were being deliberately run down and closed in favour of road transport.

Further accusations flew in an interview with the *Evening Post* on the evening of 9 February. John Ellis had obtained a copy of a letter sent by the BR (WR) estate surveyor's office to representatives

The Western GT Fuel Co. yard at Shirehampton. Had the line closed in the 1960s, the company would have liked to expand all over the site.

of Western GT oil company, which leased land in the old goods yard at Shirehampton station. The letter appeared to be advising Western GT that the entire station area was being earmarked for BR's future use. Ellis promised that he would be writing to both BR and the Ministry of Transport about this issue. Ellis saw the letter as proof that BR Western Region was intending to steamroller the closures through, despite what anyone did to try to save the line.

In response, BR's Divisional Manager, Mr Dudley Hart, issued a statement to the effect that it was Western GT that had instigated the dialogue, asking BR if, in the event of the line being closed, there was any chance of leasing further land. According to Hart, BR had told the oil company that the closure plans had to be determined by the Minister of Transport and the Transport Users Consultative Committee before any land could be considered for leasing out.

Ellis was not at all happy with this and accused BR of a 'blatant cover-up'.

Meanwhile, the closure notice for the line had been published, inviting any objectors to lodge their complaint in writing within six weeks of 25 February 1967.

Further anxiety for the docks and its workers came when local shipping company the Bristol City Line announced that it was considering pulling its business out of Bristol and instead concentrating on Newport docks. The reason for this lay in the recent decision by Barbara Castle to refuse to allow the building of a new dock at Portbury, just across the river from Avonmouth. Bristol City Line had been operating its transatlantic service for 88 years but was now thinking of switching to containers and Avonmouth had no facilities for containers. It was stressed that the plans were only under consideration and not yet finalized.

Councillor Bill Graves was in the news again on 15 February, when he accused BR of 'plotting against the docks' by planning to close the Clifton Extension. Should the line be closed, he said, all freight traffic would have to run to and from Avonmouth via Henbury. This line had recently (in 1966) been singled. Any mishap on the single line, he continued, would result in the docks traffic being held up for long periods. He claimed that this was as a result of the docks not being nationalized.

Whilst arguments over the failure to build the new deep-water docks at Portbury raged and took some of the heat off the Avonmouth railway closures, BR suddenly made an offer to those fighting to save the line. The Chairman of the British Railways Board, Sir Stanley Raymond, held a press conference in Bristol, saying that BR would keep the line open if Bristol City Council were to contribute to its running costs: 'If it is thought that the social convenience of the Avonmouth line is such that the local authority [would] like to financially help

Beeching and Marples saw off Henbury station, seen here in 1983. There are calls today to reopen it.

the railways to continue to run the line, we shall be very happy.'

Apparently, the line was failing to meet its direct costs by £70,000 per year, and it was this amount that the county council was being asked to contribute.

Sir Stanley also dismissed as 'complete nonsense' the accusations made by Bill Graves that, had the docks been nationalized, the line closure would not have been considered. He also castigated those who had made accusations against railway management: 'I think...it is quite outrageous that there should be an attack on the railway management for doing their duty. In my view the managers should be praised.' He denied that there had been any alterations or cuts to train services on the line and claimed that local managers had merely been trying to save the services by cutting costs.

It was now up to the TUCC and the Minister of Transport to come to some conclusion. As might have been expected, the TUCC received many objections to the proposed closure of the Clifton Extension to Avonmouth and the matter was passed on to the Minister of Transport for a decision.

New Plans for the Future?

On 15 March 1967, BR published its *Network for Development*, compiled by members of the same team that had served under Beeching, then approved by Barbara Castle and Sir Stanley Raymond. It set out a new plan for the future of

No longer haunted by the 'Ghost Train', Filton North platform stood forlorn for years. These days, there is support for its reopening.

Britain's railways and was quickly reviewed in the newspapers. It soon became clear that the plan was not another Beeching Report. It showed a basic rail network of 11,000 route miles, which was larger than that planned by Beeching, but West Country people were shocked to see that many major holiday resorts currently served by rail were left out of the report. Also excluded were some freight-only lines such as Yate to Thornbury (both in Gloucestershire) and the remaining section of the Cheddar branch to Cranmore (Somerset). Also missing from the report was the Bristol to Avonmouth passenger service.

Gloom settled once more over Avonmouth and staff became further demoralized. Although there had been some mention of 'socially necessary' rail services in the report, which had given Avonmouth a glimmer of hope, those hopes were dashed again in July 1967, when BR announced that Old Yard was to close.

Old Yard had always been a busy yard, but one of its main reasons for existence in post-war years had been the banana traffic. Now this was gone, BR decided to concentrate its main freight operations on Royal Edward Yard. Old Yard closed to traffic on 10 July 1967 and, less than a month later, the Dock junction between the main and Corporation lines was taken out of use, as were the Corporation lines between Gloucester Road box and Dock junction.

Gloucester Road box was closed the day after. Officially, the Corporation lines between Gloucester Road and St Andrews junction had been taken out of use in 1964 but they had often been in service afterwards for stabling wagons. Now they too were completely taken out of use, as were the GW lines between Gloucester Road and St Andrews.

Avonmouth Sidings signal box went from being a busy yard box to merely a 'Break Section' box between Dock junction and Dock station.

In another of the odd twists that occurred during this time, the Corporation lines were later reinstated when the connections at Dock junction were brought back into use in December 1967. They were just used as sidings as far as the now-lifted Old Yard.

The Late 1960s

In 1968, the new year had hardly got under way before further closure threats loomed. There had been rumours that the Bristol area was to undergo resignalling, with multiple-aspect (MAS) colour-light signals controlled from a central panel signal box. The rumours also said that the Pilning Low Level to Severn Beach line was to be closed. Signalman Brian Chaney, Avonmouth staff representative, wrote to the local management for further information (*see* below).

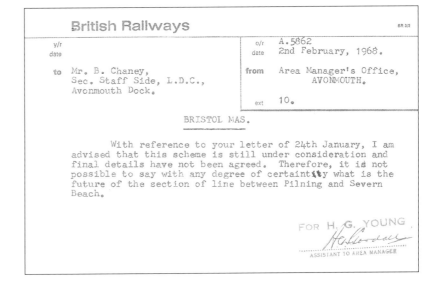

The letter that the Avonmouth staff representative received in response to his enquiry about the Bristol resignalling rumour.

At Pilning, on the GW South Wales main line, the Down goods line between Pilning station and Severn Tunnel West boxes was shortened in February 1968. The future of the branch from Pilning Branch box (known as 'Low Level') to Severn Beach – which had already lost its passenger service in 1964 – was also in doubt. When a crossing keeper on the Pilning–Severn Beach line took a day off sick, train staff were expected to open and close the crossing gates themselves. This they refused to do. Following this staff work-to-rule, and without further ado, Divisional Movements Manager Bill Bradshaw closed the line, claiming that it was 'surplus to requirements'. After 1 September 1968, the branch was not used again.

Unemployment figures released by the Ministry of Labour in April 1968 showed that there were 198 men and eighteen women out of work in Avonmouth. In the north Bristol area, unemployment rose by 215 people between April 1967 and April 1968. Many of that number were railwaymen.

Staff were aware that a resignalling of the whole area would take place at some time in the near future and their representatives were soon called to a meeting in Bristol. They attended with mixed feeling, as the future of the Avonmouth line was still under discussion at a high level.

On 29 April 1968, a meeting was held at Transport House, the Transport and General Workers Union building in Victoria Street, Bristol. The conference room there was the only one in the area that could accommodate the number of people involved, and it would be the venue for most of the ensuing meetings up to and during the resignalling scheme that was about to be announced.

The management team assembled at Transport House comprised heads of departments and managers representing the civil engineers, loco depots, signals and telecommunications, yards and depots, local managers and signalling inspectors. They faced an invited staff side of 111 representatives of the men and women employed in the areas to be affected by the proposals to build a new power signal box at Bristol. Representatives from Avonmouth, Bath, Bridgwater, Bristol, and Chipping Sodbury

were included. The meeting was chaired by Bill Bradshaw, Divisional Movements Manager, Bristol.

It was announced that the Bristol Resignalling would indeed take place and that it would happen in thirteen stages. The stage of obvious interest to the Avonmouth representatives, who included Signalman Brian Chaney and Carriage and Wagon Examiner Peter Mead, was Stage 13, which would cover the Avonmouth lines, from Clifton Down (inclusive) to Filton West and was expected to happen by June 1971.

The handout issued in conjunction with the meeting stated (amongst other things) that the date scheduled for completion of the entire scheme was June 1971. It listed sixty-one signal boxes to be closed. At Avonmouth, Holesmouth Junction box was to be retained as a ground frame, controlling the entrance into the docks and Royal Edward Yard. Dock Junction and St Andrews Junction boxes would be reduced to level-crossing ground frame status, and the level-crossing ground frames at Ableton Lane and Green Lane, on the Severn Beach-Pilning Low Level branch, would be officially closed (they were already out of use, as was the line). There had at one time been three signal boxes at Pilning. The signal box at Pilning junction, a brick-built ex-GWR box, opened in 1901, replacing an earlier 1886 box. It controlled the entrance to the Down Goods loop, the exit from an Up Goods loop from Pilning station, various sidings and the junction for the branch to Severn Beach and Avonmouth. Just over a quarter of a mile along the branch was Pilning Branch signal box. This box closed, along with the branch itself, in 1968. (In August 1970, it was still standing, along with all its signals and the level-crossing gates, as if expecting a train to appear at any moment along the weed-strewn rails.)

Some ten extra crossing keepers' posts would be required, three of which would be relief posts. The Avonmouth staff representative found the answer to his earlier question regarding the future of the Severn Beach–Pilning section of line – under the proposals contained in the handout this line, already closed, would be lifted.

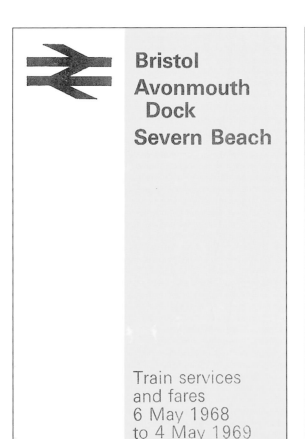

The cover of the 1968–69 timetable.

Bristol → Avonmouth Dock → Severn Beach
Weekdays

	Bristol T.M.	Bristol Lawrence Hill	Bristol Stapleton Road	Montpelier	Redland	Clifton Down	Sea Mills	Shirehampton	Avonmouth Dock	St Andrews Road	Severn Beach
	05.10	05.15	05.17	05.22	05.24	05.26	→	05.33	05.38	05.41	
	05.40	05.45	05.48	05.53	05.55	05.57	06.02	06.07	06.13	06.17	06.25
	06.38	06.43	06.45	06.50	06.52	06.54	06.59	07.04	07.09	07.12	07.20
	07.00	07.05	07.07	07.12	07.14	07.16	07.21	07.26	07.32	07.35	
	07.32	07.37	07.39	07.44	07.46	07.48	07.53	07.58	08.03	08.06	08.14
SX	08.15	08.20	08.22	08.27	08.29	08.31	08.36	08.41	08.46	08.49	08.57
SO	08.20	08.25	08.27	08.32	08.34	08.36	08.41	08.46	08.51	08.54	09.02
	09.10	09.15	09.17	09.22	09.24	09.26	09.31	09.36	09.41	09.44	09.52
	10.20	10.25	10.27	10.32	10.34	10.36	10.41	10.46	10.51	10.54	11.02
A	11.27	11.32	11.35	11.40	11.42	11.44	11.49	11.54	11.59	12.02	12.10
	13.05	13.10	13.12	13.17	13.19	13.21	13.26	13.31	13.36	13.39	13.47
	15.10	15.15	15.17	15.22	15.24	15.26	15.31	15.36	15.41	15.44	15.52
SX	15.50	15.55	15.57	16.02	16.04	16.06	16.11	16.16	16.21	16.24	
SO	16.10	16.15	16.17	16.22	16.24	16.26	16.31	16.36	16.45	16.50	16.58
SX	16.20	16.25	16.27	16.32	16.34	16.36	16.41	16.46	16.51	16.54	17.03
	16.53	16.58	17.00	17.05	17.07	17.09	17.14	17.19	17.24	17.27	17.35
B SX	17.27	17.34	17.37	17.42	17.44	17.47	17.51	17.56	18.03	18.07	18.16
	18.10	18.15	18.17	18.22	18.24	18.26	18.31	18.36	18.41	18.44	18.52
	19.10	19.15	19.17	19.22	19.24	19.26	19.31	19.36	19.41	19.44	19.52
	20.25	20.30	20.32	20.37	20.39	20.42	20.46	20.51	20.57	21.00	21.08
	21.08	21.13	21.15	21.20	21.22	21.24	21.29	21.34	21.39	21.42	21.50

Severn Beach → Avonmouth Dock → Bristol
Weekdays

	Severn Beach	St Andrews Road	Avonmouth Dock	Shirehampton	Sea Mills	Clifton Down	Redland	Montpelier	Bristol Stapleton Road	Bristol Lawrence Hill	Bristol T.M.
		06.10	06.14	06.18	06.23	06.28	06.30	06.32	06.37	06.39	06.44
C SX			06.33	06.37	06.42	06.47	06.49	06.51	06.56	06.56	06.59
	06.35	06.45	07.10a	07.14	07.19	07.24	07.26	07.28	07.33	07.35	07.40
D	07.25	07.34	07.42	07.46	07.51	07.57	07.59	08.01	08.06	08.08	08.14
		08.05	08.09	08.13	08.18	08.24	08.26	08.28	08.33	08.35	08.40
	08.21	08.29	08.33	08.37	08.42	08.47	08.49	08.51	08.56	08.58	09.03
	09.10	09.18	09.22	09.26	09.31	09.36	09.38	09.40	09.45	09.47	09.52
D	10.30	10.38	10.44	10.48	10.53	10.58	11.00	11.02	11.07	11.09	11.15
	11.08	11.16	11.20	11.24	11.29	11.34	11.36	11.38	11.43	11.45	11.51
	12.15	12.23	12.27	12.31	12.36	12.41	12.43	12.45	12.50	12.52	12.57
	14.00	14.10	14.15	14.19	14.24	14.30	14.32	14.34	14.39	14.42	14.48
	16.04	16.12	16.16	16.20	16.25	16.31	16.33	16.36	16.39	16.42	16.48
SX		16.50	16.54	16.58	17.03	17.08	17.10	17.12	17.17	17.19	17.25
SX	17.08	17.17	17.23	17.27	17.32	17.38	17.40	17.42	17.47	17.49	17.55
SX	17.40	17.48	17.52	17.56	18.01	18.06	18.08	18.10	18.15	18.17	
	18.20	18.28	18.32	18.36	18.41	18.46	18.48	18.50	18.55	18.57	19.03
	19.05	19.13	19.18	19.22	19.27	19.33	19.35	19.37	19.42	19.45	19.51
	20.05	20.13	20.20	20.24	20.29	20.35	20.37	20.39	20.44	20.46	20.52
	21.15	21.23	21.27	21.31	21.36	21.41	21.43	21.45	21.50	21.52	21.57
	22.05	22.15	22.19	22.23	22.28	22.34	22.36	22.38	22.42	22.45	22.50

Notes

a   Arrives 06.50
A   From Lawrence Hill, Saturdays (15 June to 7 September)
B   From Chippenham depart 16.40 also 16.56 Bath
C   To Keynsham & S arrive 07.19
D   Terminates Lawrence Hill, Saturdays (15 June to 7 September)
SX Saturdays excepted
SO Saturdays only
These tables are subject to alteration, particularly at Bank Holiday periods

The 1968–69 timetable.

It was bittersweet news for the Avonmouth men at this stage. Only nine months before, the Old Yard at Avonmouth had been closed and its sidings lifted, while a fierce battle had been fought to save the branch line to Severn Beach from complete closure. In May 1968, BR introduced a new, revised timetable for the line. Bristol City Council agreed to subsidize the service and things were looking up. However, it seemed that most of the signalmen and station staff in Avonmouth would still lose their jobs, either through the slimming down of resources or the planned resignalling. For the signalmen, another meeting would be called later in the year.

The new timetable came into use on 6 May 1968 and listed nineteen daily trains leaving Bristol Temple Meads for Avonmouth. Three of these trains terminated at St Andrews Road and the rest went forward to Severn Beach. Sixteen trains started back from Severn Beach to Bristol, with the 06.33 to Bristol starting from Avonmouth Dock station and the 08.05 and 16.50 returns to Bristol starting from St Andrews Road. There were seventeen trains from Bristol to Severn Beach on Saturdays; fifteen went to, and returned from, Severn Beach, whilst the 05.10 and 07.00 departures from Bristol Temple Meads ran as far as St Andrews Road.

Fares for these services were: Temple Meads to Severn Beach, 2 shillings and 3 pence (approx 11p); to Avonmouth Dock, 1 shilling and 6 pence (6p). Passengers were advised that 'if you join the train at Montpelier or Severn Beach or at any station in between you should buy your ticket from the Guard. He will issue Singles only – but the price of most of these has been reduced'. Season and Ordinary tickets were available at Temple Meads, Lawrence Hill and Stapleton Road ticket offices. Season tickets could also be bought at Severn Beach.

On 25 October 1968, the Transport Act removed the automatic closure threat from loss-making lines and replaced it with a policy that ensured that, where there would be social hardship caused by the withdrawal of a service, a separate government subsidy would be used. It was accepted that the Bristol–Avonmouth line would fall into this category and the line was reprieved. Passengers waiting at Clifton Down station on the morning when the news broke were astonished to see the signal box door open and Signalman Jack Coles run down the steps and on to the platform, where he performed a little jig of joy!

It was not all positive news, though. Stations would be unstaffed, conductor guards were to be introduced and station buildings would be demolished over the next few years, to be replaced by the ubiquitous 'bus shelter'. For the time being, however, there was still the resignalling to deal with.

At another meeting at Transport House in Bristol, on 12/13 December 1968, staff representatives were told that, as rail development plans for the Avonmouth area had not been finalized, it was now proposed to keep the existing method of working between Avonmouth Dock junction and Hallen Marsh boxes. Both would become fringe boxes to the new Panel. The existing level-crossing gates at Avonmouth station and at St Andrews junction would continue to be worked by Avonmouth Dock station ground frame and St Andrews box, respectively, for the foreseeable future. The connections into the Royal Edward Yard at Holesmouth and Avonmouth Goods Yard (Town Goods) would be simplified, and these two boxes would be closed. In the event, connections into the Royal Edward Yard at Avonmouth Goods Yard box remained unaltered until 1976 and even then the box stayed open, along with Holesmouth (which still controlled the northern entrance/exit from the sidings), until it was closed under the Avonmouth Area Resignalling in 1988.

Alterations to staffing in the Avonmouth area would be necessary as a result of these moves.

It also became apparent that the BR Freightliner Division still intended to build a Freightliner terminal on railway-owned land in Avonmouth, on the Down side of the line between Holesmouth junction and St Andrews Road. Consultation meetings would be held about this when more definite proposals had been formulated.

This new Avonmouth news was quite interesting. Not only were three boxes (Dock junction, St Andrews junction and Hallen Marsh) to remain, but there was also a good chance that the promised Freightliner depot would be sited in the area. For the Avonmouth signalling staff, at least, future employment seemed secure.

On 13 January 1969, staff representatives in Avonmouth received a letter from the Area Freight Manager. Confusingly, it was headed 'Closure of Avonmouth Old Yard', despite the fact that Old Yard had gone over a year before. It gave notice of the closure of both Avonmouth Sidings and Dock Station signal boxes, and the removal of the bay sidings at Dock station. The two sidings, which were the remains of the old light railway exchange sidings and had been controlled from Sidings box,

Severn Beach station: closed and waiting 'redevelopment' in favour of houses.

were now to be connected to a new ground frame. This was to be known as West Sidings ground frame and would be released from Dock Junction box. The work took place on Sunday 19 January 1969.

At St Andrews junction, the connection from Town Goods sidings, which had trailed into the Down GW line, was removed. Access to Town Goods yard was now only from the Goods Yard box end. Just over eight years after it was modified for the branch to ICI Severnside works, Severn Beach signal box was closed and access to the sidings and ICI branch was now by means of a ground frame, released by the Electric Train Token from Hallen Marsh box. Severn Beach station was now really just a terminus for the branch from Hallen Marsh. A short stub of the branch over Ableton Lane crossing towards Pilning was retained for extra wagon storage; stop blocks were put in just short of Green Lane crossing in December 1969. The crossing gates at Ableton Lane were operated by the guard when required. All passenger trains used the bay platform.

Stage 6 of the Resignalling

Around Bristol, resignalling work continued apace, but before Stage 6 – which would involve Avonmouth – was implemented, a further meeting was held between management and staff. The subject of this meeting, held on 12 October 1970, had direct consequences for the plans for Stage 6, and for the Avonmouth area as a whole. The staff

side of the meeting consisted of three full-time union representatives, including Bristol signalman 'Benjy' Davies, and eight drivers and guards' representatives from Bath Road depot. Pete Mead, the Avonmouth carriage and wagon examiners' representative was there, as was Signalman Brian Chaney. Fred Tuckett and R. Cockle represented yard staff. On the management side, amongst a total of seven men, were Bob Yabsley (Acting Chief Signalling Inspector), John Forrester (Signalling Inspector), Ken Watkins (Movements Assistant, Bath Road), Dick Hall (Assistant Area Manager), and two men from the Divisional Manager's office. The meeting was chaired by Mr H. Marshall, Rules and Signalling Assistant.

The purpose of this meeting was to discuss the future methods of working in the Avonmouth area. It had been agreed at the meeting held on 23 July 1970 that once again Dock Junction signal box would be closed as a signal box and reduced to a crossing ground frame. The two sidings known as the Earth Sidings, situated on the Bristol side of the level crossing, were to be removed. This plan had now been revised. Because 'retained' staff (signalmen paid at their old rate of pay but doing a lower-grade job under redundancy) were needed at Dock Junction box to operate the level-crossing barriers, this box would now be retained as a full signal box and the Earth Sidings would also be kept. Stage 6 of the resignalling would now terminate at Dock junction, which would become a fringe box to Bristol Panel. A diagram of the revised Dock

Junction layout that would come into operation at the onset of Stage 6 was now produced for the staff side to study and ask questions.

The most obvious 'modification' was the singling of the line from Stapleton Road to Clifton Down. At Clifton Down, the line was to become double through the station, creating a passing loop, then it would become single through Clifton Down tunnel. On reaching Avonmouth Dock junction, the line would become double again. The lever frame at the ex-Midland Railway box was to be altered and re-locked in a WR fashion. As could be expected from a plan that was rather hurriedly put together, there were some omissions. For example, whilst the existing fuel company sidings at Shirehampton were referred to, there was no means by which to access the sidings shown on the diagram. The management hastily explained that a ground frame was to be provided, released from Dock Junction box. It would also be necessary for trains servicing these sidings to come from the Dock junction direction only, proceeding onwards via Clifton after servicing the sidings.

To this end, from the date of the implementation of Stage 6, all freight trains for Avonmouth would be routed via Filton West and Hallen Marsh. The staff side were anxious to know if the singling of the line from Clifton would have any effect on future traffic for the Avonmouth Freightliner depot, which was still rumoured to be in the pipeline. Mr Marshall reassured them that, if the Freightliner depot plans did indeed come to fruition, the single line would have no effect whatsoever on traffic, as all freight traffic was to come from the Stoke Gifford direction. (This was also a single line and had been so since 1966. However, TCB would allow up to three trains in the same direction on the single line between Filton West junction and Hallen Marsh, so this was not thought to be a problem.) The meeting concluded with smiles all round.

From the content of this meeting, it looked very much as if the proposed resignalling of the Avonmouth area, Stage 13, was doomed. There

was no way that the BR management would spend valuable time, money and resources on modifying Stage 6 plans, keeping Dock Junction box, only to close it a year later (even though they were more or less doing that at Stoke Gifford by resignalling for the freight yards, then closing them to build a new station). It looked very much as if semaphore signalling would remain in the Avonmouth area – at least for the foreseeable future.

What had brought about this radical re-think on the part of the management? The answer was money. The cost of the resignalling was far higher than anyone had bargained for at that stage. The Temple Meads area alone had taken a large part of the allotted government funds; the bill was increasing and the scheme was not even half completed. Therefore, as the government's Grant Aid scheme required costs to be reduced as much as possible, the MAS scheme had to be modified. Shedding Stage 13 was a quick and convenient way of cutting costs without altering the main-line resignalling plans. With the original plan, even after its reduction in status to crossing ground-frame, the staff at Dock junction would most likely have been redundant signalmen and, as such, paid at their old rate of pay. This meant that the railway would save nothing at all by reducing the status of the signal box. True, it would cost them to alter the lever frame at Dock junction now that they planned to keep the box, but this was nothing compared to the cost of the plans to resignal the area throughout.

Bristol Resignalling Stage 6 took place between Stapleton Road and Filton junction and Stapleton Road and Avonmouth Dock junction over the weekend of Saturday 17 October 1970 and Monday 19 October 1970. From the beginning of the work, Clifton Down and Shirehampton boxes were closed. Both were of course relics from the Midland Railway's Clifton Extension. Clifton Down box had been built for the Midland in brick and stone by contractors McKenzie & Holland. Its MR lever frame of twenty-eight levers contained seventeen working levers at closure, having lost its coal-yard connections in 1967.

Clifton Down just before resignallng in 1971.

Shirehampton, a small wooden box of typical MR design, stood on the Down platform there. A connection on the Up side served a couple of sidings. The box had a lever frame of twenty levers in length; fifteen remained in use at closure, and there were five disused, of which numbers 9, 15, 16 and 17 were spaces. No.5 was a spare lever, which had worked the Up Intermediate Block signals (IBS) at Sea Mills until these were removed in 1967. (Sea Mills Down IB signals had been worked by lever 20 in Clifton Down box.) Crossovers 7 and 11 had been taken out of use on the Thursday morning prior to Stage 6, along with all respective ground signals and the ground signals applying to the sidings.

Under Stage 6, the line to Avonmouth was to be singled, so the existing double junction was removed and a new single junction made with the Up Relief line at Stapleton Road (the physical junction now being named Narroways Hill junction); the existing down line to Avonmouth was used to a point just beyond Montpelier station. From there, the Up line was used as the single line until Clifton Down was reached, where the line became double through the station. After passing through Clifton Down tunnel, the single line followed the old Down line formation until the approach to Sea Mills. There, it was slewed into the Up line formation to serve Sea Mills and Shirehampton platforms, thereafter following the Down line formation again

as far as Avonmouth Dock junction, where the line became double once more.

Avonmouth Dock junction box was to become a fringe box to Bristol Panel under the modified Stage 6 plans, and here the entire lever frame was subject to alteration and re-locking in the WR style (to go into details of the alterations would be outside the scope of this book). The sidings at Shirehampton were controlled by a new ground frame, which was released by Dock Junction box. Normal Absolute Block working applied between Dock junction and its neighbour, St Andrews junction, but Track Circuit Block working for single lines was brought into use between Dock junction and Clifton Down station. Operation of an acceptance lever in Dock Junction box allowed Bristol Panel to clear the signal at Clifton for trains to proceed to Avonmouth. Likewise, operation of an acceptance switch in Bristol Panel was required to allow Dock junction to clear signals towards Clifton. Train description between the two boxes was by four-character train describers.

It became apparent throughout the 1970s that the 'powers that be' had planned for a future in which freight traffic would rapidly leave the railways and transfer to the roads. Bristol East Depot yard would be closed and Bristol West Depot yard did not last long after the resignalling of that area in 1972. However, due to the Port of Bristol Authority and

BR falling out over the re-leasing of Avonmouth's Royal Edward Yard in 1978, freight traffic returned to Stoke Gifford, using the Down sidings. Traffic for Avonmouth was to be left at Stoke Gifford Down yard and moved to Avonmouth on a daily basis Monday to Saturday, using the Avonmouth 'trip' loco. This method of working continued through to privatization.

The 1970s and 1980s

During 1975, BR came to the conclusion that the industry was in financial trouble. The Labour government had made it clear that there would be no increase in the current level of state support for the railways. BR Western Region estimated that total receipts for 1976 would be around £2,000,000 lower than those of 1975, while total costs were expected to be in the region of £8,000,000. Managers reckoned that savings of £2,000,000 would need to be made. Government grant-aid contributions were to be the same as in 1975, that is to say, £350,000,000. BR came under pressure to make drastic reductions in costs and short-term savings.

In Bristol, management turned its attention once again to the Severn Beach line. In 1975, a plan was drawn up by the Area Divisional Manager's office to rationalize track and signalling in the Avonmouth area. This proposed the closure of Dock junction, Town Goods and Holesmouth signal boxes. The line was to remain single to double at Dock junction but become single again at Dock station, where only the Up platform would be used. The line would then be single all the way to Hallen Marsh, using the Down line. A ground frame, released from St Andrews box, would control connections at Town Goods, but access to the storage sidings and Fisons there would be from the Corporation lines only. A connection between the single line and the yard would be motor-worked from St Andrews. At the North End of the Royal Edward Yard, the points were to be motor-worked from Hallen Marsh and the lines would run into the old Up line, which would run as an Up/Down goods line to Hallen Marsh. Hallen would have a revised layout. St Andrews Road Down platform was to be reduced to three coaches long.

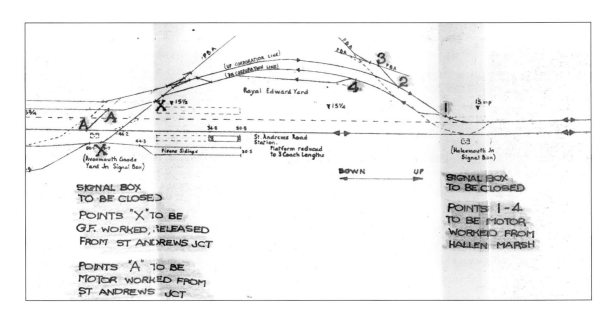

The 1975 plan.

The 1975 track and signalling reduction plan never came to fruition and no real development of the rail facilities in Avonmouth happened until the advent of the rationalization plan, which was announced in 1986.

Because of its geographical location close to Bristol and, therefore, relatively short journeys in respect of passenger miles, the passenger service on the line had been heavily subsidized. It was also subject to a high commitment of resources in the shape of trains and staff. Proposals were put forward to reduce the train service and to operate the revised service with one three-car DMU and a single power unit (SPU). To this end, the passenger service would be altered and rationalized. The 05.30 Bristol–Severn Beach would be discontinued, along with the 06.55, 09.18, 15.13, 17.03 and 20.20 services, and the 07.06 Taunton to Avonmouth St Andrews Road. In the opposite direction, the 05.58 Severn Beach to Bristol was to be discontinued, as were the 08.28, 11.13, 16.02, 18.02 and 21.30 services. The 06.17 Severn Beach to Keynsham and Somerdale would terminate at Bristol. The 09.45 St Andrews Road to Weston-super-Mare would be discontinued between Avonmouth and Bristol Temple Meads. Various other services would be retimed a few minutes either way to compensate. BR reckoned that these moves, along with re-arranging train-crew rosters, would save the wages of eighteen drivers and thirteen guards.

The altered train services were mostly put into place from January 1976, in order to avoid heavier cuts to the timetables in May 1976. Both managers and the trade unions cooperated in the plans to save the service, but the train crews were not the only workers who were affected. Bristol Bath Road diesel depot staff were also concerned that they might lose work if the DMU fleet was reduced as a result of the cuts. They were reassured that this would not be the case.

It is also worth noting that the transport issues were not confined to the railways. Even the Bristol Omnibus Company had to reduce its Avonmouth bus service during these difficult economic times.

The moves proved successful in reducing costs on the line and the situation was more or less stable for a while, with traffic remaining at a reasonable level over the next few years. However, rationalization plans were still being made.

The Royal Edward Yard had closed on 5 December 1977. BR now decided that there was a 'lack of traffic' on the night shift at Avonmouth and in April 1978 the decision was taken to close the area to traffic between 23.00 and 05.00. Hallen Marsh and Holesmouth boxes, which had worked a night shift for trains to use the Royal Edward Yard, were to close on nights. Freight trains that had, until now, run to Avonmouth between the hours of 22.00 and 05.45 would henceforth terminate at Stoke Gifford sidings and be tripped to Avonmouth next morning. All other signal boxes were already reduced to two-turn boxes.

In January 1982, decisions were taken to make further station 'improvements' along the line (in other words, cost reductions), including the

The remains of Avonmouth Dock station main building making its way out of Avonmouth for disposal.

Once a poisonous munitions site, now a trading estate: Chittening Estate seen in 1984.

LEFT: The Hallen Marsh pilot loco heads a train of UKF fertilizer 'curtain-sided' vans over the flat crossing to Chittening.

demolition of the Downside station buildings at Avonmouth Dock station and the provision of a new entrance stairway at Clifton Down. In addition, the Avonmouth telephone exchange at Dock station would close. The work at Avonmouth took place over a weekend and the train carrying the remains of the station in open wagons made its way out of Avonmouth via Hallen Marsh and Henbury.

The Royal Edward Yard had supposedly been closed but some traffic continued to use the sidings, even after the PBA (Port of Bristol Authority) had stopped using its railway system and BR had

A Class 47 dares to go to Chittening: after derailing it took a while to come back.

*BR notice of Freightliner clearance
test to Chittening.*

```
FREIGHTLINERS LTD. TEST TRAIN

WEDNESDAY 23 FEBRUARY                47011

4Z33 10.00 West Depot - Avonmouth       Special Clearance Test
(Chittening Industrial Estate)          To convey 1 x 5 set including
                                        1 x 8'6" Container.
```

discontinued its lease on the yard. Private company McGregor Cory started to make use of its Chittening warehouse for fertilizer traffic and, after clearance tests had been carried out, trips were made to Chittening trading estate from the Royal Edward. The first clearance test for BR was made on Monday 6 June 1983 with a Class 31 loco and various wagons. Another trial was to be carried out on the morning of Wednesday 8 June 1983, but this was delayed owing to a dispute between the PBA and BR over who was still providing the motive power for the tests. Eventually, a PBA Sentinel took a rake of UKF 'curtain-sided' bogie pallet wagons over to Chittening at 14.40 that afternoon. The tests proved to be successful.

Traffic for McGregor Cory came from Ince & Elton UKF fertilizer plant. A train was booked to leave Ince & Elton on Tuesday 4 October 1983, proceeding to Severn Tunnel junction yard, where it was detached for movement to Avonmouth on the following day.

On Wednesday 5 October 1983, train 6Z35 was booked to leave Severn Tunnel junction at 08.00 bound for Avonmouth Royal Edward Yard. It was made up of a locomotive and fourteen loaded 'curtain-sided' bogie pallet vans. The train was taken to the Royal Edward Yard where the vans were taken across to Chittening, seven at a time, by a Class 08 shunter that had been allocated to Hallen Marsh for such trips. (Seven pallet wagons was the maximum agreed load for a Class 08.)

In 1983, Margaret Thatcher's government set up a committee of inquiry into Britain's railway systems, headed by Sir David Serpell. Following

The platform on the 'Docky' looks a little crowded, with (left to right) Pete Mead, unknown, unknown, Guards Inspector Maurice Cornwell (with moustache), unknown. The chap on the right looks as if the cold weather is getting the better of him.

More than 10 years after Avonmouth was 'definitely getting a Freightliner terminal', this was as far as it had got!

EVENING POST, MONDAY, JUNE 22, 1987 — 9

BR ON WRONG TRACK, SAYS WATCHDOG

Bus leaflet brings rail under fire

A LEAFLET campaign advertising minibus links between Sea Mills and Shirehampton in Bristol and Parkway railway station has been criticised by a rail watchdog group.

British Rail and City Line buses joined together for a joint leaflet promotion.

But the Severn Beach Line Passenger Association has hit out at the move, saying it undermines British Rail's own service.

The new bus service will take passengers to

By Martin Powell

Parkway, but the watchdog group says passengers should be encouraged to travel there by rail on the Severn Beach line.

Secretary of the group, Mr Peter Green, said: "I couldn't believe it when I first saw the leaflet.

"Inter City are actively helping to launch a bus service which will actually operate in competition with British Rail's own service.

"How can British Rail say they are interested in the success of the Severn

Beach line if they are encouraging people to travel by other means."

But a British Rail spokesman said they are pledged to publicise all services that will help people travel by rail.

The spokesman said: "We want to increase awareness of all services to enable customers to have the widest possible choice.

"Parkway has been publicised as a "park and ride" station for those who come by car and these leaflets are to publicise the service for those who would like to use the bus."

The 1980s was not a railway-minded era.

the recommendations of the Serpell Report, which came to be known as the 'Second Beeching Plan', Avonmouth was not directly affected – although some trains were diverted via Avonmouth, when two of the four lines between Bristol Dr Day's junction and Filton junction were taken out of use. There were, however, further surreptitious attempts to close the line; it was said that Clifton Down tunnel had become unsafe and there were rumours that the tunnel would be closed and trains would run only as far as Clifton Down station, with passengers continuing to Avonmouth and Severn Beach by bus.

Industrial action in the early 1980s added to the fears for the line's future. Indeed, it was said that thirty-eight railway lines countrywide could close owing to losses of revenue that had allegedly been caused by the strikes. A report in the *Bristol Evening Post* of 24 August 1982 claimed that a new national organization known as 'Rural Voice' suspected that the Severn Beach railway was one of those at risk. A BR spokesman denied this, saying that, although the line was 'uneconomic', there were no plans to close it.

In the 1983 snow, all the staff were there but they sent no trains to Avonmouth.

Throughout the 1980s, passenger services to Severn Beach were often cancelled in favour of bus replacements – frequently at the drop of a hat. The Leyland R3 railbus was being trialled on the line, but it did not appeal to passengers. Afterwards, the BR management thanked all staff for their 'help and goodwill' during the trial and hailed it as 'an outstanding success', but most railwaymen did not agree. Apparently, there was interest in the R3 in the USA – those who had worked with it along the Avonmouth line would say that were welcome to it! It was considered by many to be a monstrosity – it could not even carry prams or bikes.

The management failed to help the cause of the line in other ways. On one snowy winter day, all members of railway staff at Avonmouth turned up for work, some travelling many miles through the difficult conditions. In spite of this, the management decided not to run the passenger service to Avonmouth and Severn Beach, as they did not want to move the points at Narroways junction. To add to the outrage, a local radio report stated that the reason the trains had not run was because the railway staff had failed to turn up for duty! Although railway staff contacted the radio station to put the record straight, no apology or correction was broadcast. They were at the time rather 'anti-railway'. Likewise, the management failed to correct its statement. Sadly, the local railway

management, presumably under pressure from a higher authority, also did their level best to discourage people from using this line in particular. Politically, railways did not enjoy much support in the 1980s.

Friends of the Railway

In the mid-1980s, a local pressure group, the Severn Beach Line Passenger Association, was formed to encourage people to use the line and to work with Bristol City Council and British Rail to improve the train service and station facilities. They also organized excursion trains from the stations along the line to bring in more revenue. They were even successful in persuading BR to lay on some Sunday services to and from the popular market held at that time at Eastville, near Stapleton Road station.

During October 1981, further charters were organized to Eastville Market from Severn Beach and Avonmouth. This time the trains were not formed by locomotive and coaches, but by three-car diesel multiple units, or DMUs. The empty train arrived at Severn Beach at 10.15 (via Filton West and Hallen Marsh) and left for Stapleton Road at 10.30, calling at all stations as before. This time the empty train ran to Marsh Junction servicing point from Stapleton Road, returning at 13.09 to form the 13.20 return to Severn Beach, calling again at all

NOTICE OF PASSENGER AND PARCELS TRAIN ARRANGEMENTS

Sunday 13 September 1981
ARRANGEMENTS IN CONNECTION WITH
CHARTER TRAIN FROM SEVERN BEACH TO
STAPLETON ROAD AND RETURN.
These trains to be formed with circuit 144.
LOAD: 10 VB/SH.
5Z12 07.55 (ECS) Malago Vale to Severn Beach
Malago Vale: 07.55
Filton West junction: 08.13
Hallen Marsh: 08.26-R/R-08.40
Severn Beach: 08.46

2Z12: 09.45 (Charter) Severn Beach to
Stapleton Road
Severn Beach (Dep) 09.45
Avonmouth: 09.54–09.55
Shirehampton: 09.58–09.59
Sea Mills: 10.02–10.03
Clifton Down: 10.08–10.09
Redland: 10.10–10.11
Montpelier: 10.12–10.13
Stapleton Road: 10.17

(The Charter ran empty to Malago Vale carriage
sidings from Stapleton Road at 10.25, returning to
Stapleton Road at 13.42, where it formed the 13.45
departure back to Severn Beach, calling all stations.
After arriving back at Severn Beach at 14.17, the
train (now empty) departed again at 15.05 and ran
to Temple Meads where the loco ran-round the
train and it left for Cardiff Canton carriage sidings via
Stapleton Road, Filton and Pilning.)

Note: VB = vacuum brake; SH = steam-heated

stations. After arriving at Severn Beach, the train returned empty to Marsh junction via Avonmouth.

Although these charter trains were well patronized, it seemed that BR was still attempting to make the Severn Beach line unpopular. In March 1985, the Severn Beach Line Passenger Association organised an excursion to Margate, to take place during August. The idea was that the train would start from Severn Beach and pick up at all stations along the Avonmouth and Clifton lines, returning the same way. All was going well with the arrangements until, on the Wednesday before the trip was due to take place, BR management announced to the Association that the excursion would not be able to start or return to Severn Beach. They

blamed the 'failure of the Avonmouth signalmen to work overtime'. Buses were instead used to make the connections with Bristol. The organizers had to hand out notices to all passengers on the excursion advising them why the Avonmouth and Severn Beach line stops were no longer to be made by rail.

Sadly, the story put out by the BR manager at the time had been untrue. The signalmen did not even know that an excursion had been planned, and were never asked to work overtime to cover the passage of the excursion. Furious Avonmouth rail staff contacted the SBLPA and put the matter straight. It transpired that BR had failed the organizers in many other ways too. The promised train formation did not happen, throwing those with reserved seats into confusion, and there was no assistance for disabled passengers. The train had not been cleaned either.

Presumably, the BR management were hoping to deter people from using the line, by making out that the staff were uncooperative. As with the snow incident, it left a nasty taste in the mouth.

Over the years, the Association morphed into the Friends of Severn Beach Railway (FOSBR), which was formed in 1995 to protest against the potential demise of the Severn Beach line. Services at the time had been reduced, with many operated by the uncomfortable Class 142 'Pacer' fixed-wheel-base railbuses – surely a retrograde step? – or replaced by buses. The first FOSBR action was on 25 September 1995, when a group of protestors met at Avonmouth Dock station with prams, push-chairs and bicycles, to demonstrate that buses were not a suitable replacement for the trains – which could not carry much in the way of prams and bikes anyway. The group later changed its name to Friends of Suburban Bristol Railways, allowing it to keep the FOSBR acronym.

The FOSBR's first campaign appealed for a better service between Bristol Temple Meads and Severn Beach. There were few trains during the week, most of which terminated at Dock station, and no service at all on Sundays. Following action by FOSBR and a string of protests, Bristol City Council agreed to subsidize a service of at least one train every 45 minutes in each direction along the line. This continued until 2007 when a 1-hour minimum service was written into the Greater Western passenger franchise. In 2007, the council unanimously agreed to pay £450,000 per year to fund extra services from May 2008 for three years, which resulted in a 60 per cent increase in passenger numbers along the line, and a 25 per cent year-on-year increase between June 2009 and June 2010. Passenger numbers on the line increased by 90 per cent over the period 2008–11, and 25 per cent in the period 2010–11. The council cut the subsidy by half, saying the extra passengers would allow the line to support itself. This prompted criticism from FOSBR, which felt that the subsidy should be used to provide evening trains and through services to Bedminster and Parson Street or Ashton Gate, something for which they had campaigned since they had started as the Severn Beach Line Passenger Association. Services were now approximately three trains every 2 hours between Avonmouth and Temple Meads, with one extending to Severn Beach. Ideally, the FOSBR wanted to see a half-hourly service, but this would need more stretches of double track. (Only three sections of the line are double track, with passing loops: Avonmouth, Clifton Down and at Dock station.)

FOSBR also campaigned for a Sunday service between Severn Beach and Weston-super-Mare, and successfully got two services each Sunday; both terminate at Severn Beach during the summer, but one terminates at Avonmouth during the winter timetable. These services are subsidized by South Gloucestershire Council and have proved very popular; during the summer of 2011, for example, more than 2000 passengers boarded Sunday trains at Severn Beach.

The group has also lobbied for the opening of a station to serve the A4 Portway Park & Ride scheme (built on land opposite the site of the old Earth Sidings at Dock junction). In August 2017, it was announced that the West of England Joint Committee, which is made up of Bristol, South Gloucestershire, Bath & North-East Somerset and North Somerset councils, had agreed to build the station. To be called 'Portway Park and Ride', it will have one platform and easy-access facilities, and will cost around £2.25 million to construct. The idea is to encourage commuters to make more use of public transport.

In other plans, the FOSBR has promoted the electrification of the Severn Beach Line, as part of the electrification scheme of the Great Western Main Line. This is highly unlikely to happen in the near future, especially as at the time of writing the scheme has halted at Chippenham. The pressure group also wants to see the re-introduction of a train service using the Henbury line, along with the reopening of stations at Henbury and North Filton. Having lost much of its traffic due to the closure of Filton airfield, North Filton still has the potential to attract passengers from the nearby Airbus works and the thousands of new houses being constructed on land on, and adjacent to, the airfield site. If Henbury were reopened, it could attract passengers to and from the Cribbs Causeway shopping area. A feasibility study is planned.

CHAPTER 17

Development of the Line

Despite clearance tests being carried out between Royal Edward Yard and Chittening trading estate in 1983 – with a PBA Sentinel 'Docky' taking a 1 × 5 Freightliner set with 8-foot 6-in containers to Chittening – the often-mentioned and much-anticipated Freightliner depot at Avonmouth never materialized.

In between then and the 1990s, passenger numbers improved as the line was promoted as part of the 'Avon Link', inaugurated on 22 June 1981. Stations between Bath and Severn Beach, Bristol and Yate all became part of the Link. In 1986, the line became known as the 'City–Severn', with fifteen departures from Bristol Temple Meads to Severn Beach between 05.15 and 21.30 Monday to Saturday. On weekdays, the trains called all stations out and back, but on Saturdays, the 11.10 departure ex-Severn Beach did not call at Lawrence Hill station. There was no Sunday service. As before, tickets could be purchased from the guard or from Temple Meads or the booking office of connecting stations. The guard could issue day return or season tickets. There was no charge for children under 5, and prams, pushchairs and bicycles could be carried for free in the guard's van.

By now, of course, there was no booking office at Lawrence Hill, Stapleton Road or Severn Beach stations. In fact, there were no station buildings at all at any of these stations.

In 1986, the management claimed that, as the signalling equipment in the area would need to be renewed within the next two years, they were going to seize the opportunity to rationalize the trackwork, close the signal boxes and introduce modern signalling. The plan was to eliminate Hallen Marsh as a junction and install a new junction between the single line from Severn Beach and the existing line at St Andrews. This would extend the single line by a further one and three-quarter miles.

In reality, this was a slightly modified version of the 1975 plan.

Between Friday 22 January and Monday 25 January 1988, the layout in Avonmouth as a whole was changed. Hallen Marsh, Holesmouth, Town Goods and Dock Junction signal boxes were closed. New signalling was brought into use between Shirehampton and Hallen Marsh (both the Severn Beach and Henbury lines). At Avonmouth Dock station, Up trains would now be able to arrive at, and start back from, the Down platform. The line between Dock junction and St Andrews would be singled, with a passing loop at Dock station.

The existing Up line between St Andrews junction and Hallen Marsh became the new Up and Down main line; the existing Down line between Hallen Marsh and St Andrews would become the Up and Down freight-only line and a continuation of the single line from Stoke Gifford. Buffer stops

It looked good on paper, but the 'new train' did not run on the line, except when it left Clifton that day and ran empty via Henbury and out of the area.

£40,000 rail link facelift unveiled

NEW-STYLE TRAIN MAKES ITS DEBUT

By Dave Baxter

A £40,000 facelift for the Avon Link rail service from Bristol to Severn Beach has been unveiled.

The Avon Link scheme, funded by Avon county council and British Rail, has set the pattern for a new drive to get passengers back on the branch line services.

The Temple Meads-Severn Beach project was carried out by youngsters under the county's work experience programme.

A prototype lightweight, two-car diesel train made its debut on the track yesterday.

The improvements along the 13¼-mile route include resurfaced platforms and improved waiting facilities at the ten stations, with a new staircase taking passengers into the heart of the Clifton Down shopping precinct.

Yesterday VIPs from Avon county and Bristol city councils, Northavon and Severn Beach saw the facelift programme being completed by the youngsters.

The old and the new . . . the latest lightweight diesel and the conventional railcar at Clifton Down Station.

Interesting article, but not quite cprrect. it gives the impression that the 'New-Style Train' was to be used on the Avon Link; it wasn't. DMUs continued for a few more years before being ousted by the Sprinters.

were erected at St Andrews and there was to be no through running between the passenger and goods lines. The tip siding ground frame was recovered and a round-round facility added to the layout here.

A new ground frame was provided at Holesmouth to work the new connections between the two single lines and into the PBA sidings. The line into Chittening trading estate would be connected to the freight line at Hallen Marsh.

A new control panel would be installed at St Andrews box and the levers there removed. The existing Block working was withdrawn and the line between Shirehampton and St Andrews worked by Track Circuit Block. The Up and Down passenger line between St Andrews and Severn Beach was worked by No Signalman Key Token (NSKT), with an intermediate token machine situated at Holesmouth ground frame. St Andrews would also

Table 133

Local Train Services

**Severn Beach
Avonmouth
Bristol**

AVON LINK

From 13 May 1985 to 10 May 1986

The cover of the 1985–86 'Avon Link' timetable.

AVON LINK Timetable

Until 10 May 1986

Mondays to Saturdays (no Sunday service)

2nd class only on this branch line (unless otherwise shown)

		BHX	BHX	BHX		BHX SX			A				B	FO	C SO	D	MFSX	BHX MO	BHX		BHX			
Severn Beach	d	0558	–	0650	–	–	0756	0858	0953	1110	1210	1303	1410	–	1540	1545	–	–	1645	1726	–	1830	1900	2033	2212
St Andrew's Road	d	0606	–	0658	–	0730	0804	0906	1001	1118	1218	1311	1418	–	1548	1553	–	–	1701b	1734	–	1838	1908	2041	2220
Avonmouth	d	0609	–	0701	–	0733	0807	0909	1004	1121	1221	1314	1421	–	1551	1556	–	–	1704	1737	–	1841	1911	2044	2223
Shirehampton	d	0613	–	0705	–	0737	0811	0913	1008	1125	1225	1318	1425	–	1555	1600	–	–	1708	1741	–	1845	1915	2048	2227
Sea Mills	d	0617	–	0709	–	0741	0815	0917	1012	1129	1229	1322	1429	–	1559	1604	–	–	1712	1745	–	1849	1919	2052	2231
Clifton Down	d	0623	–	0715	–	0747	0823	0923	1018	1135	1235	1328	1435	–	1605	1610	–	–	1718	1752	–	1855	1925	2058	2237
Redland	d	0625	–	0717	–	0749	0825	0925	1020	1137	1237	1330	1437	–	1607	1612	–	–	1720	1754	–	1857	1927	2100	2239
Montpelier	d	0627	–	0719	–	0751	0827	0927	1022	1139	1239	1332	1439	–	1609	1614	–	–	1722	1756	–	1859	1929	2102	2241
Stapleton Road	d	0631	0654	0723	0734	0755	0831	0931	1026	1143	1243	1336	1443	1556	1613	1618	1622	1652	1727	1802	1901	1904	1933	2106	2245
Lawrence Hill	d	0634	–	0726	0737	0758	0834	0934	1029	1146	1246	1339	1446	1559	1616	1621	1625	1655	1730	1805	–	1907	1936	2109	2248
Bristol Temple Meads	a	0641	0701	0730	0742	0802	0838	0938	1032	1153	1251	1345	1450	1602	1620	1625	1628	1658	1733	1808	1906	1910	1940	2113	2252
connection for																									
London Paddington	a	0835	–	0910	–	0943	1015	1151	–	1337	1519	1558	1711	–	–	1824	–	–	1946	–	–	–	2216	2311	–
Plymouth	a	–	–	1017	–	–	1113	–	1258	–	1525	1624	1721	–	–	–	2036	–	–	2244	–	–	–
Birmingham	a	–	–	0925	–	–	1056	–	1211	1357	1456	–	–	–	–	–	–	–	2105	–	2331	–	–
Weston-super-Mare	a	0734	–	0832	–	0947	1033	1057	**1227**	1354	1427	**1524**	–	1720	–	–	1814	1926	–	–	2036	–	0002

						BHX SX				A					C SO	D	C SO	D	SX	SO	SX	C SO	BHX D		BHX			SO	D
Weston-super-Mare	d	–	–	–	0625	–	0710	–	0920	1040	–	–	**1235**	1325	–	–	1513	1525	–	–	1730	1845	2040	–	–
Birmingham	d	–	–	–	–	–	0732	–	0917	–	1019	–	1130	1226	–	–	1358	–	–	1544	–	1944	–	–
Plymouth	d	–	–	–	–	–	0833	–	0944	–	1125	1234	–	–	–	1508	–	1711	1900	–	–
London Paddington	d	–	–	–	–	0640	–	0905	–	1005	–	1045	–	1245	–	1405	1430	–	1535	1605	1805	1930	–	–
connection into		BHX	BHX	BHX	BHX SX						C SO	D	C SO	D	SX	SO	SX	C SO	BHX D		BHX			SO	D
Bristol Temple Meads	d	0515	0603	0608	0645	0700	0730	0808	0908	1003	1120	1212	1220	1305	1313	1420	1417	1458	1550	1555	1635	1723	1737	1812	1950	2130	2135	2330
Lawrence Hill	d	0518	0606	0611	0649	0703	0734	0811	0911	1006	1123	1215	1223	1308	1316	1423	1420	1501	1553	1558	1638	–	1740	1815	1953	2133	–
Stapleton Road	d	0521	0610a	0614	0651a	0706	0738a	0814	0914	1009	1126	1218	1226	1311	1319	1426	1423	1504	1556	1601	1641	1727a	1743	1818	1956	2136	2140a	2334a
Montpelier	d	0525	–	0618	–	0710	–	0818	0918	1013	1130	1222	1230	1315	1323	1430	1427	1508	1600	1605	1645	–	1747	1822	2000	2140	–
Redland	d	0527	–	0620	–	0712	–	0820	0920	1015	1132	1224	1232	1317	1325	1432	1429	1510	1602	1607	1647	–	1749	1824	2002	2142	–
Clifton Down	d	0530	–	0623	–	0715	–	0823	0923	1018	1135	1235d	1235	1328c	1328	1435	1435f	1513	1605	1610	1650	–	1752	1827	2005	2145	–
Sea Mills	d	0534	–	0628	–	0720	–	0828	0928	1023	1140	1240	1240	1333	1333	1440	1440	1517	1610	1615	1654	–	1757	1831	2009	2149	–
Shirehampton	d	0538	–	0632	–	0724	–	0832	0932	1027	1144	1244	1244	1337	1337	1444	1444	1521	1614	1619	1658	–	1801	1835	2013	2153	–
Avonmouth	d	0542	–	0635	–	0727	–	0835	0935	1030	1147	1247	1247	1340	1340	1447	1447	1525	1617	1622	1702	–	1804	1839	2017	2157	–
St. Andrew's Road	d	0545	–	0639	–	0731	–	0839	0939	1034	1151	1251	1251	1344	1344	1451	1451	1528a	1621	1626	1705	–	1808	1842	2020	2200	–
Severn Beach	d	0554	–	0647	–	0739	–	0847	0947	1042	1159	1259	1259	1352	1352	1459	1459	–	1629	1634	1714	–	1816	1851	2029	2209	–

A	All Mondays to Fridays, also Saturdays from 5 October, to Weston-super-Mare	**MFSX**	Mondays, Fridays and Saturdays excepted
B	All Mondays to Fridays, also Saturdays from 5 October, to Taunton arrive 1604	**FO**	Fridays only
C	Until 28 September	**SX**	Saturdays excepted
D	Not Saturdays 18 May to 28 September	**SO**	Saturdays only
MO	Mondays only	**BHX**	Bank Holidays excepted

a	Arrival time
b	Arrive 1653
c	Arrive 1320
d	Arrive 1227
f	Arrive 1432
▲	First and second class

Please enquire for full details of connections shown, before travelling. NB. Connections shown apply Mondays to Fridays only

Subject to alteration or cancellation at short notice, especially during public holidays.

The 1985–86 timetable.

Railcards

Senior Citizen Railcard
Reduced rate travel to almost anywhere. There is a choice of two cards—one for Day Return tickets only, the other for Day Return plus standard and Saver tickets. The cards are valid a year from date of issue and full details are in the special folder which includes an application form.

Family Railcard
The card permits one or two nominated adults plus two other adults to purchase standard and Saver Single, standard and Saver Return or Day and Saver tickets at a discount. Valid for one year from the date of issue, the card is ideal for days out, holidays, family visits and much, much more.

Young Persons Railcard
A Young Persons Railcard is issued for 12 months and is available for students aged 14 years and over and to anyone under 24 years of age. It entitles the holder to second class travel at a reduced rate, subject to certain conditions. Ask for a folder giving full details.

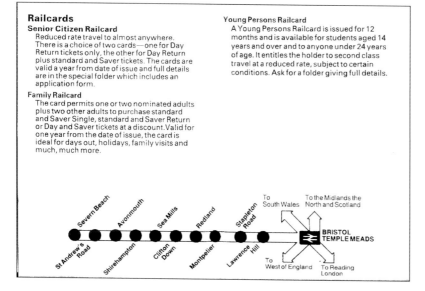

The back cover of the 1985–86 timetable, giving rather useful information.

Even the closed Severn Beach station building became part of the 'Avon Link' for a while – at least, that is how it appeared.

Shirehampton station in 1983.

take over the issue of Electric Train Tokens for the Severn Beach line. The line between Filton West and Hallen Marsh was to continue to be worked as TCB.

St Andrews was to take over control of the level crossing at Dock junction in addition to those at Dock station and St Andrews. All level crossings were to be supervised by CCTV.

Further expansion of the Avonmouth facilities took place in 1994, when the Avonmouth bulk-handling terminal was built on the site of the Royal Edward Yard. This facility was designed to bring imported coal from ships into a bulk silo via a conveyer system, and then to unload it into trains beneath. Freight trains are moved auto-matically under the bunkers and permit a train to be fully and automatically loaded in under 36 minutes. Loads from Royal Portbury dock could also unload on to conveyors and the load moved to trains at the Royal Edward via an underground tunnel system equipped with two 2,500-tonne rapid bulk-handling conveyors. At first, quarry company Foster-Yeoman was interested in using the silo to move stone, which it intended to bring to the Royal Portbury dock by ship from Scotland, then move it to the silo. In the end, Yeoman decided

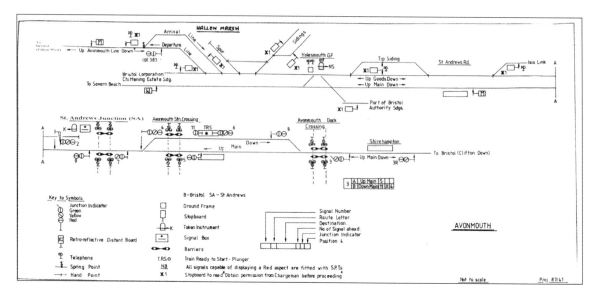

The plan of the 1988 Avonmouth resignalling and rationalization.

against using the scheme. However, it was used to handle coal, which was imported from places such as South Africa to fill the gap in the need for fossil fuel for power stations after the closure of most of the UK's mines. The bulk coal terminal discharges imported coal from ships docked at both the Royal Edward and Royal Portbury docks via the rail-loading system. Merry-go-round trains were employed on this work. At the Royal Edward, a Gottwald Harbour Crane can unload up to 10,000 tonnes of coal per day.

The building of the bulk-handling terminal meant that the line between Filton West and Hallen Marsh was once again doubled. Work began on this when, on 26 April 1992, a new 'signal box' (really a Portakabin) was opened at the crossing. In May 1992, the line between Filton West and the Brabazon aircraft crossing was slewed into the old Down line formation to allow new ballast and track to be laid on the Up line formation. The line between Brabazon Crossing box and the eastern end of Charlton tunnel was slewed into the Down

The 1989 view north from St Andrews box – no Corporation lines and only a single passenger line to Severn Beach. Town Goods has gone as well and the weeds are threatening to take over.

The entire line from Clifton was now controlled from St Andrews.

ABOVE: 'Brabazon' crossing signal box – the temporary cabin during the 1994 doubling of the line.

BELOW: 10 years after the last 'Ghost Train', North Filton platform is still there and now has two tracks again.

line formation by 29 June 1992, and new track was laid on the Up line formation.

By April 1993, the line was doubled between Filton West and a point just west of the site of Blaise sidings. Here, there was a physical junction where the double line that was now in use became single again. Brabazon Crossing box was closed on 4 April 1993 and a new (Portakabin) box known as 'Henbury West' (what was wrong with 'Blaise'?) was brought into use at the same time.

Just over half a mile down the line towards Avonmouth was another junction, this time controlled by a ground frame, which provided access to a new siding on the formation of the Down line. Adjacent to Moorhouse Lane, the siding was used for offloading stone brought in from the Frome quarries. The stone was destined for the building of the Second Severn Crossing and the approaches to a new railway bridge, which would stand adjacent to the existing one that carried the Filton West to Hallen Marsh line over the M5 motorway. This was known as 'Hallen Moor stone terminal'.

Once the new bridge had been built, the ground frame was taken out of use, on 13 April 1994, and the Down line between 'Henbury West' and the junction at the ground frame was laid and connected. By 28 June 1994, the line was double all the

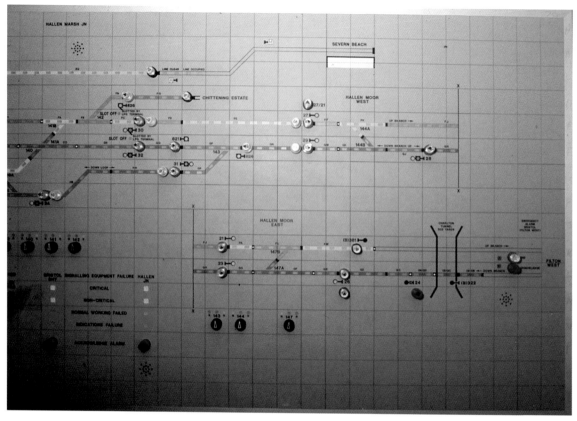

The Hallen Marsh end of the Westinghouse panel installed in St Andrews box.

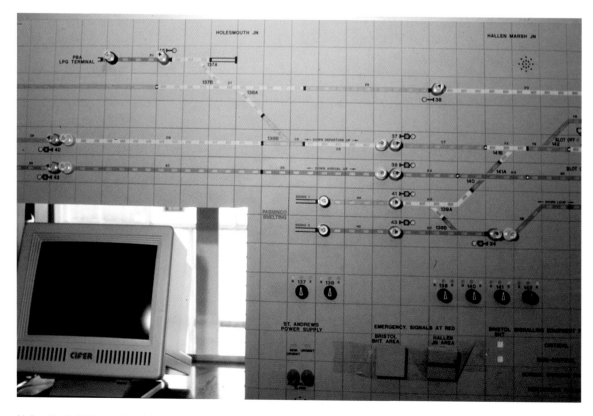

Hallen Marsh, Holesmouth and the smelting works sidings as depicted on the panel.

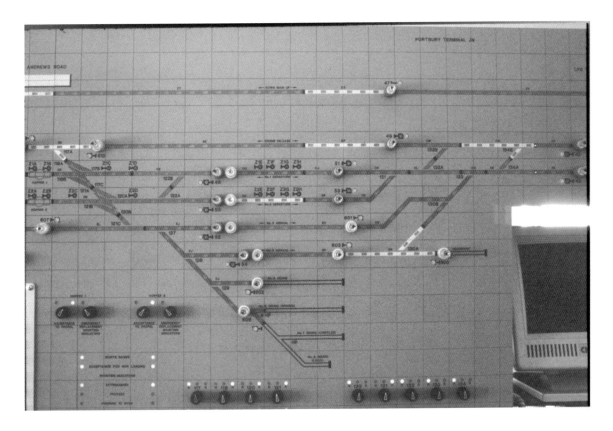

The bulk-handling terminal as shown on the panel.

Looking north again from St Andrews box, the bulk-handling terminal is being put together.

LEFT: The bulk-handling terminal conveyor dwarfs Sprinter 150248 as the 1990s change Avonmouth.

BELOW: Signalman Malcolm Eggleton passes the single-line token to the Guard of 'Burger Van' class 143, as it limps its way to Severn Beach.

way to Hallen Marsh. 'Henbury West' signal box was closed. Two new trailing crossovers were laid in – one just west of the old ground frame at Hallen Moor and another just over 1,000 yards nearer to Hallen. These were known as the East Crossover and the West Crossover, respectively. Both lines between the West Crossover and Hallen Marsh were signalled for bi-directional working. The whole was signalled from a huge Westinghouse control panel installed in St Andrews signal box.

As the twenty-first century progresses, the future of the Clifton Extension, Avonmouth and Henbury railway lines seems assured. South Gloucestershire Council continues to fund the service, freight uses the bulk terminal and passengers use the trains. Hopefully, before long the passenger service via Henbury will be restored and there will be stations once more at Henbury and North Filton. The heyday of the Avonmouth line may have gone, but thankfully the line has not.

Avonmouth Station, January 2017.

RIGHT: Shirehampton station has lost its buildings but has a tidy shelter and a nice coat of paint.

BELOW: A First Great Western service at Avonmouth Dock station. The bulk-handling terminal dominates the skyline.

The eco age: wind turbines now dominate the Hallen Marsh skyline. ICI has gone, Sevalco has gone. The smelting works has gone. Even most of the fuel pipes have gone. There is no more fertilizer traffic but there are more weeds than ever before. The trains still run to Severn Beach though.

References

Avon County Council, Railway Stations and Halts: A Photographic Record in Avon (Author, 1984)

Avonmouth and Portishead Docks, *Rules for the Movement of Trains and Locomotives,* rev. edn (Author, 1963)

Back-Track magazine (March 2003)

Bristol Evening Post (various, 1968)

British Railway Board, *The Reshaping of British Railways* (HMSO, 1963/National Archives and HarperCollins, 2013)

British Railways Magazine: Western Region, vol.6, no.7 (July 1955)

— vol.6, no.8 (August 1955)

— vol.6, no.9 (September 1955)

— vol.6, no.10 (October 1955)

British Railways Rule Book (1950)

British Transport Commission, *Sectional Appendix to the Rule Book (Western Region)* (Author, 1948)

Cooke, R.A., *Track Layout Diagrams of the Great Western Railway: Section 19B, Avonmouth Lines,* 2nd edn (Lightmoor Press, n.d.)

humanities.uwe.ac.uk

Jones, R., *Beeching: The Inside Track* (Heritage Railway, 2012)

Maggs, C.G., *Rail Centres: Bristol* (Ian Allan, 1981)

Ministry of Transport, 'Report into the Collision between Two Freight Trains at Hallen Marsh in 1947' (23 June 1947)

Railway magazine (December 1954)

— (August 1968)

— (December 1969)

Railway World magazine (October 1970)

Rendall, P.D., *Starting Something Big at Bristol– the Story of the 1970 Bristol Resignalling* (Past-Track Publications, 2007)

Rendall, P.D., *The South Wales Direct Line: History and Working* (Crowood, 2014)

'Report on Explosion and Fire at Regent Oil Co. Ltd Premises, Avonmouth, Bristol on 7th September 1951' (HMSO, 1952)

South Gloucestershire News (various)

Index